# Moving Target Defense

# Advances in Information Security

## Sushil Jajodia

*Consulting Editor*
*Center for Secure Information Systems*
*George Mason University*
*Fairfax, VA 22030-4444*
*email: jajodia@gmu.edu*

The goals of the Springer International Series on ADVANCES IN INFORMATION SECURITY are, one, to establish the state of the art of, and set the course for future research in information security and, two, to serve as a central reference source for advanced and timely topics in information security research and development. The scope of this series includes all aspects of computer and network security and related areas such as fault tolerance and software assurance.

ADVANCES IN INFORMATION SECURITY aims to publish thorough and cohesive overviews of specific topics in information security, as well as works that are larger in scope or that contain more detailed background information than can be accommodated in shorter survey articles. The series also serves as a forum for topics that may not have reached a level of maturity to warrant a comprehensive textbook treatment.

Researchers, as well as developers, are encouraged to contact Professor Sushil Jajodia with ideas for books under this series.

For further volumes:
http://www.springer.com/series/5576

Sushil Jajodia • Anup K. Ghosh • Vipin Swarup
Cliff Wang • X. Sean Wang
Editors

# Moving Target Defense

## Creating Asymmetric Uncertainty for Cyber Threats

 Springer

*Editors*

Sushil Jajodia
Center for Secure Information Systems
George Mason University
Fairfax, VA, USA

Vipin Swarup
Information Security Division
The MITRE Corporation
McLean, VA, USA

X. Sean Wang
Division of Information & Intelligent
System
National Science Foundation
Arlington, VA, USA

Anup K. Ghosh
Center for Secure Information Systems
George Mason University
Fairfax, VA, USA

Cliff Wang
Computing and Information Science Division
Engineering Sciences Directorate
PO Box 12211
Triangle Park, NC, USA

ISSN 1568-2633
ISBN 978-1-4614-2991-3          ISBN 978-1-4614-0977-9 (eBook)
DOI 10.1007/978-1-4614-0977-9
Springer New York Dordrecht Heidelberg London

Printed on acid-free paper

Springer is part of Springer Science+Business Media (www.springer.com)

# Preface

In May 2010, at the IEEE Security & Privacy Conference in Oakland, CA, the President's Cyber Policy Review announced three "game-changing" themes to cyber security: (1) Tailored Trustworthy Spaces, (2) Moving Target Defense, and (3) Cyber Economic Incentives. These three themes emerged after a summit convened under the theme of National Cyber Leap Year held in August 2009 sponsored by the White House's Office of Science and Technology Policy (OSTP) and coordinated by the agencies that comprise the Federal Networking and Information Technology Research and Development (NITRD) program.

In this book, we focus on Moving Target Defense (MTD). Moving Target Defense is motivated by the asymmetric costs borne by cyber defenders. In current systems, bloated software consisting of millions of lines of code need have only a single vulnerability to enable 20 lines of script code to completely "own" the system. From a defensive position, those million lines of code must be properly coded or adequately protected to prevent that single flaw from being exploited. From an offensive perspective, an attacker needs to find only a single flaw to break the system. The annual Pwn2Own contest held at CanSecWest illustrates the attacker's and defender's relative positions well. At the 2011 Pwn2Own contest, Apple's Safari browser was completely "owned" in less than 5 seconds.[1]

Unlike prior efforts in cybersecurity, MTD does not attempt to build flawless systems to prevent attack. Rather, the vision of Moving Target Defense is to:

"Create, evaluate, and deploy mechanisms and strategies that are diverse, continually shift, and change over time to increase complexity and costs for attackers, limit the exposure of vulnerabilities and opportunities for attack, and increase system resiliency."[2]

Moving Target Defenses take an advantage afforded to attackers and reverse it to advantage defenders. Attackers must learn of a particular vulnerability in a system

---

[1] http://www.bgr.com/2011/03/10/apples-safari-browser-embarrassed-at-pwn2own-hacked-in-5-seconds/

[2] "Cybersecurity Game-Change Research & Development Recommendations", NITRD CSIA IWG. Available online: http://www.nitrd.gov/pubs/CSIA_IWG_%20Cybersecurity_%20GameChange_RD_%20Recommendations_20100513.pdf

to exploit it. The longer a system is exposed, the longer an adversary has to study it to discover its vulnerabilities. Newly discovered vulnerabilities are often unpublished and exploits of those vulnerabilities are known as zero-day exploits. Zero-day exploits present a significant risk to system owners because without knowledge of the vulnerability, they have no way to patch it.

Current approaches to system defense are three-fold: (a) attempt to remove bugs from software at the source, (b) patch software as rapidly and uniformly as possible across affected systems, and (c) identify attack code and infections. The first approach is necessary but insufficient because the complexity of software precludes flawless released software. The second approach of patch distribution is standard practice in large enterprises, but has proven difficult to keep ahead of the threat, nor does it provide protection against zero-day attacks. The last approach is predicated on having a signature or definition of the malicious attack in order to find it and potentially block it or remediate. However, the speed and agility of adversaries as well as simple polymorphic mechanisms that continuously change the signatures of attacks renders signature-based approaches largely ineffective.

Observe that for attackers to exploit a system today, they rely on a system's properties and code to be static and persistent long enough to discover and exploit vulnerabilities. Likewise for defenders to detect these attacks today, they must develop a signature of the malware or attacks and hope the attack code is static long enough to detect and block that attack. Malware writers have observed this and have developed mechanisms to rapidly change malware in order to defeat detection mechanisms. To reverse the asymmetric advantage of attackers, defenders must build systems that rapidly change its properties and code such that attackers do not have adequate time to discover its vulnerabilities and code an exploit. In other words, Moving Target Defenses are able to automatically change one or more system attributes such that the attack surface area available to adversaries is unpredictable.

Moving Target Defense is enabled by technical trends in recent years, including virtualization and workload migration on commodity systems, widespread and redundant network connectivity, instruction set and address space layout randomization, just-in-time compilers, among other techniques. However, many challenging research problems remain to be solved, e.g., the security of virtualization infrastructures, secure and resilient techniques to move systems within a virtualized environment, automatic diversification techniques, automated ways to dynamically change and manage the configurations of systems and networks, quantification of security improvement and potential degradation.

The goal of this edited book is to explore the following questions:

- What scientific understanding is lacking in this topic area?
- What research is needed to achieve that understanding?
- What are the fundamental technical challenges to implementing moving target defenses?
- What recent scientific breakthroughs or accomplishments would now enable us to do so?
- How does one quantify the improvement or degradation caused by a moving target defense?

- What are classes of systems that are ideal candidates or conversely poor candidates for moving target defenses?
- What is a roadmap for making progress in Moving Target Defense?

In this book, a group of leading researchers describe the fundamental challenges facing the research community and identify promising solution paths.

Fairfax, VA                                                                                  *Sushil Jajodia*
*Anup K. Ghosh*
*Vipin Swarup*
*Cliff Wang*
*X. Sean Wang*

# About the Book

Chapters in this book can be roughly divided into three areas: MTD foundations (Chapters 1-2), MTD approaches based on software transformations (Chapters 3-7), and MTD approaches based on network and software stack configurations (Chapters 8-10).

In Chapter 1, Manadhata and Wing introduce the measure of a software system's attack surface as an indicator of the system's security. Moving target defenses seek to vary the attack surface dynamically in an unpredictable manner, with the goal of improving system security. In Chapter 2, Evans et al. analyze the moving target defense approach and identify scenarios where moving target defenses are and are not effective.

Chapters 3 through 6 describe moving target defense approaches based on software transformation. In Chapter 3, Portokalidis and Keromytis propose the adoption of instruction-set randomization across the entire software stack, thus preventing the execution of unauthorized binaries and scripts regardless of their origin. In Chapter 4, Franz et al. propose techniques that compilers can utilize to diversify software, and two execution models that utilize such compilers to make it exponentially harder for attackers to run successful attacks. In Chapter 5, Cui and Stolfo propose a new poly-culture architecture that provides complete uniqueness for each distinct device, and a new security paradigm based on perpetual mutation and diversity, driven by symbiotic defensive mutualism. In Chapter 6, Rinard describes and evaluates mechanisms that can change the functionality of the program in ways that may eliminate security vulnerabilities while still leaving the program able to provide acceptable functionality. This approach leverages the observation that many software systems provide substantially more functionality than users require, desire, or are even aware of. In Chapter 7, Christodorescu et al. present an end-to-end software diversification proposal in a multitiered system, typified by Internet services.

In Chapter 8, Huang and Ghosh present an approach based on diverse virtual servers (VSs), each configured with a unique software mix, producing diversified attack surfaces. A rotational scheme maintains a set of online virtual servers that are randomly selected and replaced dynamically, with the offline virtual servers being reverted to predefined pristine states. In Chapter 9, Al-Shaer investigates a network approach that enables end-hosts and network devices to change their con-figuration such as IP address, port numbers, routes and IPSec tunnels randomly and dynamically while preserving the integrity of network operation. In Chapter 10, Kant discusses how the moving target defense principle can be exploited to harden configuration management against hacker attacks.

# Acknowledgements

We are extremely grateful to the numerous contributors to this book. In particular, it is a pleasure to acknowledge the authors for their contributions. Special thanks go to Susan Lagerstrom-Fife, Senior Publishing Editor for Springer, and Jennifer Maurer, Editorial Assistant at Springer for their support of this project. We also wish to thank the Army Research Office for their financial support under the grant number W911NF-10-1-0470.

# Contents

# Chapter 1
# A Formal Model for a System's Attack Surface

Pratyusa K. Manadhata and Jeannette M. Wing

**Abstract** Practical software security metrics and measurements are essential for secure software development. In this chapter, we introduce the measure of a software system's *attack surface* as an indicator of the system's security. The larger the attack surface, the more insecure the system. We formalize the notion of a system's attack surface using an I/O automata model of the system and introduce an *attack surface metric* to measure the attack surface in a systematic manner. Our metric is agnostic to a software system's implementation language and is applicable to systems of all sizes. Software developers can use the metric in multiple phases of the software development process to improve software security. Similarly, software consumers can use the metric in their decision making process to compare alternative software.

## 1.1 Introduction

Measurement of security, both qualitatively and quantitatively, has been a long standing challenge to the research community and is of practical import to software industry today [7, 28, 22, 29]. There is a growing demand for secure software as we are increasingly depending on software in our day-to-day life. The software industry has responded to the demands by increasing effort for creating "more secure" products and services (e.g., Microsoft's Trustworthy Computing Initiative and SAP's Software LifeCycle Security efforts). How can industry determine whether this effort is paying off and how can consumers determine whether industry's effort has made a difference? We need security metrics and measurements to gauge progress with respect to security; software developers can use metrics to quantify

Pratyusa K. Manadhata
HP Labs, 5 Vaughn Dr, Princeton, NJ 08540, e-mail: manadhata@cmu.edu

Jeannette M. Wing
Computer Science Department, Carnegie Mellon University, Pittsburgh, PA 15213 e-mail: wing@cs.cmu.edu

the improvement in security from one version of their software to another and software consumers can use metrics to compare alternative software that provide the same functionality.

In this chapter, we formalize the notion of a system's *attack surface* and use the measure of a system's attack surface as an indicator of the system's security. Intuitively, a system's attack surface is the set of ways in which an adversary can enter the system and potentially cause damage. Hence the larger the attack surface, the more insecure the system. We also introduce an *attack surface metric* to measure a system's attack surface in a systematic manner.

Our metric does not preclude future use of the attack surface notion to define other security metrics and measurements. In this chapter, we use the attack surface metric in a *relative* manner, i.e., given two systems, we compare their attack surface measurements to indicate whether one is more secure than another with respect to the attack surface metric. Also, we use the attack surface metric to compare only *similar* systems, i.e., different versions of the same system (e.g., different versions of the Windows operating system) or different systems with similar functionality (e.g., different File Transfer Protocol (FTP) servers). We leave other contexts of use for both notions—attack surface and attack surface metric—as future work.

## 1.1.1 Motivation

Our attack surface metric is useful to both software developers and software consumers.

Software vendors have traditionally focused on improving code quality to improve software security and quality. The code quality improvement effort aims toward reducing the number of design and coding errors in software. An error causes software to behave differently from the intended behavior as defined by the software's specification; a vulnerability is an error that can be exploited by an attacker. In principle, we can use formal correctness proof techniques to identify and remove all errors in software with respect to a given specification and hence remove all its vulnerabilities. In practice, however, building large and complex software devoid of errors, and hence security vulnerabilities, remains a very difficult task. First, specifications, in particular explicit assumptions, can change over time so something that was not an error can become an error later. Second, formal specifications are rarely written in practice. Third, formal verification tools used in practice to find and fix errors, including specific security vulnerabilities such as buffer overruns, usually trade soundness for completeness or vice versa. Fourth, we do not know the vulnerabilities of the future, i.e., the errors present in software for which exploits will be developed in the future.

Software vendors have to embrace the hard fact that their software will ship with both known and future vulnerabilities in them and many of those vulnerabilities will be discovered and exploited. They can, however, minimize the risk associated with the exploitation of these vulnerabilities. One way to minimize the risk is by reducing the attack surfaces of their software. A smaller attack surface makes the exploitation of the vulnerabilities harder and lowers the damage of exploitation and hence mitigates the security risk. As shown in Figure 1.1, the code quality effort and the attack surface reduction approach are complementary; a complete risk mitigation strategy requires a combination of both. Hence software developers can use our metric as a tool in the software development process to reduce their software's attack surfaces.

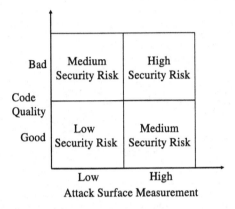

**Fig. 1.1** Attack Surface Reduction and Code Quality Improvement are complementary approaches for mitigating security risk and improving software security.

Software consumers often face the task of choosing one software product from a set of competing and alternative products that provide similar functionality. For example, system administrators often make a choice between different available operating systems, web servers, database servers, and FTP servers for their organization. Several factors such as ease of installation, maintenance, and use, and interoperability with existing enterprise software are relevant to software selection; security, however, is a quality that many consumers care about today and will use in choosing one software system over another. Hence software consumers can use our metric to measure the attack surfaces of alternative software and use the measurements as a guide in their decision making process.

## 1.1.2 Attack Surface Metric

We know from the past that many attacks, e.g., exploiting a buffer overflow error, on a system take place by sending data from the system's operating environment into the system. Similarly, many other attacks, e.g., symlink attacks, on a system take place because the system sends data into its environment. In both these types of attacks, an attacker connects to a system using the system's *channels* (e.g., sockets), invokes the system's *methods* (e.g., API), and sends *data items* (e.g., input strings) into the system or receives data items from the system. An attacker can also send data indirectly into a system by using data items that are persistent (e.g., files). An attacker can send data into a system by writing to a file that the system later reads. Similarly, an attacker can receive data indirectly from the system by using shared persistent data items. Hence an attacker uses a system's methods, channels, and data items present in the system's environment to attack the system. We collectively refer to a system's methods, channels, and data items as the system's *resources* and thus define a system's attack surface in terms of the system's resources (Figure 1.2).

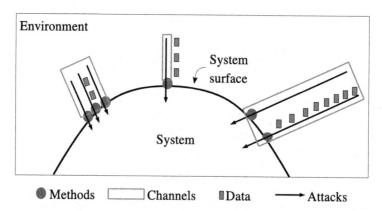

**Fig. 1.2** Intuitively, a system's attack surface is the subset of the system's resources (methods, channels, and data) used in attacks on the system.

Not all resources, however, are part of the attack surface and not all resources contribute equally to the attack surface measurement. In order to measure a system's attack surface, we need to identify the relevant resources that are part of the system's attack surface and to determine the contribution of each such resource to the system's attack surface measurement. A resource is part of the attack surface if an attacker can use the resource in attacks on the system; we introduce an *entry point and exit point framework* to identify these relevant resources. A resource's contribution to the attack surface measurement reflects the likelihood of the resource being used in attacks. For example, a method running with `root` privilege is more likely to be used in attacks than a method running with `non-root` privilege. We introduce the notion of a *damage potential-effort ratio* to estimate a resource's contribution to the attack surface measurement. A system's attack surface measurement is the total contribution of the resources along the methods, channels, and data dimensions; the measurement indicates the level of damage an attacker can potentially cause to the system and the effort required for the attacker to cause such damage. Given two systems, we compare their attack surface measurements to indicate, along each of the three dimensions, whether one is more secure than the other with respect to the attack surface metric.

A system's attack surface measurement does not represent the system's code quality; hence a large attack surface measurement does not imply that the system has many vulnerabilities and having few vulnerabilities in a system does not imply a small attack surface measurement. Instead, a larger attack surface measurement indicates that an attacker is likely to exploit the vulnerabilities present in the system with less effort and cause more damage to the system. Since a system's code is likely to contain vulnerabilities, it is prudent for software developers to reduce their software's attack surfaces and for software consumers to choose software with smaller attack surfaces to mitigate security risk.

### *1.1.3 Roadmap*

The rest of this chapter is organized as follows. We briefly discuss the inspiration behind our research in Section 1.2. In Section 1.3, we introduce the *entry point and exit point framework* based on the I/O automata model and define a system's attack surface in terms of the framework. In Section 1.4, we introduce the notions of *damage potential* and *effort* to estimate a resource's contribution to the attack surface; we also define a qualitative measure of the attack surface. We define a *quantitative* measure of the attack surface and introduce an *abstract method* to quantify the attack surface in Section 1.5. In Section 1.6, we briefly discuss empirical attack surface measurement results and validation studies. We compare our work with related work in Section 1.7 and conclude with a discussion of future work in Section 1.8.

## 1.2 Motivation

Our research on attack surface measurement is inspired by Michael Howard's Relative Attack Surface Quotient (RASQ) measurements [12]. We generalized Howard's method and applied the method to four versions of the Linux operating system [20].

### *1.2.1 Windows Measurements*

Michael Howard of Microsoft informally introduced the notion of attack surface for the Windows operating system and Pincus and Wing further elaborated on Howard's informal notion [11]. The first step in Howard's method is the identification of the *attack vectors* of Windows, i.e., the features of Windows often used in attacks on Windows. Examples of such features are services running on Windows, open sockets, dynamic web pages, and enabled guest accounts. Not all features, however, are equally likely to be used in attacks on Windows. For example, a service running as SYSTEM is more likely to be attacked than a service running as an ordinary user. Hence the second step in Howard's method is the assignment of weights to the attack vectors to reflect their *attackability*, i.e., the likelihood of a feature being used in attacks on Windows. The weight assigned to an attack vector is the attack vector's contribution to the attack surface. The final step in Howard's method is the estimation of the total attack surface by adding the weighted counts of the attack vectors; for each instance of an attack vector, the attack vector's weight is added to the total attack surface.

Howard, Pincus, and Wing applied Howard's measurement method to seven versions of the Windows operating system. They identified twenty attack vectors for Windows based on the history of attacks on Windows and then assigned weights to the attack vectors based on their expert knowledge of Windows. The measurement method was adhoc in nature and was based on intuition; the measurement results, however, confirmed perceived belief about the relative security of the seven versions of Windows. For example, Windows 2000 was perceived to have improved security compared to Windows NT [16]. The measurement results showed that Windows 2000 has a smaller attack surface than Windows NT; hence the measurements reflected the general perception. Similarly, the measurements showed that Windows Server 2003 has the smallest attack surface among the seven versions. The measurement is consistent with observed behavior in several ways, e.g., the relative susceptibility of the versions to worms such as Code Red and Nimda.

### 1.2.2 Linux Measurements

We applied Howard's measurement method to four versions of Linux (three RedHat and one Debian) to understand the challenges in applying the method and then to define an improved measurement method.

Howard's method did not have a formal definition of a system's attack vectors. Hence there was no systematic way to identify Linux's attack vectors. We used the history of attacks on Linux to identify Linux's attack vectors. We identified the features of Linux appearing in public vulnerability bulletins such MITRE Common Vulnerability and Exposures (CVE), Computer Emergency Response Team (CERT) Advisories, Debian Security Advisories, and Red Hat Security Advisories; these features are often used in attacks on Linux. We categorized these features into fourteen attack vectors.

Howard, Pincus, and Wing used their intuition and expertise of Windows security to assign weights in the Windows measurements. Their method, however, did not include any suggestions on assigning weights to other software systems' attack vectors. We could not determine a systematic way to assign weights to Linux's attack vectors. Hence we did not assign explicit numeric weights to the attack vectors; we assumed that each attack vector has the same weight. We then counted the number of instances of each attack vector for the four versions of Linux and compared the numbers to get a relative measure of the four versions' attack surfaces.

Our measurements showed that the attack surface notion held promise; e.g., Debian was perceived to be a more secure OS and that perception was reflected in our measurement. We, however, identified two shortcomings in the measurement method. First, Howard's method is based on informal notions of a system's attack surface and attack vectors; hence there is no systematic method to identify the attack vectors and to assign weights to them. Second, the method requires a security expert (e.g., Howard for Windows), minimally to enumerate attack vectors and assign weights to them. Thus, taken together, non-experts cannot systematically apply his method easily.

Our research on defining a *systematic* attack surface measurement method is motivated by our above findings. We use the entry point and exit point framework to identify the relevant resources that contribute to a system's attack surface and we use the notion of the damage potential-effort ratio to estimate the weights of each such resource. Our measurement method entirely avoids the need to identify the attack vectors. Our method does not require a security expert; hence software developers with little security expertise can use the method. Furthermore, our method is applicable, not just to operating systems, but also to a wide variety of software such as web servers, IMAP servers, and application software.

## 1.3 I/O Automata Model

In this section, we introduce the entry point and exit point framework and use the framework to define a system's attack surface. Informally, a system's *entry points* are the ways through which data "enters" into the system from its environment and *exit points* are the ways through which data "exits" from the system to its environment. Many attacks on software systems require an attacker either to send data into a system or to receive data from a system; hence a system's entry points and the exit points act as the basis for attacks on the system.

### 1.3.1 I/O Automaton

We model a system and the entities present in its environment as I/O automata [18]. We chose I/O automata as our model for two reasons. First, our notions of entry points and exit points map naturally to an I/O automaton's *input actions* and *output actions*. Second, the I/O automaton's *composition* property allows us to easily reason about a system's attack surface in a given environment.

An I/O automaton, $A = \langle sig(A), states(A), start(A), steps(A) \rangle$, is a four tuple consisting of an *action signature*, $sig(A)$, that partitions a set, $acts(A)$, of *actions* into three disjoint sets, $in(A)$, $out(A)$, and $int(A)$, of *input, output* and *internal* actions, respectively, a set, $states(A)$, of *states*, a non-empty set, $start(A) \subseteq states(A)$, of *start states*, and a *transition relation*, $steps(A) \subseteq states(A) \times acts(A) \times states(A)$. An I/O automaton's environment generates input and transmits the input to the automaton using input actions. In contrast, the automaton generates output actions and internal actions autonomously and transmits output to its environment. Our model does not require an I/O automaton to be *input-enabled*, i.e., unlike a standard I/O automaton, input actions are not always enabled in our model. Instead, we assume that every action of an automaton is enabled in at least one reachable state of the automaton.

We construct an I/O automaton modeling a complex system by *composing* the I/O automata modeling the system's simpler components. When we compose a set of automata, we identify different automata's same-named actions; we identify an automaton's output action, $m$, with the input action $m$ of each automaton having $m$ as an input action. When an automaton having $m$ as an output action performs $m$, all automata having $m$ as an input action perform $m$ simultaneously. The composition of a set of I/O automata results in an I/O automaton.

### *1.3.2 Model*

Consider a set, $S$, of systems, a user, $U$, and a data store, $D$. For a given system, $s \in S$, we define its environment, $E_s = \langle U, D, T \rangle$, to be a three-tuple where $T = S \setminus \{s\}$ is the set of systems excluding $s$. The system $s$ interacts with its environment $E_s$; hence we define the entry points and exit points of $s$ with respect to $E_s$. Figure 1.3 shows a system, $s$, and its environment, $E_s = \langle U, D, \{s_1, s_2, \} \rangle$. For example, $s$ could be a web server and $s_1$ and $s_2$ could be an application server and a directory server, respectively.

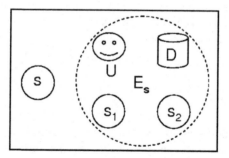

**Fig. 1.3** A system, $s$, and its environment, $E_s$.

We model every system $s \in S$ as an I/O automaton, $\langle sig(s), states(s), start(s), steps(s) \rangle$. We model the methods in $s$'s codebase as actions of the I/O automaton. We specify the actions using pre and post conditions: for an action, $m$, $m.pre$ and $m.post$ are the pre and post conditions of $m$, respectively. A state, $st \in states(s)$, of $s$ is a mapping of the state *variables* to their *values*: $st: Var \rightarrow Val$. An action's pre and post conditions are first order predicates on the state variables. A state transition, $\langle st, m, st' \rangle \in steps(s)$, is the invocation of an action $m$ in state $st$ resulting in state $st'$. An *execution* of $s$ is an alternating sequence of actions and states beginning with a start state and a *schedule* of an execution is a subsequence of the execution consisting only of the actions appearing in the execution.

Every system has a set of *communication channels*. A system, $s$'s, channels are the means by which the user $U$ or any system $s_1 \in T$ communicates with $s$. Specific examples of channels are TCP/UDP sockets and named pipes. We model each channel of a system as a special state variable of the system.

We also model the user $U$ and the data store $D$ as I/O automata. The user $U$ and the data store $D$ are global with respect to the systems in $S$. For simplicity, we assume only one user $U$ present in the environment. $U$ represents the adversary who attacks the systems in $S$.

We model the data store $D$ as a separate entity to allow sharing of data among the systems in $S$. The data store $D$ is a set of typed *data items*. Specific examples of data items are strings, URLs, files, and cookies. For every data item, $d \in D$, $D$ has an output action, $read_d$, and an input action, $write_d$. A system, $s$, or the user $U$ reads $d$ from the data store through the invocation of $read_d$ and writes $d$ to the data store through the invocation of $write_d$. To model global sharing of the data items, corresponding to each data item $d \in D$, we add a state variable, $d$, to every system, $s \in S$, and the user $U$. When the system $s$ (or $U$) reads the data item $d$ from the data store, the value of the data item is written to the state variable $d$ of $s$ (or $U$). Similarly, when $s$ (or $U$) writes the data item $d$ to the data store, the value of the state variable $d$ of $s$ (or $U$) is written to the data item $d$ of the data store.

### 1.3.3 Entry Points

The methods in a system's codebase that receive data from the system's environment are the system's entry points. A system's methods can receive data directly or indirectly from the environment. A method, $m$, of a system, $s$, receives data items *directly* if either (i.) the user $U$ (Figure 1.4.a) or a system, $s'$, (Figure 1.4.b) in the environment invokes $m$ and passes data items as input to $m$, or (ii.) $m$ reads data items from the data store (Figure 1.4.c), or (iii.) $m$ invokes a method of a system, $s'$, in the environment and receives data items as results returned (Figure 1.4.d). A method is a *direct entry point* if it receives data items directly from the environment. Examples of the direct entry points of a web server are the methods in the API of the web server, the methods of the web server that read configuration files, and the methods of the web server that invoke the API of an application server.

In the I/O automata model, a system, $s$, can receive data from the environment if $s$ has an input action, $m$, and an entity in the environment has a same-named output action, $m$. When the entity performs the output action $m$, $s$ performs the input action $m$ and data is transmitted from the entity to $s$. We formalize the scenarios when a system, $s' \in T$, invokes $m$ (Figure 1.4.b) or when $m$ invokes a method of $s'$ (Figure 1.4.d) the same way, i.e., $s$ has an input action, $m$, and $s'$ has an output action, $m$.

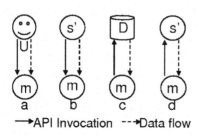

**Fig. 1.4** Direct Entry Point.          **Fig. 1.5** Indirect Entry Point.

**Definition 1.1.** A *direct entry point* of the system $s$ is an input action, $m$, of $s$ such that either (i.) the user $U$ has the output action $m$ (Figure 1.4.a), or (ii.) a system, $s' \in T$, has the output action $m$ (Figure 1.4.b and Figure 1.4.d), or (iii.) the data store $D$ has the output action $m$ (Figure 1.4.c).

A method, $m$, of $s$ receives data items *indirectly* if either (i.) a method, $m_1$, of $s$ receives a data item, $d$, directly, and either $m_1$ passes $d$ as input to $m$ (Figure 1.5.a) or $m$ receives $d$ as result returned from $m_1$ (Figure 1.5.b), or (ii.) a method, $m_2$, of $s$ receives a data item, $d$, indirectly, and either $m_2$ passes $d$ as input to $m$ (Figure 1.5.c) or $m$ receives $d$ as result returned from $m_2$ (Figure 1.5.d). A method is an *indirect entry point* if it receives data items indirectly from the environment. For example, a method in the API of the web server that receives login information from a user might pass the information to another method in the authentication module; the method in the API is a direct entry point and the method in the authentication module is an indirect entry point.

In the I/O automata model, a system's internal actions are not visible to other systems in the environment. Hence we use an I/O automaton's internal actions to formalize the system's indirect entry points. We formalize data transmission using the pre and post conditions of a system's actions. If an input action, $m$, of a system, $s$, receives a data item, $d$, directly from the environment, then the subsequent behavior of the system $s$ depends on the value of $d$; hence $d$ appears in the post condition of $m$ and we write $d \in Res(m.post)$ where $Res : predicate \rightarrow 2^{Var}$ is a function such that for each post condition (or pre condition), $p$, $Res(p)$ is the set of resources appearing in $p$. Similarly, if an action, $m$, of $s$ receives a data item $d$ from another action, $m_1$, of $s$, then $d$ appears in the post condition of $m_1$ and in the pre condition of $m$. Similar to the direct entry points, we formalize the scenarios Figure 1.5.a and Figure 1.5.b the same way and the scenarios Figure 1.5.c and Figure 1.5.d the same way. We define indirect entry points recursively.

**Definition 1.2.** An *indirect entry point* of the system $s$ is an internal action, $m$, of $s$ such that either (i.) $\exists$ direct entry point, $m_1$, of $s$ such that $m_1.post \Rightarrow m.pre$ and $\exists$ a data item, $d$, such that $d \in Res(m_1.post) \wedge d \in Res(m.pre)$ (Figure 1.5.a and Figure 1.5.b), or (ii.) $\exists$ indirect entry point, $m_2$, of $s$ such that $m_2.post \Rightarrow m.pre$ and $\exists$ data item, $d$, such that $d \in Res(m_2.post) \wedge d \in Res(m.pre)$ (Figure 1.5.c and Figure 1.5.d).

The set of entry points of $s$ is the union of the set of direct entry points and the set of indirect entry points of $s$.

## 1.3.4 Exit Points

A system's methods that send data to the system's environment are the system's exit points. For example, a method that writes into a log file is an exit point. A system's methods can send data directly or indirectly into the environment. A method, $m$, of a system, $s$, sends data items *directly* if either (i.) the user $U$ (Figure 1.6.a) or a system, $s'$, (Figure 1.6.b) in the environment invokes $m$ and receives data items as results returned from $m$, or (ii.) $m$ writes data items to the data store (Figure 1.6.c), or (iii.) $m$ invokes a method of a system, $s'$, in the environment and passes data items as input (Figure 1.6.d).

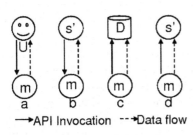

**Fig. 1.6** Direct Exit Point.                    **Fig. 1.7** Indirect Exit Point.

In the I/O automata model, a system, $s$, can send data to the environment if $s$ has an output action, $m$, and an entity in the environment has a same-named input action, $m$. When $s$ performs the output action $m$, the entity performs the input action $m$ and data is transmitted from $s$ to the entity.

**Definition 1.3.** A *direct exit point* of the system $s$ is an output action, $m$, of $s$ such that either (i.) the user $U$ has the input action $m$ (Figure 1.6.a), or (ii.) a system, $s' \in T$, has the input action $m$ (Figure 1.6.b and Figure 1.6.d) , or (iii.) the data store $D$ has the input action $m$ (Figure 1.6.c).

A method, $m$, of $s$ sends data items *indirectly* to the environment if either (i.) $m$ passes a data item, $d$, as input to a direct exit point, $m_1$ (Figure 1.7.a), or $m_1$ receives a data item, $d$, as result returned from $m$ (Figure 1.7.b), and $m_1$ sends $d$ directly to the environment, or (ii.) $m$ passes a data item, $d$, as input to an indirect exit point, $m_2$ (Figure 1.7.c), or $m_2$ receives a data item, $d$, as result returned from $m$ (Figure 1.7.d), and $m_2$ sends $d$ indirectly to the environment. A method $m$ of $s$ is an *indirect exit point* if $m$ sends data items indirectly to the environment.

Similar to indirect entry points, we formalize indirect exit points of a system using an I/O automaton's internal actions. If an output action, $m$, sends a data item, $d$, to the environment, then the subsequent behavior of the environment depends on the value of $d$. Hence $d$ appears in the pre condition of $m$ and in the post condition of the same-named input action $m$ of an entity in the environment. Again we define indirect exit points recursively.

**Definition 1.4.** An *indirect exit point* of the system $s$ is an internal action, $m$, of $s$ such that either (i.) $\exists$ a direct exit point, $m_1$, of $s$ such that $m.post \Rightarrow m_1.pre$ and $\exists$ a data item, $d$, such that $d \in Res(m.post) \wedge d \in Res(m_1.pre)$ (Figure 1.7.a and Figure 1.7.b), or (ii.) $\exists$ an indirect exit point, $m_2$, of $s$ such that $m.post \Rightarrow m_2.pre$ and $\exists$ a data item, $d$, such that $d \in Res(m.post) \wedge d \in Res(m_2.pre)$ (Figure 1.7.c and Figure 1.7.d).

The set of exit points of $s$ is the union of the set of direct exit points and the set of indirect exit points of $s$.

### 1.3.5 Channels

An attacker uses a system's channels to connect to the system and invoke a system's methods. Hence a system's channels act as another basis for attacks on the system. An entity in the environment can invoke a method, $m$, of a system, $s$, by using a channel, $c$, of $s$; hence in our I/O automata model, $c$ appears in the pre condition of a direct entry point (or exit point), $m$, i.e., $c \in Res(m.pre)$. In our model, every channel of $s$ must appear in the pre condition of at least one direct entry point (or exit point) of $s$. Similarly, at least one channel must appear in the pre condition of every direct entry point (or direct exit point).

### 1.3.6 Untrusted Data Items

The data store $D$ is a collection of persistent and transient data items. The data items that are visible to both a system, $s$, and the user $U$ across $s$'s different executions are $s$'s persistent data items. Specific examples of persistent data items are files, cookies, database records, and registry entries. The persistent data items are shared between $s$ and $U$, hence $U$ can use the persistent data items to send (receive) data indirectly into (from) $s$. For example, $s$ might read a file from the data store after $U$ writes the file to the data store. Hence the persistent data items act as another basis for attacks on $s$. An *untrusted data item* of a system, $s$, is a persistent data item, $d$, such that a direct entry point of $s$ reads $d$ from the data store or a direct exit point of $s$ writes $d$ to the data store.

**Definition 1.5.** An *untrusted data item* of a system, $s$, is a persistent data item, $d$, such that either (i.) $\exists$ a direct entry point, $m$, of $s$ such that $d \in Res(m.post)$, or (ii.) $\exists$ a direct exit point, $m$, of $s$ such that $d \in Res(m.pre)$.

Notice that an attacker sends (receives) the transient data items directly into (from) $s$ by invoking $s$'s direct entry points (direct exit points). Since $s$'s direct entry points (direct exit points) act as a basis for attacks on $s$, we do not consider the transient data items as a different basis for attacks on $s$. The transient data items are untrusted data items; they are, however, already "counted" in our definition of direct entry points and direct exit points.

### 1.3.7 Attack Surface Definition

A system's attack surface is the subset of its resources that an attacker can use to attack the system. An attacker can use a system's entry points and exit points, channels, and untrusted data items to send (receive) data into (from) the system to attack the system. Hence the set of entry points and exit points, the set of channels, and the set of untrusted data items are the relevant subset of resources that are part of the attack surface.

**Definition 1.6.** Given a system, $s$, and its environment, $E_s$, $s$'s attack surface is the triple, $\langle M^{E_s}, C^{E_s}, I^{E_s} \rangle$, where $M^{E_s}$ is the set of entry points and exit points, $C^{E_s}$ is the set of channels, and $I^{E_s}$ is the set of untrusted data items of $s$.

Notice that we define $s$'s entry points and exit points, channels, and data items with respect to the given environment $E_s$. Hence $s$'s attack surface, $\langle M^{E_s}, C^{E_s}, I^{E_s} \rangle$, is with respect to the environment $E_s$. We compare the attack surfaces of two similar systems (i.e., different versions of the same software or different software that provide similar functionality) along the methods, channels, and data dimensions with respect to the same environment to determine if one has a larger attack surface than another.

**Definition 1.7.** Given an environment, $E = \langle U, D, T \rangle$, the attack surface, $\langle M_A^E, C_A^E, I_A^E \rangle$, of a system, $A$, is larger than the attack surface, $\langle M_B^E, C_B^E, I_B^E \rangle$, of a system, $B$, iff either (i.) $M_A^E \supset M_B^E \wedge C_A^E \supseteq C_B^E \wedge I_A^E \supseteq I_B^E$, or (ii.) $M_A^E \supseteq M_B^E \wedge C_A^E \supset C_B^E \wedge I_A^E \supseteq I_B^E$, or (iii.) $M_A^E \supseteq M_B^E \wedge C_A^E \supseteq C_B^E \wedge I_A^E \supset I_B^E$.

### 1.3.8 Relation between Attack Surface and Potential Attacks

Consider a system, $A$, and its environment, $E_A = \langle U, D, T \rangle$. We model $A$'s interaction with the entities present in its environment as parallel composition, $A \| E_A$. Notice that an attacker can send data into $A$ by invoking $A$'s input actions and the attacker can receive data from $A$ when $A$ executes its output actions. Since an attacker attacks a system either by sending data into the system or by receiving data from the system, any schedule of the composition of $A$ and $E_A$ that contains $A$'s input actions or output actions is a potential attack on $A$. We denote the set of potential attacks on $s$ as $attacks(A)$.

**Definition 1.8.** Given a system, $s$, and its environment, $E_s = \langle U, D, T \rangle$, a *potential attack* on $s$ is a schedule, $\beta$, of the composition, $P = s || U || D || (||_{t \in T} t)$, such that an input action (or output action), $m$, of $s$ appears in $\beta$.

Note that $s$'s schedules may contain internal actions, but in order for a schedule to be an attack, the schedule must contain at least one input action or output action.

We model an attacker by a set of attacks in our I/O automata model. In other models of security, e.g., for cryptography, an attacker is modeled not just by a set of attacks but also by its power and privilege [6]. Examples of an attacker's power and privilege are the attacker's skill level (e.g., script kiddies, experts, and government agencies) and the attacker's resources (e.g., computing power, storage, and tools). We, however, do not model the attacker's power and privilege in our I/O automata model. Hence our notion of attack surface is independent of the attacker's power and privilege and is dependent only on a system's design and inherent properties.

We show that with respect to the same attacker and operating environment, if a system, $A$, has a larger attack surface compared to a similar system, $B$, then the number of potential attacks on $A$ is larger than $B$. Since $A$ and $B$ are similar systems, we assume both $A$ and $B$ have the same set of state variables and the same sets of resources except the ones appearing in the attack surfaces.

**Theorem 1.1.** *Given an environment,* $E = \langle U, D, T \rangle$, *if the attack surface,* $\langle M_A^E, C_A^E, I_A^E \rangle$, *of a system, $A$, is larger than the attack surface,* $\langle M_B^E, C_B^E, I_B^E \rangle$, *of a system, $B$, then the rest of the resources of $A$ and $B$ being equal* $attacks(A) \supset attacks(B)$.

*Proof.* (Sketch)

- Case i: $M_A^E \supset M_B^E \wedge C_A^E \supseteq C_B^E \wedge I_A^E \supseteq I_B^E$
  Without loss of generality, we assume that $M_A^E \setminus M_B^E = \{m\}$. Consider the compositions $P_A = A || U || D || (||_{t \in T} t)$ and $P_B = B || U || D || (||_{t \in T} t)$. Any method, $m \in M_B^E$, that is enabled in a state, $s_B$, of $B$ is also enabled in the corresponding state $s_A$ of $A$ and for any transition, $\langle s_B, m, s_B' \rangle$, of $P_B$, there is a corresponding transition, $\langle s_A, m, s_A' \rangle$, of $P_A$. Hence for any schedule $\beta \in attacks(B)$, $\beta \in attacks(A)$ and $attacks(A) \supseteq attacks(B)$.

  - Case a: $m$ is a direct entry point (or exit point) of $A$.
    Since $m$ is a direct entry point (or exit point), there is an output (or input) action $m$ of either $U$, $D$, or a system, $t \in T$. Hence there is at least one schedule, $\beta$, of $P_A$ containing $m$. Moreover, $\beta$ is not a schedule of $P_B$ as $m \notin M_B^E$. Since $\beta$ is a potential attack on $A$, $\beta \in attacks(A) \wedge \beta \notin attacks(B)$. Hence $attacks(A) \supset attacks(B)$.
  - Case b: m is an indirect entry point (or exit point) of $A$.
    Since $m$ is an indirect entry point (or exit point) of $A$, there is a direct entry point (or exit point), $m_A$, of $A$ such that $m_A.post \Rightarrow m.pre$ (or $m.post \Rightarrow$

$m_A.pre$). Hence there is at least one schedule, $\beta$, of $P_A$ such that $m$ follows $m_A$ (or $m_A$ follows $m$) in $\beta$. Moreover, $\beta$ is not an schedule of $P_B$ as $m \notin M_B^E$. Since $\beta$ is a potential attack on $A$, $\beta \in attacks(A) \wedge \beta \notin attacks(B)$. Hence $attacks(A) \supset attacks(B)$.

- Case ii: $M_A^E \supseteq M_B^E \wedge C_A^E \supset C_B^E \wedge I_A^E \supseteq I_B^E$
  Without loss of generality, we assume that $C_A^E \backslash C_B^E = \{c\}$. We know that $c$ appears in the pre condition of a direct entry point (or exit point), $m \in M_A^E$. But $c \notin C_B^E$, hence $m$ is never enabled in any state of $B$ and $m \notin M_B^E$. Hence $M_A^E \supset M_B^E$ and from Case i, $attacks(A) \supset attacks(B)$.
- Case iii: $M_A^E \supseteq M_B^E \wedge C_A^E \supseteq C_B^E \wedge I_A^E \supset I_B^E$
  The proof is similar to case ii.

Theorem 1.1 has practical significance in the software development process. The theorem shows that if we create a software system's newer version by only adding more resources to an older version, then assuming all resources are counted equally (see Section 1.4), the newer version has a larger attack surface and hence a larger number of potential attacks. Software developers should ideally strive towards reducing their software's attack surface from one version to another or if adding resources to the software (e.g., adding methods to an API), then do so knowingly that they are increasing the attack surface.

## 1.4 Damage Potential and Effort

Not all resources contribute equally to the measure of a system's attack surface because not all resources are equally likely to be used by an attacker. A resource's contribution to a system's attack surface depends on the resource's *damage potential*, i.e., the level of harm the attacker can cause to the system in using the resource in an attack and the *effort* the attacker spends to acquire the necessary access rights in order to be able to use the resource in an attack. The higher the damage potential or the lower the effort, the higher the contribution to the attack surface. In this section, we use our I/O automata model to formalize the notions of damage potential and effort. We model the damage potential and effort of a resource, $r$, of a system, $s$, as the state variables $r.dp$ and $r.ef$, respectively.

In practice, we estimate a resource's damage potential and effort in terms of the resource's attributes. Examples of attributes are method privilege, access rights, channel protocol, and data item type. Our estimation method is a specific instantiation of our general measurement framework. Our estimation of damage potential includes only technical impact (e.g., privilege elevation) and not business impact (e.g., monetary loss) though our framework does not preclude this generality. We do not make any assumptions about the attacker's capabilities or resources in estimating damage potential or effort.

We estimate a method's damage potential in terms of the method's *privilege*. An attacker gains the privilege of a method by using the method in an attack. For exam-

ple, the attacker gains `root` privilege by exploiting a buffer overflow in a method
running as `root`. The attacker can cause damage to the system after gaining `root`
privilege. The attacker uses a system's channels to connect to a system and send (receive) data to (from) a system. A channel's *protocol* imposes restrictions on the data
exchange allowed using the channel, e.g., a `TCP socket` allows raw bytes to be
exchanged whereas an `RPC endpoint` does not. Hence we estimate a channel's
damage potential in terms of the channel's protocol. The attacker uses persistent data
items to send (receive) data indirectly into (from) a system. A persistent data item's
*type* imposes restrictions on the data exchange, e.g., a `file` can contain executable
code whereas a `registry entry` can not. The attacker can send executable code
into the system by using a `file` in an attack, but the attacker can not do the same
using a `registry entry`. Hence we estimate a data item's damage potential in
terms of the data item's type. The attacker can use a resource in an attack if the
attacker has the required *access rights*. The attacker spends effort to acquire these
access rights. Hence for the three kinds of resources, i.e., method, channel, and data,
we estimate the effort the attacker needs to spend to use a resource in an attack in
terms of the resource's access rights.

We assume that we have a total ordering, $\succ$, among the values of each of the
six attributes, i.e., method privilege and access rights, channel protocol and access
rights, and data item type and access rights. In practice, we impose these total orderings using our knowledge of a system and its environment. For example, an attacker
can cause more damage to a system by using a method running with `root` privilege than a method running with `non-root` privilege; hence `root` $\succ$ `non-root`.
We use these total orderings to compare the contributions of resources to the attack
surface. Abusing notation, we write $r_1 \succ r_2$ to express that a resource, $r_1$, makes a
larger contribution to the attack surface than a resource, $r_2$.

**Definition 1.9.** Given two resources, $r_1$ and $r_2$, of a system, $A$, $r_1 \succ r_2$ iff either
(i.) $r_1.dp \succ r_2.dp \wedge r_2.ef \succ r_1.ef$, or (ii.) $r_1.dp = r_2.dp \wedge r_2.ef \succ r_1.ef$, or (iii.)
$r_1.dp \succ r_2.dp \wedge r_2.ef = r_1.ef$.

**Definition 1.10.** Given two resources, $r_1$ and $r_2$, of a system, $A$, $r_1 \succeq r_2$ iff either (i.)
$r_1 \succ r_2$ or (ii.) $r_1.dp = r_2.dp \wedge r_2.ef = r_1.ef$.

### 1.4.1 Modeling Damage Potential and Effort

In our I/O automata model, we use an action's pre and post conditions to formalize
effort and damage potential, respectively. We present a parametric definition of an
action, $m$, of a system, $s$, below. For simplicity, we assume that the entities in the
environment connect to $s$ using only one channel, $c$, to invoke $m$ and $m$ either reads
or writes only one data item, $d$.

$m(MA,CA,DA,MB,CB,DB)$
$\quad pre : P_{pre} \wedge MA \succeq m.ef \wedge CA \succeq c.ef \wedge DA \succeq d.ef$

$$post : P_{post} \wedge MB \succeq m.dp \wedge CB \succeq c.dp \wedge DB \succeq d.dp$$

The parameters $MA$, $CA$, and $DA$ represent the highest method access rights, channel access rights, and data access rights acquired by an attacker so far, respectively. Similarly, the parameters $MB$, $CB$, and $DB$ represent the benefit to the attacker in using the method $m$, the channel $c$, and the data item $d$ in an attack, respectively. $R_{pre}$ is the part of $m$'s pre condition that does not involve access rights. The clause, $MA \succeq m.ef$, captures the condition that the attacker has the required access rights to invoke $m$; the other two clauses in the pre condition are analogous. Similarly, $R_{post}$ is the part of $m$'s post condition that does not involve benefit. The clause, $MB \succeq m.dp$, captures the condition that the attacker gets the expected benefit after the execution of $m$; the rest of the clauses are analogous.

We use the total orderings $\succ$ among the values of the attributes to define the notion of weaker (and stronger) pre conditions and post conditions. We first introduce a predicate, $\langle m_1, c_1, d_1 \rangle \succ_{at} \langle m_2, c_2, d_2 \rangle$, to compare the values of an attribute, $at \in \{dp, ef\}$, of the two triples, $\langle m_1, c_1, d_1 \rangle$ and $\langle m_2, c_2, d_2 \rangle$. We later use the predicate to compare pre and post conditions.

**Definition 1.11.** Given two methods, $m_1$ and $m_2$, two channels, $c_1$ and $c_2$, two data items, $d_1$ and $d_2$, and an attribute, $at \in \{dp, ef\}$, $\langle m_1, c_1, d_1 \rangle \succ_{at} \langle m_2, c_2, d_2 \rangle$ iff either (i.) $m_1.at \succ m_2.at \wedge c_1.at \succeq c_2.at \wedge d_1.at \succeq d_2.at$, or (ii.) $m_1.at \succeq m_2.at \wedge c_1.at \succ c_2.at \wedge d_1.at \succeq d_2.at$ or (iii.) $m_1.at \succeq m_2.at \wedge c_1.at \succeq c_2.at \wedge d_1.at \succ d_2.at$.

Consider two methods, $m_1$ and $m_2$. We say that $m_1$ has a weaker pre condition than $m_2$ iff $(m_1.R_{pre} = m_2.R_{pre}) \wedge (m_2.pre \Rightarrow m_1.pre)$. We only compare the parts of the pre conditions involving the access rights and assume that the rest of the pre conditions are the same for both $m_1$ and $m_2$. Notice that if $m_1$ has a lower access rights level than $m_2$, i.e., $m_2.ef \succ m_1.ef$, then for all access rights levels $MA$, $(MA \succeq m_2.ef) \Rightarrow (MA \succeq m_1.ef)$; the rest of the clauses in the pre conditions are analogous. Hence we define the notion of weaker pre condition as follows.

**Definition 1.12.** Given the pre condition, $m_1.pre = (R_{pre} \wedge MA \succeq m_1.ef \wedge CA \succeq c_1.ef \wedge DA \succeq d_1.ef)$, of a method, $m_1$, and the pre condition, $m_2.pre = (R_{pre} \wedge MA \succeq m_2.ef \wedge CA \succeq c_2.ef \wedge DA \succeq d_2.ef)$, of a method, $m_2$, $m_2.pre \Rightarrow m_1.pre$ if $\langle m_2, c_2, d_2 \rangle \succ_{ef} \langle m_1, c_1, d_1 \rangle$.

We say that $m_1$ has a weaker post condition than $m_2$ iff $(m_1.R_{post} = m_2.R_{post}) \wedge (m_1.post \Rightarrow m_2.post)$.

**Definition 1.13.** Given the post condition, $m_1.post = (R_{post} \wedge MB \succeq m_1.dp \wedge CB \succeq c_1.dp \wedge DB \succeq d_1.dp)$, of a method, $m_1$ and the post condition, $m_2.post = (R_{post} \wedge MB \succeq m_2.dp \wedge CB \succeq c_2.dp \wedge DB \succeq d_2.dp)$, of a method, $m_2$, $m_1.post \Rightarrow m_2.post$ if $\langle m_1, c_1, d_1 \rangle \succ_{dp} \langle m_2, c_2, d_2 \rangle$.

### 1.4.2 Attack Surface Measurement

Given two systems, $A$ and $B$, if $A$ has a larger attack surface than $B$ (Definition 1.7), then everything else being equal, it is easy to see that $A$ has a larger attack surface measurement than $B$. It is also possible that even though $A$ and $B$ both have the same attack surface, if a resource, $A.r$, belonging to $A$'a attack surface makes a larger contribution than the same-named resource, $B.r$, belonging to $B$'s attack surface, then everything else being equal $A$ has a larger attack surface measurement than $B$.

Given the attack surface, $\langle M_A^E, C_A^E, I_A^E \rangle$, of a system, $A$, we denote the set of re-sources belonging to $A$'s attack surface as $R_A = M_A^E \cup C_A^E \cup I_A^E$. Note that from Definition 1.7, if $A$ has a larger attack surface than $B$, then $R_A \supset R_B$.

**Definition 1.14.** Given an environment, $E = \langle U, D, T \rangle$, the attack surface, $\langle M_A^E, C_A^E, I_A^E \rangle$, of a system, $A$, and the attack surface, $\langle M_B^E, C_B^E, I_B^E \rangle$, of a system, $B$, $A$ has a larger attack surface measurement than $B$ ($A \gg B$) iff either

1. $A$ has a larger attack surface than $B$ (i.e., $R_A \supset R_B$) and $\forall r \in R_B.A.r \succeq B.r$, or
2. $M_A^E = M_B^E \wedge C_A^E = C_B^E \wedge I_A^E = I_B^E$ (i.e., $R_A = R_B$) and there is a nonempty set, $\mathbb{R}_{AB} \subseteq R_B$, of resources such that $\forall r \in \mathbb{R}_{AB}.A.r \succ B.r$ and $\forall r \in (R_B \setminus \mathbb{R}_{AB}).A.r = B.r$.

From Definitions 1.7 and 1.14, $\gg$ is transitive. For example, given three systems, $A$, $B$, and $C$, if $A$ has a larger attack surface measurement than $B$ and $B$ has a larger attack surface measurement than $C$, then $A$ has a larger attack surface measurement than $C$.

**Theorem 1.2.** *Given an environment,* $E = \langle U, D, T \rangle$, *the attack surface,* $R_A$, *of a system,* $A$, *the attack surface,* $R_B$, *of a system,* $B$, *and the attack surface,* $C$, *of a system,* $R_C$, *if* $A \gg B$ *and* $B \gg C$, *then* $A \gg C$.

*Proof.* (Sketch) From Definition 1.14, $A$'s attack surface measurement can be larger than $B$'s in two different ways. Similarly, $B$'s attack surface measurement can be larger than $C$'s in two different ways. Hence we consider four different cases in proving the theorem.

- Case 1: $R_A \supset R_B$ and $\forall r \in R_B.A.r \succeq B.r$.

    - Case 1.1: $R_B \supset R_C$ and $\forall r \in R_C.B.r \succeq C.r$.
      Since $R_A \supset R_B$ and $R_B \supset R_C$, $R_A \supset R_C$. Also, since $R_B \supset R_C$ and $\forall r \in R_B.A.r \succeq B.r$, $\forall r \in R_C.A.r \succeq B.r$. From the assumptions of Case 1.1, $\forall r \in R_C.B.r \succeq C.r$. Hence $\forall r \in R_C.A.r \succeq B.r \succeq C.r$. Hence $A \gg C$.
    - Case 1.2: $R_B = R_C$ and there is a nonempty set, $\mathbb{R}_{BC} \subseteq R_C$, of resources such that $\forall r \in \mathbb{R}_{BC}.B.r \succ C.r$ and $\forall r \in (R_C \setminus \mathbb{R}_{BC}).B.r = C.r$.
      Since $R_A \supset R_B$ and $R_B = R_C$, $R_A \supset R_C$. Consider a resource, $r \in R_C$. From the assumptions of Case 1.2, if $r \in \mathbb{R}_{BC}$, then $B.r \succ C.r$, and if $r \in (R_C \setminus \mathbb{R}_{BC})$, then $B.r = C.r$. Hence $\forall r \in R_C.B.r \succeq C.r$. Also, from the assumptions of Case 1, $\forall r \in R_B.A.r \succeq B.r$. Since $R_B = R_C$, $\forall r \in R_C.A.r \succeq B.r \succeq C.r$. Hence $A \gg C$.

- Case 2: $R_A = R_B$ and there is a nonempty set, $\mathbb{R}_{AB} \subseteq R_B$, of resources such that $\forall r \in \mathbb{R}_{AB}.A.r \succ B.r$ and $\forall r \in (R_B \setminus \mathbb{R}_{AB}).A.r = B.r$.

  - Case 2.1: $R_B \supset R_C$ and $\forall r \in R_C.B.r \succeq C.r$.
    The proof is similar to Case 1.2.
  - Case 2.2: $R_B = R_C$ and there is a nonempty set, $\mathbb{R}_{BC} \subseteq R_C$, of resources such that $\forall r \in \mathbb{R}_{BC}.B.r \succ C.r$ and $\forall r \in (R_C \setminus \mathbb{R}_{BC}).B.r = C.r$.
    Since $R_A = R_B$ and $R_B = R_C$, $R_A = R_C$. Consider the set, $\mathbb{R}_{AC} = \mathbb{R}_{AB} \cup \mathbb{R}_{BC}$, of resources. We shall prove that $\forall r \in \mathbb{R}_{AC}.A.r \succ C.r$. Consider a resource, $r \in \mathbb{R}_{AC}$. If $r \in \mathbb{R}_{AB} \cap \mathbb{R}_{BC}$, then $A.r \succ B.r \succ C.r$. If $r \in \mathbb{R}_{AB} \setminus \mathbb{R}_{BC}$, then $A.r \succ B.r = C.r$. Similarly, if $r \in \mathbb{R}_{BC} \setminus \mathbb{R}_{AB}$, then $A.r = B.r \succ C.r$. Hence $\forall r \in \mathbb{R}_{AC}.A.r \succ C.r$. Also, from the assumptions of Case 2 and Case 2.2, $\forall r \in R_C \setminus \mathbb{R}_{AC}.A.r = C.r$. Hence $A \gg C$.

The transitivity of $\gg$ has practical implications for attack surface reduction; while reducing $A$'s attack surface measurement compared to $C$'s, software developers should focus on the set $\mathbb{R}_{AC}$ of resources instead of either the set $\mathbb{R}_{AB}$ or the set $\mathbb{R}_{BC}$.

### 1.4.3 Relation Between Attack Surface Measurement and Potential Attacks

We show that with respect to the same attacker and operating environment, if a system, $A$, has a larger attack surface measurement compared to a system, $B$, then the number of potential attacks on $A$ is larger than $B$.

**Theorem 1.3.** *Given an environment, $E = \langle U, D, T \rangle$, if the attack surface of a system $A$ is the triple $\langle M_A^E, C_A^E, I_A^E \rangle$, the attack surface of of a system, $B$, is the triple $\langle M_B^E, C_B^E, I_B^E \rangle$, and $A$ has a larger attack surface measurement than $B$, then $attacks(A) \supseteq attacks(B)$.*

*Proof.* (Sketch)

- Case 1: This is a corollary of Theorem 1.1.
- Case 2: $M_A^E = M_B^E \wedge C_A^E = C_B^E \wedge I_A^E = I_B^E$
  Without loss of generality, we assume that $R = \{r\}$ and $A.r \succ B.r$.

  - Case i: $(B.r).ef \succ (A.r).ef \wedge (A.r).dp \succ (B.r).dp$
    From definitions 1.12 and 1.13, there is an action, $m_A \in M_A^E$, that has a weaker precondition and a stronger post condition than the same-named action, $m_B \in M_B^E$, i.e.,

    $$(m_B.pre \Rightarrow m_A.pre) \wedge (m_A.post \Rightarrow m_B.post). \tag{1.1}$$

    Notice that any schedule of the composition $P_B$ (as defined in the proof sketch of Theorem 1.1) that does not contain $m_B$ is also a schedule of the composition

$P_A$. Now consider a schedule, $\beta$, of $P_B$ that contains $m_B$ and the following sequence of actions that appear in $\beta$:..$m_1 m_B m_2$... Hence,

$$(m_1.post \Rightarrow m_B.pre) \wedge (m_B.post \Rightarrow m_2.pre). \qquad (1.2)$$

From equations (1) and (2), $(m_1.post \Rightarrow m_B.pre \Rightarrow m_A.pre) \wedge (m_A.post \Rightarrow m_B.post \Rightarrow m_2.pre)$. Hence, $(m_1.post \Rightarrow m_A.pre) \wedge (m_A.post \Rightarrow m_2.pre)$. That is, we can replace the occurrences of $m_B$ in $\beta$ with $m_A$. Hence $\beta$ is also a schedule of the composition $P_A$ and $attacks(A) \supseteq attacks(B)$.

- Case ii and Case iii: The proof is similar to Case i.

Theorem 1.3 also has practical significance in the software development process. The theorem shows that if software developers modify the values of a resource's attributes and hence increase the resource's damage potential and/or decrease the resource's effort in their software's newer version, then all else being the same between the two versions, the newer version's attack surface measurement becomes larger and the number of potential attacks on the software increases.

## 1.5 A Quantitative Metric

In the previous section, we introduced a qualitative measure of a system's attack surface (Definition 1.14). The qualitative measure is an ordinal scale [5]; given two systems, we can only determine if one system has a relatively larger attack surface measurement than another. We, however, can not quantify the difference in the measurements.

We need a quantitative measure of the attack surface to quantify the difference in the attack surface measurements. We can also measure the absolute attack surface using the quantitative measure. In this section, we introduce a quantitative measure of the attack surface; the measure is a ratio scale. We quantify a resource's contribution to the attack surface in terms of a *damage potential-effort ratio*.

### 1.5.1 Damage Potential-Effort Ratio

In the previous section, in estimating a resource's contribution to the attack surface, we consider the resource's damage potential and effort in isolation. From an attacker's point of view, however, damage potential and effort are related; if the attacker gains higher privilege by using a method in an attack, then the attacker also gains the access rights of a larger set of methods. For example, the attacker can access only the methods with `authenticated` user access rights by gaining `authenticated` privilege, whereas the attacker can access methods with `authenticated` user and `root` access rights by gaining `root` privilege. The attacker might be willing to spend more effort to gain a higher privilege level that then enables the attacker to cause damage as well as gain more access rights. Hence we consider a resource's damage potential and effort in tandem and quantify a resource's contribution to the attack surface as a damage potential-effort ratio. The damage potential-effort ratio is similar to a cost-benefit ratio; the damage potential is the benefit to the attacker in using a resource in an attack and the effort is the cost to the attacker in using the resource.

We assume a function, $der_m$: method $\rightarrow \mathbb{Q}$, that maps each method to its damage potential-effort ratio belonging to the set, $\mathbb{Q}$, of rational numbers. Similarly, we assume a function, $der_c$: channel $\rightarrow \mathbb{Q}$, for the channels and a function, $der_d$: data item $\rightarrow \mathbb{Q}$, for the data items. In practice, however, we compute a resource's damage potential-effort ratio by assigning numeric values to the resource's attributes. For example, we compute a method's damage potential-effort ratio from the numeric values assigned to the method's privilege and access rights. We assign the numeric values according to the total orderings imposed on the attributes and based on our knowledge of a system and its environment. For example, we assume a method running as `root` has a higher damage potential than a method running as `non-root` user; hence `root` > `non-root` user in the total ordering and we assign a higher number to `root` than `non-root` user. The exact choice of the numeric values is subjective and depends on a system and its environment. Hence we cannot automate the process of numeric value assignment. We, however, provide guidelines to our users for numeric value assignment using parameter sensitivity analysis [20].

In terms of our formal I/O automata model, a method, $m$'s, damage potential determines how strong $m$'s post condition is. $m$'s damage potential determines the potential number of methods that $m$ can call and hence the potential number of methods that can follow $m$ in a schedule; the higher the damage potential, the larger the number of methods. Similarly, $m$'s effort determines the potential number of methods that can call $m$ and hence the potential number of methods that $m$ can follow in a schedule; the lower the effort, the larger the number of methods. Hence $m$'s damage potential-effort ratio, $der_m(m)$, determines the potential number of schedules in which $m$ can appear. Given two methods, $m_1$ and $m_2$, if $der_m(m_1) > der_m(m_2)$ then $m_1$ can potentially appear in more schedules (and hence more potential attacks) than $m_2$. Similarly, if a channel, $c$, (or a data item, $d$) appears in the pre condition of a method, $m$, then the damage potential-effort ratio of $c$ (or $d$) determines the potential number of schedules in which $m$ can appear. Hence we estimate a resource's contribution to the attack surface as the resource's damage potential-effort ratio.

### 1.5.2 Quantitative Attack Surface Measurement Method

We quantify a system's attack surface measurement along three dimensions: methods, channels, and data. We estimate the total contribution of the methods, the total contribution of the channels, and the total contribution of the data items to the attack surface.

**Definition 1.15.** Given the attack surface, $\langle M^{E_s}, C^{E_s}, I^{E_s} \rangle$, of a system, $s$, $s$'s attack surface measurement is the triple $\langle \sum_{m \in M^{E_s}} der_m(m), \sum_{c \in C^{E_s}} der_c(c), \sum_{d \in I^{E_s}} der_d(d) \rangle$.

We quantitatively measure a system's attack surface in the following three steps.

1. Given a system, $s$, and its environment, $E_s$, we identify a set, $M^{E_s}$, of entry points and exit points, a set, $C^{E_s}$, of channels, and a set, $I^{E_s}$, of untrusted data items of $s$.
2. We estimate the damage potential-effort ratio, $der_m(m)$, of each method $m \in M^{E_s}$, the damage potential-effort ratio, $der_c(c)$, of each channel $c \in C^{E_s}$, and the damage potential-effort ratio, $der_d(d)$, of each data item $d \in I^{E_s}$.
3. The measure of $s$'s attack surface is $\langle \sum_{m \in M^{E_s}} der_m(m), \sum_{c \in C^{E_s}} der_c(c), \sum_{d \in I^{E_s}} der_d(d) \rangle$.

Our measurement method is analogous to the risk estimation method used in risk modeling [9]. A system's attack surface measurement is an indication of the system's risk from attacks on the system. In risk modeling, the risk associated with a set, $E$, of events is $\sum_{e \in E} p(e)C(e)$ where an event, $e$'s, probability of occurrence is $p(e)$ and consequence is $C(e)$. The events in risk modeling are analogous to a system's resources in our measurement method. The probability of occurrence of an event is analogous to the probability of a successful attack on the system using a resource; if the attack is not successful, then the attacker does not benefit from the attack. For example, a buffer overrun attack using a method, $m$, will be successful only if $m$ has an exploitable buffer overrun vulnerability. Hence the probability, $p(m)$, associated with a method, $m$, is the probability that $m$ has an exploitable vulnerability. Similarly, the probability, $p(c)$, associated with a channel, $c$, is the probability that the method that receives (or sends) data from (to) $c$ has an exploitable vulnerability and the probability, $p(d)$, associated with a data item, $d$, is the probability that the method that reads or writes $d$ has an exploitable vulnerability. The consequence of an event is analogous to a resource's damage potential-effort ratio. The pay-off to the attacker in using a resource in an attack is proportional to the resource's damage potential-effort ratio; hence the damage potential-effort ratio is the consequence of a resource being used in an attack. The risk along $s$'s three dimensions is the triple, $\langle \sum_{m \in M^{E_s}} p(m)der_m(m), \sum_{c \in C^{E_s}} p(c)der_c(c), \sum_{d \in I^{E_s}} p(d) der_d(d) \rangle$, which is also the measure of $s$'s attack surface.

In practice, however, it is difficult to predict defects in software [4] and to estimate the likelihood of vulnerabilities in software [8]. Hence we take a conservative approach in our attack surface measurement method and assume that $p(m) = 1$ for all methods, i.e., every method has an exploitable vulnerability. We assume that even if a method does not have a known vulnerability now, it might have a future vulnerability not discovered so far. We similarly assume that $p(c) = 1$ for all channels and $p(d) = 1$ for all data items. With our conservative approach, the measure of $s$'s attack surface is the triple $\langle \sum_{m \in M^{E_s}} der_m(m), \sum_{c \in C^{E_s}} der_c(c), \sum_{d \in I^{E_s}} der_d(d) \rangle$.

Given two similar systems, $A$ and $B$, we compare their attack surface measurements along each of the three dimensions to determine if one system is more secure than another along that dimension. There is, however, a seeming contradiction in our measurement method with our intuitive notion of security. For example, consider a system, $A$, that has 1000 entry points each with a damage potential-effort ratio of 1 and a system, $B$, that has only one entry point with a damage potential-effort ratio of 999. A has a larger attack surface measurement whereas A is intuitively more secure. This contradiction is due to the presence of *extreme events*, i.e., events that have a significantly higher consequence compared to other events [9]. An entry point with a damage potential-effort ratio of 999 is analogous to an extreme event. In the presence of extreme events, the shortcomings of the risk estimation method used in the previous paragraph is well understood and the partitioned multiobjective risk method is recommended [2]. In our attack surface measurement method, however, we compare the attack surface measurements of similar systems, i.e., systems with comparable sets of resources and comparable damage potential-effort ratios of the resources; hence we do not expect extreme events such as the example shown to arise in practice.

## 1.6 Empirical Results

In this section, we briefly discuss our empirical attack surface measurements and exploratory validation studies. Our discussion focuses on the reasons behind each study; please see Manadhata and Wing for details about the studies [21].

### 1.6.1 Attack Surface Measurement Results

We introduced an abstract attack surface measurement method in the previous section. We instantiated the method for software implemented in the C programming language and demonstrated that our method is applicable to real world software. We measured the attack surfaces of two open source IMAP servers: Courier-IMAP 4.0.1 and Cyrus 2.2.10; we chose the IMAP servers due to their popularity. We considered only the code specific to the IMAP daemon in our measurements to obtain a fair comparison. The Courier and the Cyrus code bases contain nearly 33K and 34K lines of code specific to the IMAP daemon, respectively. We also measured the attack surfaces of two open source FTP daemons: ProFTPD 1.2.10 and Wu-FTPD 2.6.2. The ProFTP codebase contains 28K lines of C code and the Wu-FTP codebase contains 26K lines of C code. The measurement results conformed to our intuition. For example, the ProFTP project grew out of the Wu-FTP project and was designed and implemented from the ground up to be a more secure and configurable FTP server. Our measurements showed that ProFTPD is more secure than Wu-FTPD along the method dimension.

## 1.6.2 Validation Studies

A key challenge in security metrics research is the validation of a metric. Validating a software attribute's measure is hard in general [14]; security is a software attribute that is hard to measure and hence even harder to validate. To validate our metric, we conducted three exploratory empirical studies inspired by the software engineering research community's software metrics validation approaches [5].

In practice, validation approaches are based on distinguishing *measures* from *prediction systems*; measures are used to numerically characterize software attributes whereas prediction systems are used to predict software attributes' values. For example, lines of code (LOC) is a measure of software "length;" the measure becomes a prediction system if we use LOC to predict software "complexity." A software measure is validated by establishing that the measure is a proper numerical characterization of an attribute. Similarly, prediction systems are validated by establishing their accuracy via empirical means.

Our attack surface metric plays a dual role: the metric is a measure of a software attribute, i.e., the attack surface and also a prediction system to indicate the security risk of software. Hence we took a two-step approach for validation. First, we validated the measure by validating our attack surface measurement method. Second, we validated the prediction system by validating attack surface measurement results.

We conducted two empirical studies to validate our measurement method: a statistical analysis of data collected from Microsoft Security Bulletins and an expert user survey. Our approach is motivated by the notion of *convergent evidence* in Psychology [10]; since each study has its own strengths and weaknesses, the convergence in the studies' findings enhances our belief that the findings are valid and not methodological artifacts. Also, the statistical analysis is with respect to Microsoft Windows whereas the expert survey is with respect to Linux. Hence our validation approach is agnostic to operating system and system software.

We validated our metric's prediction system by establishing a positive correlation between attack surface measurements and software's security risk. First, we formally showed that a larger attack surface leads to a larger number of potential attacks on software in the I/O automata model (Section 1.3.8 and Section 1.4.3). Second, we established a relationship between attack surface measurements and security risk by analyzing vulnerability patches in open source software. A vulnerability patch reduces a system's security risk by removing an exploitable vulnerability from the system; hence we expect the patch to reduce the system's attack surface measurement. We demonstrated that a majority of patches in open source software, e.g., Firefox and ProFTP server, reduce the attack surface measurement. Third, we gathered anecdotal evidence from software industry to show that attack surface reduction mitigates security risk; for example, the Sasser worm, the Zotob worm, and the Nachi worm did not affect some versions of Windows due to reduction in their attack surfaces [13].

## *1.6.3 SAP Software Systems*

Our C measurements focused on software that are small in their code size and simple in their architectural design. We collaborated with SAP, the world's largest enterprise software company, to apply our method to SAP's enterprise-scale software implemented in Java. Our motivation behind the collaboration was two-fold. First, we wanted to demonstrate that our method scales to enterprise-scale software and is agnostic to implementation language. Second, we had the opportunity to interact closely with SAP's software developers and architects and get their feedback on improving our measurement method.

We instantiated our abstract measurement method for the Java programming language and implemented a tool to measure the attack surfaces of SAP software implemented in Java. We applied our method to three versions of a core SAP component. The measurement results conformed to the three versions' perceived relative security. We also identified multiple uses of attack surface measurements in the software development process. For example, attack surface measurements are useful in the design and development phase to mitigate security risk, in the testing and code inspection phase to guide manual effort, in the deployment phase to choose a secure configuration, and in the maintenance phase to guide vulnerability patch implementation.

## 1.7 Related Work

Our attack surface metric differs from prior work in three key aspects. First, our attack surface measurement is based on a system's inherent properties and is independent of any vulnerabilities present in the system. Previous work assumes the knowledge of the known vulnerabilities present in the system [1, 30, 25, 27, 23, 15]. In contrast, our identification of all entry points and exit points encompasses all known vulnerabilities as well as potential vulnerabilities not yet discovered or exploited. Moreover, a system's attack surface measurement indicates the security risk of the exploitation of the system's vulnerabilities; hence our metric is complementary to and can be used in conjunction with previous work.

Second, prior research on measurement of security has taken an *attacker-centric approach* [25, 27, 23, 15]. In contrast, we take a *system-centric approach*. The attacker-centric approach makes assumptions about attacker capabilities and resources whereas the system-centric approach assesses a system's security without reference to or assumptions about attacker capabilities [24]. Our attack surface measurement is based on a system's design and is independent of the attacker's capabilities and behavior; hence our metric can be used as a tool in the software design and development process.

Third, many of the prior works on quantification of security are conceptual in nature and haven't been applied to real software systems [1, 17, 15, 19, 26]. In contrast, we demonstrate the applicability of our metric to real systems by measuring the attack surfaces of two FTP servers, two IMAP servers, and three versions of an SAP software system.

Alves-Foss et al. use the System Vulnerability Index (SVI)–obtained by evaluating factors such as system characteristics, potentially neglectful acts, and potentially malevolent acts–as a measure of a system's vulnerability [1]. They, however, identify only the relevant factors of operating systems; their focus is on operating systems and not individual or generic software applications. Moreover, they assume that they can quantify all the factors that determine a system's SVI. In contrast, we assume that we can quantify a resource's damage potential and effort.

Littlewood et al. explore the use of probabilistic methods used in traditional reliability analysis in assessing the operational security of a system [17]. In their conceptual framework, they propose to use the effort made by an attacker to breach a system as an appropriate measure of the system's security. They, however, do not propose a concrete method to estimate the attacker effort.

Voas et al. propose a relative security metric based on a fault injection technique [30]. They propose a Minimum-Time-To-Intrusion (MTTI) metric based on the predicted period of time before any simulated intrusion can take place. The MTTI value, however, depends on the threat classes simulated and the intrusion classes observed. In contrast, the attack surface metric does not depend on any threat class. Moreover, the MTTI computation assumes the knowledge of system vulnerabilities.

Ortalo et al. model a system's known vulnerabilities as a privilege graph [3] and combine assumptions about the attacker's behavior with the privilege graphs to obtain attack state graphs [25]. They analyze the attack state graphs using Markov techniques to estimate the effort an attacker might spend to exploit the vulnerabilities; the estimated effort is a measure of the system's security. Their technique, however, assumes the knowledge of the system's vulnerabilities and the attacker's behavior. Moreover, their approach focuses on assessing the operational security of operating systems and not individual software applications.

Schneier uses attack trees to model the different ways in which a system can be attacked [27]. Given an attacker goal, Schneier constructs an attack tree to identify the different ways in which the goal can be satisfied and to determine the cost to the attacker in satisfying the goal. The estimated cost is a measure of the system's security. Construction of an attack tree, however, assumes the knowledge of the following three factors: system vulnerabilities, possible attacker goals, and the attacker behavior.

McQueen et al. use an estimate of a system's expected time-to-compromise (TTC) as an indicator of the system's security risk [23]. TTC is the expected time needed by an attacker to gain a privilege level in a system; TTC, however, depends on the system's vulnerabilities and the attacker's skill level.

## 1.8 Summary and Future Work

There is a pressing need for practical security metrics and measurements today. In this chapter, we formalized the notion of a system's attack surface and introduced a systematic method to measure it. Our pragmatic attack surface measurement approach is useful to both software developers and software consumers.

Our formal model can be extended in two directions. First, we do not make any assumptions about an attacker's resources, capabilities, and behavior in our I/O automata model. In terms of an attacker profile used in cryptography, we do not characterize an attacker's power and privilege. A useful extension of our work would be to include an attacker's power and privilege in our formal I/O automata model.

Second, our I/O automata model is not expressive enough to include attacks such as side channel attacks, covert channel attacks, and attacks where one user of a software system can affect other users (e.g., fork bombs). We could extend the current formal model by extending our formalization of damage potential and attacker effort to include such attacks.

We view our work as a first step in the grander challenge of security metrics. We believe that no single security metric or measurement will be able to fulfill our requirements. We certainly need multiple metrics and measurements to quantify different aspects of security. We also believe that our understanding over time would lead us to more meaningful and useful quantitative security metrics.

## References

1. J. Alves-Foss and S. Barbosa. Assessing computer security vulnerability. *ACM SIGOPS Operating Systems Review*, 29(3), 1995.
2. E. Asbeck and Y. Y. Haimes. The partitioned multiobjective risk method. *Large Scale Systems*, 6(1):13–38, 1984.
3. M. Dacier and Y. Deswarte. Privilege graph: An extension to the typed access matrix model. In *Proc. of European Symposium on Research in Computer Security*, 1994.
4. N. E. Fenton and M. Neil. A critique of software defect prediction models. *IEEE Transactions on Software Engineering*, 25(5), 1999.
5. Norman E. Fenton and Shari Lawrence Pfleeger. *Software Metrics: A Rigorous and Practical Approach*. PWS Publishing Co., Boston, MA, USA, 1998.
6. Virgil D. Gligor. Personal communication, 2008.
7. Seymour E. Goodman and Herbert S. Lin, editors. *Toward a Safer and More Secure Cyberspace*. The National Academics Press, 2007.
8. R. Gopalakrishna, E. Spafford, , and J. Vitek. Vulnerability likelihood: A probabilistic approach to software assurance. Technical Report 2005-06, CERIAS, Purdue Univeristy, 2005.
9. Y. Y. Haimes. *Risk Modeling, Assessment, and Management*. Wiley, 2004.
10. Curtis P. Haugtvedt, Paul M. Herr, and Frank R. Kardes, editors. *Handbook of Consumer Psychology*. Psychology Press, 2008.
11. M. Howard, J. Pincus, and J.M. Wing. Measuring relative attack surfaces. In *Proc. of Workshop on Advanced Developments in Software and Systems Security*, 2003.
12. Michael Howard. Fending off future attacks by reducing attack surface. http://msdn.microsoft.com/library/default.asp?url=/library/en-us/dncode/html/secure02132003.asp, 2003.

13. Michael Howard. Personal communication, 2005.
14. Barbara Kitchenham, Shari Lawrence Pfleeger, and Norman Fenton. Towards a framework for software measurement validation. *IEEE Transactions on Software Engineering*, 21(12):929–944, 1995.
15. David John Leversage and Eric James Byres. Estimating a system's mean time-to-compromise. *IEEE Security and Privacy*, 6(1), 2008.
16. Jason Levitt. Windows 2000 security represents a quantum leap. http://www.informationweek.com/834/winsec.htm, April 2001.
17. B. Littlewood, S. Brocklehurst, N. Fenton, P. Mellor, S. Page, D. Wright, J. Dobson J. McDermid, and D. Gollman. Towards operational measures of computer security. *Journal of Computer Security*, 2(2/3):211–230, 1993.
18. N. Lynch and M. Tuttle. An introduction to input/output automata. *CWI-Quarterly*, 2(3), September 1989.
19. Bharat B. Madan, Katerina Goseva-Popstojanova, Kalyanaraman Vaidyanathan, and Kishor S. Trivedi. Modeling and quantification of security attributes of software systems. In *DSN*, pages 505–514, 2002.
20. Pratyusa K. Manadhata. *An Attack Surface Metric*. PhD thesis, Carnegie Mellon University, December 2008.
21. Pratyusa K. Manadhata and Jeannette M. Wing. An attack surface metric. *IEEE Transactions on Software Engineering*, 99(PrePrints), 2010.
22. Gary McGraw. From the ground up: The DIMACS software security workshop. *IEEE Security and Privacy*, 1(2):59–66, 2003.
23. Miles A. McQueen, Wayne F. Boyer, Mark A. Flynn, and George A. Beitel. Time-to-compromise model for cyber risk reduction estimation. In *ACM CCS Workshop on Quality of Protection*, September 2005.
24. David M. Nicol. Modeling and simulation in security evaluation. *IEEE Security and Privacy*, 3(5):71–74, 2005.
25. R. Ortalo, Y. Deswarte, and M. Kaâniche. Experimenting with quantitative evaluation tools for monitoring operational security. *IEEE Transactions on Software Engineering*, 25(5), 1999.
26. Stuart Edward Schechter. *Computer Security Strength & Risk: A Quantitative Approach*. PhD thesis, Harvard University, 2004.
27. Bruce Schneier. Attack trees: Modeling security threats. *Dr. Dobb's Journal*, 1999.
28. Sean W. Smith and Eugene H. Spafford. Grand challenges in information security: Process and output. *IEEE Security and Privacy*, 2:69–71, 2004.
29. Rayford B. Vaughn, Ronda R. Henning, and Ambareen Siraj. Information assurance measures and metrics - state of practice and proposed taxonomy. In *Proc. of Hawaii International Conference on System Sciences*, 2003.
30. J. Voas, A. Ghosh, G. McGraw, F. Charron, and K. Miller. Defining an adaptive software security metric from a dynamic software failure tolerance measure. In *Proc. of Annual Conference on Computer Assurance*, 1996.

# Chapter 2
# Effectiveness of Moving Target Defenses

David Evans, Anh Nguyen-Tuong, John Knight

**Abstract** Moving target defenses have been proposed as a way to make it much more difficult for an attacker to exploit a vulnerable system by changing aspects of that system to present attackers with a varying attack surface. The hope is that constructing a successful exploit requires analyzing properties of the system, and that in the time it takes an attacker to learn those properties and construct the exploit, the system will have changed enough by the time the attacker can launch the exploit to disrupt the exploit's functionality. This is a promising and appealing idea, but its security impact is not yet clearly understood. In this chapter, we argue that the actual benefits of the moving target approach are in fact often much less significant than one would expect. We present a model for thinking about dynamic diversity defenses, analyze the security properties of a few example defenses and attacks, and identify scenarios where moving target defenses are and are not effective.

## 2.1 Introduction

The idea of security through diversity is to automatically generate variants of a target program or system that alter certain properties of the system. These alterations are designed to preserve the essential semantics of the original program on normal inputs, but to alter its behavior on malicious inputs. A widely deployed example is address space randomization, forms of which are included in most modern operating systems including Mac OS X, Ubuntu, Windows Vista, and Windows 7. Address space randomization thwarts exploits that depend on known absolute addresses for objects in memory by randomizing the locations of those objects. As we discuss in Section 2.4, although address space randomization does disrupt many attacks, it is vulnerable to brute force attacks because of the limited entropy used in many address space randomization implementations, and vulnerable to probing attacks.

University of Virginia
e-mail: [evans,nguyen,knight]@virginia.edu

Moving target defenses seek to overcome the limitations of static diversity defenses by dynamically altering properties of programs. For long-running server processes, this requires dynamically altering the running execution (or, more disruptively, periodically restarting the process with a new randomization). If the attack surface changes rapidly enough, the hope is that dynamic diversity defenses can protect systems even in situations where static diversity would be vulnerability to low entropy or probing attacks.

In this chapter we develop a model for moving target defenses, and analyze their effectiveness against sophisticated attackers. We argue that in many cases the added security a dynamic diversity defense provides against such attackers is quite limited and can be quantified. In other scenarios, where there are good reasons to believe the time required to develop an effective exploit is high, dynamic diversity defenses can provide significant benefits over static diversity.

## 2.2 Diversity Defenses

The goal of a diversity defense is to present attackers with an unpredictable target, thereby making it difficult for an exploit to have the desired malicious behavior. Diversity techniques may be applied at a low-level, where the standard semantics of the programming language are preserved but its undefined semantics altered. This has the advantage that it can be done automatically, without needing any behavioral specification of the target program other than belief that its behavior does not depend on undefined language semantics. The limitation of such low-level diversity techniques is that they can only change behavior for exploits that exploit the altered undefined semantics. This covers many important classes of attacks including most code injection and memory corruption attacks, but does not include any attacks that exploit the application's higher-level semantics.

The other type of diversity defense attempts to alter that applications' higher-level behavior. This depends on a sufficiently clear understanding of the application's required behavior to be able to alter the application's semantics in ways that may disrupt attacks but do not impact its essential functionality. The drawback of higher-level diversity defenses is that they typically require manual effort to produce the variants, and because they are constructed in ad hoc ways it is much more difficult to reason about the security they provide. It is also difficult to use such an approach in a dynamic diversity scenario since it requires a large number of variants to provide a moving target.

In this chapter, we focus on low-level, automatic, diversity defenses. The idea of automatically generating diverse variants of a program to disrupt exploits was introduced by Forrest et al. [32], and many subsequent works considered various ways for automatically generating useful diversity in program executions. Here we describe three common types of automatic diversity techniques. Although the model and analysis we present applies to a wide range of diversity techniques, our examples focus on the most commonly used techniques described here.

## 2.2.1 Address Space Randomization

Address space randomization or *address space layout randomization* (ASLR) is the most successful and widely deployed diversity technique. The basic idea is simple: randomize the locations of objects in memory so an attack that depends on knowing the address of these objects will fail. Address space randomization was first implemented by PaX for Linux [35] in 2000, and has since been implemented in most major operating systems including Windows (first in Windows Vista in 2007, and later in Windows Server 2008 and Windows 7), Linux (partially included in the Linux kernel since 2005, and more complete implementations in most hardened Linux distributions), and Mac OS (in a limited form since OS X 10.5).

The simplest ASLR implementations just randomize the base address for large memory areas. For example, PaX randomizes the base addresses for the executable area containing the program's code and static data structures, the stack area containing the execution stack, and the mapped memory area containing the heap as well as shared memory and dynamically-loaded libraries. The address of each of these areas is randomized by adding a randomly generated offset to the address. Within each area, though, the layout is unchanged. The advantage of such an approach is it can be implemented by the loader without any changes needed to the executable.

Other implementations of ASLR more comprehensively randomize the address layout. For example, address obfuscation randomizes the both the absolute locations of data and code as well as their relative locations [3]. This can be done by randomly permuting the order of variables on the stack or in a structure, as well as by adding random padding between objects. Unlike randomizing segment base addresses, however, making such changes requires deeper analysis of the target program.

## 2.2.2 Instruction Set Randomization

Instruction set randomization is a general technique for thwarting code injection attacks by obscuring the instruction set of the target [14, 12, 13]. An attacker who knows an exploit that allows code constructed by the attacker to be injected into the target application will not be able to create code that has the desired behavior without knowing the target instruction set.

An example implementation of instruction set randomization is Barrantes et al.'s RISE [12]. The instruction set is randomized by generating a sequence of random bytes and XORing each instruction in the program with a corresponding random byte when the code text is loaded. Then, the program is executed in an emulator that XORs the instruction with the random byte to obtain the original instruction. A code injection attack that does not know the randomization key will not be able to generate the desired behavior, since the injected instructions will be XORed with random bytes before they are executed.

Other implementations of instruction set randomization us block encryption instead of bytewise XORs. For example, Hu et al. implemented a form of instruction set randomization by encrypting program code with AES at the granularity of 128-bit blocks [36]. Higher-level instruction sets can also be randomized. For example, SQL injection attacks can be thwarted by adding random nonces to SQL commands [33] and Perl injection attacks can be thwarted by randomizing parts of the Perl language [4].

### 2.2.3 Data Randomization

Another type of low-level diversification is altering how data is stored in memory. An early instantiation of this idea was PointGuard [8], which attempts to thwart pointer corruption attacks by storing pointers in memory XORed with a random key. When a pointer value is loaded into a register, it is XORed with the key to produce the actual pointer value. A more general technique we developed by Cadar et al. [10]. They XORed data in memory with random masks, selected based on the memory object's class. This requires a static analysis of the program to determine memory regions that are associated with particular objects, so that attempts to write outside objects will be disrupted since different random masks are applied.

## 2.3 Model

We consider a model involving two players: an attacker and a defender. The defender's goal is to provide a service, $S$, with a high reliability and performance. The attacker's goal is to successfully exploit the server. We assume the service has at least one vulnerability which is known to the attacker but not to the defender. An attacker with knowledge of the full state of the system can launch an exploit that compromises the server. We define $t_e$ as the time between starting to launch the exploit and the system compromise. For our purposes, it is not necessary to specify the actual harm the compromise causes, but we can think of this as obtaining confidential account information from the server.

In a static diversity defense, instead of running $S$, the defender generates a random secret key, $k \in K$, and executes $S_{\mathcal{T}_k}$ where $\mathcal{T}$ is a key-dependent transformation. The transform preserves the essential semantic of $S$; that is, for all legitimate inputs $x \in \mathcal{N}$, $S(x) \approx S_{\mathcal{T}_k}(x)$, where $\approx$ indicates a loose semantic equivalence test that may be service-specific. The intent of the transformation is to alter the service's response to attack inputs. For a particular targeted class of attack inputs, $a \in \mathcal{A}$, $S(a) \neq S_{\mathcal{T}_k}(a)$. In particular, while $S(a)$ constitutes compromise behavior, $S_{\mathcal{T}_k}(a)$ is harmless behavior.

An attacker who can determine $k$, or possibly only determine some information about $k$, can construct an exploit $a_k$ that achieves the desired compromise:

$S(a) \approx S_{\mathcal{T}_k}(a_k)$. Thus, the diversity defense succeeds when all the attacker's exploits are in the target class of attack input $\mathscr{A}$ and the attacker has not learned enough information about $k$ to construct the exploit $a_k$.

Consider the lifetime of a particular service, shown in Figure 2.1. At time $t_0$, the defender has generated a random key $k_0$ and launches the diversified service, $S_{\mathcal{T}_{k_0}}$. The attacker knows a vulnerability in $S$ and an attack $a \in \mathscr{A}$ that exploits that vulnerability but is thwarted by the diversification. Starting at time $t_0$, the attacker attempts to exploit the running service. This may be done by generating variants of $a$ transformed around guessed randomization keys. It may also involve sending probe packets designed to leak information about $k$.

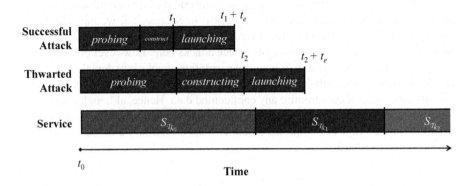

**Fig. 2.1** Attack Lifetime

The probability of the attack succeeding is a function of the amount of information the attacker has obtained about $k$. Assuming a simple defense where the attacker needs to guess all bits of $k$ completely for the attack to succeed, but has zero probability of success otherwise:

$$Pr[S_{\mathcal{T}_k}(a_{k_g}) \approx S(a)] = Pr[k_g = k] \qquad (2.1)$$

If the attacker has no information about $k$ but must guess $k$ exactly to construct a successful attacks, when $|K| = 2^N$ (that is, $k$ has $N$ bits of entropy) $Pr[k_g = k] = \frac{1}{2^N}$.

The attacker may be able to obtain information about $k$ by sending probes. This increases $Pr[k_g = k]$ over time as the attacker learns more about the target service. At some later time, $t_1$, the attacker finds a successful exploit against $S_{\mathcal{T}_{k_0}}$ and launches that exploit against the service. This exploit compromises the service at time $t_1 + t_e$.

If dynamic diversity is employed, the service is periodically rediversified with a new key. If that transformation happens during the probing phase or the exploit execution phase, it changes the target system to a new target $S_{\mathcal{T}_{k'}}$. This disrupts the attack $a_{k_g}$ since although $k_g = k$ the system is now diversified with $k' \neq k_g$. In the case of the second attack, $t_2 + t_e$ is past when the service has been rediversified, so although the constructed attack would succeeded if it had been launched at time $t_1$, it fails when it is launched at time $t_2$.

Our goal is to understand what types of diversity and attacks can be disrupted by such a strategy, and how the rate if re-diversification impacts the attacker's success probability.

## 2.4 Attack Strategies

The effectiveness of a moving target defense depends on the attacker's capabilities, resources, and strategy. Here, we consider several different broad strategies an attacker may employ against diversity defenses. In Section 2.5, we consider how much additional advantage dynamic diversity provides against each attack strategy. Note that we do not consider denial-of-service attacks here. Low-level diversity defenses often turn code injection or memory corruption attacks into denial-of-service attacks, which are generally less harmful than injection and corruption attacks since they do not expose or compromise any confidential data. Hence, although denial-of-service is undesirable, we consider it a successful attack disruption if an attack that would normal corrupt or compromise data is transformed into a denial-of-service by the diversity defense.

### 2.4.1 Circumvention Attacks

The first attacker strategy is to circumvent the diversification entirely. This can be done if the attacker finds any exploit that does not depend on the properties of the server that are altered by the diversification. For example, an attacker may be able to circumvent a instruction set randomization defense by avoiding the need to inject code. Instead, the attacker repurposes code already provided by the executing binary. An early form of this strategy is the *return-to-libc* attack [1], in which the attacker replaces the return address on the stack with an address to an exploitable function in libc and loads the appropriate arguments on the stack. Shacham et al. introduced a more general form of this attack strategy known as *return-oriented programming*. Instead of relying on the functions provided intentionally by libc, return-oriented programming exploits fragments of code found in the binary (including fragments that start in the middle of intended instructions) to provide a Turing-complete programming system without needing to inject any code. A recent exploit against Adobe Reader/Acrobat used return-oriented programming to circumvent ASLR in Windows 7 and Windows Vista [21].

Another type of circumvention attack exploits incomplete randomization. For example, the Mac OS X Snow Leopard implementation of ASLR randomizes libraries but does not apply any randomization to the stack, heap, or program code [6]. An attacker can exploit a vulnerability in a program by taking advantage of non-randomized portions of memory. The Windows 7 and Ubuntu implementations of ASLR randomize the operating system components completely, but only randomize the program image when developers set the appropriate (non-default) compiler flag. For Ubuntu, this is due to the relatively high performance overhead of position independent executables on 32-bit architectures, as well as uncertainty about compatibility with all programs. Hence, only certain programs included in Ubuntu that are deemed to be security critical are compiled as position independent executables, and other programs are executed without randomizing the program image [18]. Müller provides examples of many forms of circumvention attacks against PaX ALSR that find ways to return into non-randomized portions of memory including the program text, static variable storage (BSS), and heap [20].

Another example of a circumvention attack that exploits incomplete randomization is to alter an exploit to depend only on the local relative addresses instead of global addresses. Standard ASLR implementations may change the absolute address of a target memory location, but not its relative position to some other objects. For example, if the value an attacker wants to corrupt is a field in a structure, it may be possible to overwrite this value by exploiting a buffer overflow vulnerability on a buffer that is stored as a different field in the same structure. It is not necessary for the attacker to know the absolute address of either object, only to know their relative locations. Some proposed implementations of ASLR do provide randomization at this level such as Bhatkar et al.'s [3], but it is not done by standard implementations and cannot be done safely in general without a deeper analysis of the program.

Finally, an attacker may circumvent randomization defenses by exploiting the program at a higher semantic level that is not effected by the randomization. For example, randomizing the instruction set and address space layout of a web server provides no mitigation against a SQL injection attack that is exploiting vulnerabilities in the high-level application logic. Randomizing the instruction set to prevent code injection provides no defense against memory corruption attacks that do not need to inject any code such as the attacks describe by Chen et al. [7].

## 2.4.2 Deputy Attacks

In a *confused deputy attack* [16], an attacker finds a way to use a benign program in a malicious way. For randomization defenses, the main fear is that an attacker will be able to find a way to use the program to apply the randomizing transformation to the attacker's data.

For many diversity defenses, the randomization transformation is done at runtime by the program itself. Hence, the code to perform the transformation (and the randomization key) is present somewhere in the running program.

One attacker strategy avoids the need to break the diversification entirely. Instead, the attacker either finds a way to exploit the target system that does not depend on any properties altered by the diversification, or finds a way to deputize code included in the executing program that performs the transformation to transform the injected attack.

An attack that is somewhat like a deputy attack is a partial overwrite attack. Unlike a deputy attack which repurposes existing code to launch an attack, the partial overwrite attack coopts existing data. Consider a program that is protected by a coarse-grained variant of address-space randomization. A partial overwrite attack that modifies the least-significant byte of an address $A$ so that the program transfers control flow to a targeted function $F$ would bypass any protection afforded by address-space randomization. The address of the targeted function, while randomized, would still be at a known offset from $A$. Durden descries a partial overwriting attacks against PaX ALSR [11].

### 2.4.3 Brute Force and Entropy Reduction Attacks

A *brute force attack* simply attempts all possible randomization keys until an exploit is found that succeeds. If the key space is small enough, such an attack may be practical. For example, Shacham et al. demonstrated an effective brute force attack against an Apache server protected using PaX ASLR [29]. A 32-bit architecture provides at most 32 bits of entropy for address randomization, but because of limitations on address mapping that actual entropy provided by PaX is only 16 bits for the executable and memory mapped areas, and 24 bits for the stack. Since the shared libc library is stored in a memory mapped area, is it only necessary to search 16 bits to locate the library and launch a return-to-libc attack. On average, their attack succeeds against a vulnerable Apache server in approximately 216 seconds on average.

For larger key spaces, attackers may find ways to reduce the effective key space by designing attacks that work for a set of possible keys. This changes the success probability in the original model from Equation 2.1 to:

$$Pr[S_{\mathcal{T}_k}(a_{k_g}) \approx S(a)] = Pr[k \in \mathcal{W}_a(k_g)]$$

where $\mathcal{W}_a(k)$ is the set of keys that are equivalent to $k$ with respect to attack $a$. The attacker's goal is to construct an attack $a$ for which

$$\bigcup_{k_g \in \mathcal{G}} \mathcal{W}_a(k_g) = K$$

for the smallest possible set $\mathcal{G}$.

A longstanding example of an entropy reduction attack is a *NOP sled*, widely used in standard stack smashing buffer overflow attacks to overcome uncertainty about memory layout even without the use of ASLR. With a NOP sled, the attacker inserts a series of one-byte NOP (No Operation Performed) instructions before the attack code. To avoid intrusion detection systems that alert on suspected NOP sleds, attackers can use other instructions that have no or limited sematic impact, or sequences of multi-byte instructions that can be interpreted as NOPs starting at any of their bytes [25, 24].

Since each instruction in the NOP sled is choosen to have no semantic effect, if the attacker can redirect execution to jump to any location in the NOP sled it will have the same behavior as jumping to the specific location where the attack code begins. The longer the NOP sled, the higher the probability a jump to a randomized location will land within the NOP sled and reach the attack code. For example, if a 127-byte NOP sled is used, $|\mathscr{W}_a(k_g)| \approx 128$, effectively reducing the randomization entropy by up to 7 bits (the actual reduction is probably less, for example, if the randomization offsets must be word-aligned).

A more extensive form of entropy reduction is *heap spraying* in which an attacker attempts to fill up a large fraction of memory in a way that increases the likelihood of reaching a target object. An early example of heap spraying was Govindavajhala and Appel's attack to circumvent type safety mechanisms on Java virtual machines [15]. The attack was not designed to overcome intentional address space randomization, but instead to take advantage of random bit errors (caused, by example, by heating up memory until there is a high liklihood of single bit errors).

Several recent attacks have used heap spraying from JavaScript to launch attacks on ASLR-protected web browsers [38, 19]. In a JavaScript heap spraying attack, the attacker uses JavaScript code executed by the browser to allocate a large number of objects in the heap [26]. Each object is constructed to include a NOP sled, followed by the attack code. This increases the likelihood that a jump to a randomized address will reach one of the copies in memory of the exploit code. A sophisticated version of the attack known as *heap feng shui* takes advantage of the way the heap allocator and garbage collector work to control more of memory and how the attack objects are arranged [30].

The effectiveness of randomization defenses is severely reduced by these types of entropy reduction attacks. In many cases, a well constructed heap sprying exploit succeeds on the first attempt with high probability.

### 2.4.4 Probing Attacks

A probing attack attempts to overcome a diversity defense by using probe packets to learn properties of the randomized execution needed to construct an attack. A probe attack is distinguished from a standard entropy reduction attack in that the probe packets are designed only to obtain information about the target, rather than to produce the desired malicious behavior.

Shacham et al.'s attack on ASLR used probes to find the randomization offset for the memory map region, which could then be used to learn the locations of all libc functions and construct the attack [29]. The probe packets attempted to find the usleep function in libc by jumping to randomized addresses. The remoted attacker could observe when the usleep function was found since the call to usleep causes the connection to hang; if the guessed address is incorrect the server child process will (most likely) crash. Once the usleep address is obtained, the attacker has enough information to compute the address of all the other libc functions, including the system function used to obtain a shell. In this case, probing does not have much advantage over just sending the guessed attack directly (that is, it is not any easier to guess the location of usleep than it is to guess the location of system), but does enable an attacker to use smaller, possibly harder to detect, packets to probe the system to learn the randomization key rather than needing to send the full attack payload with each guess attempt.

For the previous example, the amount of information the attacker receives for each probe attempt is very limited — if the guess is incorrect the server crashes and the attacker learns nothing more other than that this guess was not the correct offset. In some cases, though, probe attacks may be possible where each probe obtains a great deal of information. It may be possible to use information contained in server error messages returned to the attacker to learn addresses, or to exploit a format string vulnerability to obtain the address of a targeted object. Müller provides two examples based on pointer redirecting to obtain addresses of randomized functions [20].

Strackx et al. developed *buffer overread attacks* to expose randomized addresses in memory [34]. The attack takes advantage of a property of the strncpy library function, as well as other similar functions in the standard C library. These functions take a size parameter indicating the size of the output buffer to protect against buffer overflows, but do not automatically add a null terminator at the end of the result if the string being copied exceeds the size of the output buffer. Thus, when the string is printed, it will contain subsequent data in memory until the next NULL byte. This data may contain addresses, revealing the actual locations of randomized addresses. Similar attacks are also possible against instruction set randomization [37].

### 2.4.5 Incremental Attacks

An increment attack is a form of probing attack where more than one successful probe is needed to obtain sufficient information to construct the exploit. For example, this occurs when the randomization key is many bytes long, but each successful probe packet obtains only a single key byte. This is the case for implementations of instruction set randomization that use an XOR mask to randomize the instructions. In Kc et al.'s proposed hardware design, the XOR mask is a four-byte value that is stored in a dedicated register [14]; in Barrantes et al.'s software implementation, RISE, the XOR mask can be as long as the program text [12].

Sovarel et al. developed an incremental attack against instruction set randomization [31]. The attack uses probes to determine key bytes until a large enough region of key bytes is known to inject the attack code. In one version of the attack, a single byte instruction (the 0xc3 return instruction) is guessed, and for some vulnerabilities it may be possible to incrementally break the randomization key one byte at a time. For most vulnerabilities, though, the difference in behavior from a correct and incorrect guess of the return instruction is indistinguishable (both are likely to cause the server to crash, since the return instruction leaves the stack in a corrupted state). An alternate attack uses the two-byte short jump instruction with offset -2 (0xebfe) which jumps back to itself, causing the server to enter an infinite loop which can be distinguished by the attacker from the crash that usually results from an incorrect. By this method, a many byte key can be broken incrementally in two-byte chunks.

## 2.5 Analysis

The value of a moving target defense depends on the class of attack. For each attack strategy described in Section 2.4, we consider the impact of dynamic diversity over static diversity. In the first three cases, dynamic diversity appears to have little benefit; for incremental probing attacks, however, the situation is more interesting and dynamic diversity appears to have substantial value.

### 2.5.1 Circumvention Attacks

In a circumvention attack, the transformation $\mathcal{T}_k$ does not diversify any aspects of $S$ that is required for a successful attack. Hence, there is no benefit to changing the diversification. Since the diversity transformation does not cover the attack class, reapplying the transformations with varying keys yields no benefits.

### 2.5.2 Deputy Attacks

In a deputy attack, an attacker is able to induce the target program to apply the diversity transformation to the attack input. If the diversification key changes, this has no impact on the attack since the attacker is exploiting the actual transformation code in the program. Similarly to circumvention attacks, dynamic diversity provides no advantage for deputy attacks.

### 2.5.3 Brute Force and Entropy Reduction Attacks

As noted in Section 2.4.3, Shacham et al. showed that PaX ASLR provides only enough entropy to slow the spread of a worm. Dynamic diversity provides modest benefit against a brute force or entropy reduction attack. Even if the target is rerandomized after every attack attempt, the maximum impact on the attacker is changing the random search from random sampling without replacement to random sampling with replacement. This adds at most a single bit of entropy to the search space.

Hence, dynamic diversity provides little benefit as a defense mechanism against these attacks above and beyond the baseline static version. If the effective entropy of a diversity transform is low, the expected time to mount a successful attack would be relatively short, and therefore a factor of two would be of little value. When entropy is high, the expected time to mount a successful attack would be long, and again a factor of two provides limited additional benefit.

As we discuss in Section 2.6.1, if multiple diversity techniques are composed in a way that requires an attacker to incrementally break each of them, there may be more substantial gains possible by dynamically re-diversifying each technique in an interleaved way.

### 2.5.4 Probing Attacks

Dynamic diversity could be useful against a probing attack if the time between a successful probe and completing an exploit is long. In practice, however, exploits can be constructed automatically based on the probe information, so the time between the probe and attack launch is effectively just the network latency for two round trips between the server and attacker's client. If the re-randomization can be done frequently enough, it may be possible to ensure that the system has always been re-randomized between the probe and exploit. Such frequent re-randomization is too expensive for most services, but perhaps could be done in some scenarios. This would be most effective against probing attacks such as the buffer overread attack that depend on using a first request to leak information about the randomization, and use that information to construct a targeted attack.

### 2.5.5 Incremental Attacks

Dynamic diversity seems most promising against incremental attacks since these attacks require a lot of preparation by the attacker before enough information about the randomization is obtained to construct the attack. Here, we develop a model to analyze the effectiveness of dynamic diversity against incremental attacks. Our model applies to the Sovarel et al. attack described in Section 2.4.5, but should also apply to any incremental attack that involves sending a large number of probe packets to gradually acquire information about the randomization.

We model an incremental attack as a series of $b$ state-space searches where the states are of the same size $s$. A state-space search is carried out as a series of probes, and each state-space search is designed to reveal a single key fragment. Hence the key length is $b$ fragments. We define a successful attack as a sequence of successful state-space searches of the $b$ spaces.

We assume that:

- the adversary proceeds sequentially from space to space determining one fragment for each space,
- the adversary knows when a fragment has been revealed, and,
- each probe of a space requires the same time.

These assumptions simplify the analysis, but do not meaningfully limit the class of incremental attacks.

In this case, the quantity of interest is the probability of a successful attack occurring in some specific number of probes, say $L$, or less. With that probability known, re-randomization could be triggered after the adversary had an opportunity to perform $L$ probes and thereby limit the probability of a successful attack. Thus, our first goal in the analysis is to determine this probability. Clearly, we cannot know how many probes have occurred, but we can estimate the number of opportunities that the adversary had.

Searching each space will terminate with a successful probe, and each successful probe will be preceded by from zero to $s-1$ probes that fail. The initial step in the model is to determine the probability of a successful attack in exactly $L$ probes. Such an attack will experience a total of $k-b$ probe failures across all $b$ spaces together with $b$ successful probes. Thus, the total number of different sequences of probes that can lead to a successful attack in $L$ probes is the number of ways that $L-b$ failing probes can be distributed across $b$ spaces with no more than $s-1$ occurring in any single space. This number can be derived using the *Balls In Bins* analysis [5]:

$$N(L) = \sum_{t=0}^{b} (-1)^t \binom{b}{t} \binom{L-ts-1}{b-1}$$

In this expression, binomial coefficients are defined to be zero if the upper operand is smaller than the lower operand.

The probability of a successful attack occurring in exactly $L$ probes for $b \leq L \leq sb$ is:

$$p(L) = \frac{N(L)}{2^{sb}}$$

The probability of a successful attack occurring in $L$ probes or less for $b \leq L \leq sb$ is:

$$P(L) = \sum_{i=b}^{L} p(i)$$

This is the probability we sought, and with this probability we can determine the effect of periodic re-randomization as a defense against an incremental attack.

We model the effect of re-randomization by treating an attack as a series of independent trials by the adversary each of length $m$ probes where the key is changed after each trial, i.e., after $m$ probes. Thus, the effect of re-randomization is to force

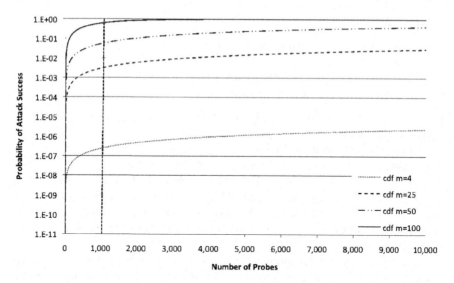

**Fig. 2.2** Effectiveness of dynamic diversity

the adversary to restart the attack after each series of $m$ probes if the attack was not successful at that point.

The probability of a successful attack in $m$ or fewer probes is $P(m)$. With re-randomization after each trial (each $m$ probes), the probability of an attack succeeding in $jm$ probes or fewer is:

$$M(jm) = 1 - (1 - P(m))^j$$

Note that this probability is defined only for every $m$ probes. In order to derive the probability of a successful attack in $L$ or fewer probes, we need to add the probability of a successful trial (determining a single fragment of the key) in $L - jm$ probes where $L - jm$ lies between 0 and $m - 1$, i.e., between the points at which the key is changed. Adding this yields:

$$M(L) = 1 - (1 - P(m))^j (1 - P(L - jm))$$

$M(L)$ is the probability of a successful attack in $L$ or fewer probes with re-randomizing every $m$ probes and $P(L)$ is that probability without re-randomization. With these two probabilities, we can determine the effectiveness of dynamic diversity.

As an example, consider the case in which $b = 4$ and $s = 256$. This corresponds to a key that is four bytes long which would be expected to have a search space of size $2^{32}$. However, the incremental attack proceeds one byte at a time so that there are four searches each of spaces of size 256. Obviously, the probability of success in 1024 probes or less is one.

Figure 2.2 shows the probability of attack success, $M(L)$, for values of $m = 4, 25,$ 50, and 100. Note that the Y axis is a logarithmic scale. The dashed vertical line is 1024 on the X axis. This is the point at which an attack is expected to succeed without dynamic diversity, and the intersection of the dashed line with the four curves shows the relative advantage of re-randomization. The case in which $m$ is set to 4 is the limiting case in this example. Four is the least number of probes within which an attack might succeed since there are four bytes in the key and the adversary has to determine all four in sequence. Thus, the curve in Figure 2.2 for $m = 4$ is the best that dynamic diversity can do in this example.

The effectiveness of dynamic diversity against incremental attacks in this case depends critically on the rate of re-randomization. Varying this rate from every $100^{th}$ probe to every $4^{th}$ probe spans 6 orders of magnitude. Moreover, the probability of attack success when re-randomizing only every $100^{th}$ or $50^{th}$ probe quickly exceeds 90%, i.e., dynamic diversity in these cases is ineffective.

For a server responding to network inputs, a network message corresponds to a probe in the model. Re-randomizing on every $4^{th}$ or $25^{th}$ network messages would seem prohibitively costly. However, our results show that it is possible to re-randomize XOR keys used in instruction-set randomization at the rate of every 100 ms with an average cost of 14% overhead over native execution [23]. Re-randomization may be triggered based on events instead of the current time-based scheme. For example, many probe attacks result in process crashes when the guess is incorrect, so it makes sense to rerandomize after a crash. Rerandomization may also be triggered by particular system calls (e.g., opening a file) or when an anomaly detector flags a packet as suspicious. The risk in any event-based rerandomization scheme is that a sophisticated attacker may be able to develop a probe attack that does not produce the trigger event. Hence, some combination of time-based and event-based rerandomization seems most promising.

## 2.5.6 Summary

Table 2.1 summarizes the effectiveness of dynamic diversity against the five attack classes. For circumvention and deputy attacks, dynamic diversity yields no benefit since the attack does not depend on guessing the randomization key. For brute force and entropy reduction attacks, the benefits of dynamic diversity are marginal and only increase the attacker's workload by at most a factor of two. Dynamic diversity holds the most promise for probing and incremental attacks. The rate of re-diversification required to obtain tangible benefits, especially against probing attacks, appears to be very high, but for some types of implementation it may be possible to achieve such a high rate of re-randomization without excessive performance overhead [23].

| Circumvention attacks | No advantage |
|---|---|
| Deputy attacks | No advantage |
| Entropy reducing attacks | At most doubles expected attack time |
| Probing attacks | Very high rate of rerandomization may thwart attack |
| Incremental attacks | May provide significant advantage |

**Table 2.1** Impact of Dynamic Diversity

## 2.6 Discussion

The limited effectiveness of adding dynamic rerandomization to low-level diversity defenses suggests the need for alternate approaches to increase the effectiveness of diversity defenses. Some of these depend on designing implementations to maximize entropy and avoid vulnerabilities, but since the goal of these defenses is to harden systems that have unknown vulnerabilities it is unsatisfying to rely solely on this approach. In addition, for schemes like address space randomization the maximum amount of entropy available is limited by properties of the hardware and underlying operating system. Next, we discuss two approaches that can improve the effectiveness of diversity defenses. The first, composition, amplifies the value of rerandomization; the second requires an attacker to simultaneously compromise multiple variants, avoid the need to keep any secret key.

### 2.6.1 Composition

Our analysis so far assumed a single diversity defense was deployed, and an attacker who can overcome that defense will succeed. One way to substantially increase the attacker's difficulty is to compose multiple diversity defenses. If the defenses are orthogonal, they will compose multiplicatively not additively. That is, it will be necessary for the attacker to simultaneously break both defenses, so the effective search space is the product of each defense's search space individually. This assumes the attacker cannot probe each defense separately, making the attack difficulty the sum of the two defenses. Worse, if the composition is not done in a careful way, the composed defense may provide the attacker with new opportunities that would not be effective against either defense individually.

Address space randomization and instruction set randomization can be composed. This would thwart many attacks on instruction set randomization, since the attacker cannot probe for the ISR key without also knowing the target address. If either the key or target address is incorrect, the server is likely to crash and the attacker does not learn if either key guess by itself is correct. Simplistically, if the address space randomization has 24 bits of entropy and the attacker can use a one-byte incremental probing attack, the combined defense provides 32 bits of entropy. On the other hand, combining address space randomization with instruction set randomization does not provide any benefit against attacks such as return-oriented programming that do not need to inject code. The problem for the attacker is the same as with address space randomization alone, since there is no need for the attacker to break both defenses.

If defenses can be composed multiplicatively, however, many low-entropy defense may be combined to provide a high-entropy defense. Holland et al. proposed schemes for randomizing many properties of an execution using a virtual machine [17]. Many of the individual diversification strategies provided little entropy (for example, altering the number of registers and machine word size), but they argued that by composing them they could provide a large machine space where attackers may need to guess all the diversification parameters.

It is difficult to reason precisely about the orthogonality and multiplicity of a composition of diversity defenses, but it is a promising way to increase the entropy facing an attacker. Adding dynamic rerandomization to composed defenses is promising, since if the composition does have the property that an attacker much simultaneously break all of the diversity techniques, it is only necessary to schedule the rerandomizations of each defense in a tiled way to limit the amount of time all of the diversity parameters are unchanged.

## 2.6.2 N-Variant Systems

Whereas composition strategies attempt to require the attacker to simultaneously break multiple different diversity defenses, the *N-Variant Systems* approach is designed to require an attacker to simultaneously break multiple variants of the same diversity defense [9]. The idea is to run multiple instantiations of the server in synchrony, each of which is diversified using a different randomization key. The variants are run in a framework that sends the same inputs to each variant, and monitors that they behave similarly. Any divergence considered a signal of a possible attack, since the variants should behave identically on non-attack inputs. This requires that the variants are kept closely synchronized and that any other sources of nondeterminism are removed.

If the attack spaces for the variants are disjoint with respect to some attack class, then no single input can simultaneously compromise all the variants. A simple example is to use two variants with disjoint address spaces (for example, one variant has only addresses beginning with a 0, and the other variant has only addresses starting with a 1). Then, any attack that depends on injecting an absolute address must fail — there is no address that is simultaneously valid in both variants. Several opportunities for disjoint attack spaces are possible including address spaces [9], instruction sets [9], and how data is represented [22]. When fully disjoint attack spaces cannot be found, a similar approach can also be used probabilistically. Examples include changing the direction of the stack [27] or diversifying the relative positions in memory (as done by DieHard [2], which focused on software debugging rather than attack detection).

A key advantage of this approach (at least for disjoint attack spaces) is that it eliminates the need to keep any secrets at all. This means brute force, entropy reduction, probing, and incremental attacks all fail. The main remaining worries are circumvention attacks, which are possible against any diversity defense if the diversification does not impact properties needed by the exploit, and deputy attacks, especially since each variant includes its own derandomization code or differently randomized data so may be simultaneously exploited across the variants. There are, however, a number of challenges to deploying N-Variant systems in practice. The first is the close monitoring requires eliminating all causes of nondeterminism. This is particularly difficult in multi-threaded applications where the interleaving of threads may lead to divergence. Performance overhead is also a concern, since the approach requires duplicating each request. This overhead can be fairly low for I/O bound servers [9], and it may be further reduced by using parallel execution on multi-core machines [28].

## 2.7 Conclusion

Diversity defenses are a promising mechanisms for making vulnerable servers more difficult for attackers to exploit. The effectiveness of a diversity defense depends on what properties of the execution it alters, the amount of entropy in the randomization, and how resistant the diversity defense is to attempts to probe the system or to circumvent or deputize the diversity mechanisms. Dynamic diversity can enhance the effectiveness of these defenses by rerandomizing the system periodically or based on trigger events. The effectiveness of dynamic diversity, however, is limited to scenarios where the attack requires an extended sequence of requests to probe the system and develop an attack. For many scenarios, dynamic rerandomization provides less benefit than expected. It provides no benefit against circumvention and deputy attacks, and against entropy reduction attacks provides at most a factor of two increase in difficulty. Against other classes of attack, dynamic diversity defense may provide more substantial advantages, but the defenses must be crafted carefully to provide the intended benefits.

## Acknowledgment

This research has been partially supported by grants from the National Science Foundation and the US Department of Defense under AFOSR MURI grant FA9550-07-1-0532. The views and conclusions contained herein are those of the authors and should not be interpreted as necessarily representing the official policies or endorsements, either expressed or implied, of the sponsoring agencies.

# References

1. Alexander Peslyak (Solar Designer). Return-to-libc Attack. Bugtraq Mailing List, August 1997.
2. Emery D. Berger and Benjamin G. Zorn. DieHard: Probabilistic Memory Safety for Unsafe Languages. In *ACM SIGPLAN Conference on Programming Language Design and Implementation (PLDI)*, June 2006.
3. Sandeep Bhatkar, Daniel DuVarney, and R. Sekar. Address Obfuscation: An Efficient Approach to Combat a Broad Range of Memory Error Exploits. In *USENIX Security Symposium*, 2003.
4. Stephen W. Boyd, Gaurav S. Kc, Michael E. Locasto, Angelos D. Keromytis, and Vassilis Prevelakis. On The General Applicability of Instruction-Set Randomization. *IEEE Transactions on Dependable and Secure Computing*, 7(3), 2010.
5. Kevin Brown. Balls In Bins with Limited Capacity. http://www.mathpages.com/home/kmath337.htm.
6. Brian X. Chen. Apple's Snow Leopard Is Less Secure Than Windows, But Safer. *Wired*, September 2009.
7. Shuo Chen, Jun Xu, Emre C. Sezer, Prachi Gauriar, and Ravishankar K. Iyer. Non-Control-Data Attacks Are Realistic Threats. In *USENIX Security Symposium*, 2005.
8. Crispin Cowan, Steve Beattie, John Johansen, and Perry Wagle. PointGuard: Protecting Pointers from Buffer Overflow Vulnerabilities. In *12th USENIX Security Symposium*, 2003.
9. Benjamin Cox, David Evans, Adrian Filipi, Jonathan Rowanhill, Wei Hu, Jack Davidson, John Knight, Anh Nguyen-Tuong, and Jason Hiser. N-Variant Systems: A Secretless Framework for Security through Diversity. In *USENIX Security Symposium*, 2006.
10. Cristian Cadar and Periklis Akritidis and Manuel Costa and Jean-Phillipe Martin and Miguel Castro. Data Randomization. Technical Report TR-120-2008, Microsoft Research, 2008.
11. Tyler Durden. Bypassing PaX ASLR protection. http://www.phrack.com/issues.html?issue=59\&id=9/, 2009.
12. Elena Gabriela Barrantes and David Ackley and Stephanie Forrest and Trek Palmer and Darko Stefanovic and Dino Dai Zovi. Intrusion Detection: Randomized Instruction Set Emulation to Disrupt Binary Code Injection Attacks. In *10th ACM Conference on Computer and Communications Security (CCS)*, 2003.
13. Elena Gabriela Barrantes and David H. Ackley and Stephanie Forrest and Darko Stefanovic. Randomized Instruction Set Emulation. *ACM Transactions on Information and System Security*, February 2005.
14. Gaurav S. Kc and Angelos D. Keromytis and Vassilis Prevelakis. Countering Code-Injection Attacks with Instruction-Set Randomization. In *10th ACM Conference on Computer and Communications Security (CCS)*, 2003.
15. Sudhakar Govindavajhala and Andrew W. Appel. Using Memory Errors to Attack a Virtual Machine. In *IEEE Symposium on Security and Privacy (Oakland)*, 2003.
16. Norman Hardy. The Confused Deputy (or why capabilities might have been invented). *ACM SIGOPS Operating Systems Review*, 22(4), October 1988.
17. David Holland, Ada Lim, and Margo Seltzer. An Architecture A Day Keeps The Hacker Away. In *Workshop on Architectural Support for Security and Anti-Virus*, April 2004.
18. Kubuntu Wiki. Supported Position Independent Executables. https://wiki.kubuntu.org/SecurityTeam/KnowledgeBase/BuiltPIE, 2011.
19. Microsoft Corporation. Microsoft Security Advisory (961051): Vulnerability in Internet Explorer Could Allow Remote Code Execution. http://www.microsoft.com/technet/security/advisory/961051.mspx, December 2008.
20. Tilo Müller. ASLR Smack and Laugh Reference. Seminar on Advanced Exploitation Techniques, February 2008.
21. Ryan Naraine. Adobe PDF Exploits Using Signed Certificates, Bypasses ASLR/DEP. *ZDNet Zero Day*, September 2010.

22. Anh Nguyen-Tuong, David Evans, John C. Knight, Benjamin Cox, and Jack W. Davidson. Security through Redundant Data Diversity. In *IEEE/IFPF International Conference on Dependable Systems and Networks*, June 2008.

23. Anh Nguyen-Tuong, Andrew Wang, Jason D. Hiser, John C. Knight, and Jack W. Davidson. On the effectiveness of the metamorphic shield. In *Proceedings of the Fourth European Conference on Software Architecture: Companion Volume*, ECSA '10, pages 170–174, New York, NY, USA, 2010. ACM.

24. Pratap V. Prahbu and Yingbo Song and Salvatore J. Stolfo. Smashing the Stack with Hydra: The Many Heads of Advanced Polymorphic Shellcode. Technical Report CUCS-037-09, Columbia University, August 2009.

25. Rapid7 LLC. Metasploit. http://www.metasploit.com/, 2003–2011.

26. Paruj Ratanaworabhan, Benjamin Livshits, and Benjamin Zorn. Nozzle: A Defense Against Heap-spraying Code Injection Attacks. In *USENIX Security Symposium*, 2009.

27. Babak Salamat, Andreas Gal, and Michael Franz. Reverse Stack Execution in a Multi-Variant Execution Environment. In *Workshop on Compiler and Architectural Techniques for Application Reliability and Security*, June 2008.

28. Babak Salamat, Todd Jackson, Andreas Gal, and Michael Franz. Orchestra: Intrusion Detection using Parallel Execution and Monitoring of Program Variants in User-Space. In *ACM European Conference on Computer Systems (EuroSys)*, 2009.

29. Hovav Shacham, Matthew Page, Ben Pfaff, Eu-Jin Goh, Nagendra Modadugu, and Dan Boneh. On the effectiveness of address-space randomization. In *ACM Conference on Computer and Communications Security (CCS)*, CCS '04, pages 298–307, New York, NY, USA, 2004. ACM.

30. Alexander Sotirov. Heap Feng Shui in JavaScript. http://www.blackhat. com/presentations/bh-europe-07/Sotirov/Presentation/ bh-eu-07-sotirov-apr19.pdf, 2007.

31. Ana Nora Sovarel, David Evans, and Nathanael Paul. Where's the feep? the effectiveness of instruction set randomization. In *14th USENIX Security Symposium*, Berkeley, CA, USA, 2005. USENIX Association.

32. Stephanie Forrest and Anil Somayaji and David Ackley. Building Diverse Computer Systems. In *Hot Topics in Operating Systems*, 1997.

33. Stephen W. Boyd and Angelos D. Keromytis. SQLrand: Preventing SQL Injection Attacks. In *Applied Cryptography and Network Security (ACNS)*, 2004.

34. Raoul Strackx, Yves Younan, Pieter Philippaerts, Frank Piessens, Sven Lachmund, and Thomas Walter. Breaking the Memory Secrecy Assumption. In *Second European Workshop on System Security*, 2009.

35. PaX Team. PaX Homepage. http://pax.grsecurity.net/, 2000.

36. Wei Hu and Jason Hiser and Dan Williams and Adrian Filipi and Jack W. Davidson and David Evans and John C. Knight and Anh Nguyen-Tuong and Jonathan Rowanhill. Secure and Practical Defense Against Code-injection Attacks Using Software Dynamic Translation. In *Second International Conference on Virtual Execution Environments*, 2006.

37. Yoav Weiss and Elena Gabriela Barrantes. Known/Chosen Key Attacks against Software Instruction Set Randomization. In *Annual Computer Security Applications Conference (ACSAC)*, 2006.

38. Berend-Jan "SkyLined" Wever. MS Internet Explorer (IFRAME Tag) Buffer Overflow Exploit. http://www.exploit-db.com/exploits/612/, 2004.

# Chapter 3
# Global ISR: Toward a Comprehensive Defense Against Unauthorized Code Execution

Georgios Portokalidis and Angelos D. Keromytis

**Abstract**

Instruction-set randomization (ISR) obfuscates the "language" understood by a system to protect against code-injection attacks by presenting an ever-changing target. ISR was originally motivated by code injection through buffer overflow vulnerabilities. However, Stuxnet demonstrated that attackers can exploit other vectors to place malicious binaries into a victim's filesystem and successfully launch them, bypassing most mechanisms proposed to counter buffer overflows. We propose the holistic adoption of ISR across the software stack, preventing the execution of unauthorized binaries and scripts regardless of their origin. Our approach requires that programs be randomized with different keys during a user-controlled installation, effectively combining the benefits of code whitelisting/signing and runtime program integrity. We discuss how an ISR-enabled environment for binaries can be implemented with little overhead in hardware, and show that higher-overhead software-only alternatives are possible. We use Perl and SQL to demonstrate the application of ISR in scripting environments with negligible overhead.

## 3.1 Introduction

Code-injection attacks occur when an attacker implants arbitrary code into a vulnerable program to gain unauthorized access on a system, acquire elevated privileges, or extract sensitive information like passwords. In the past, code-injection (CI) attacks accounted for almost half of the advisories released by CERT [1]. Because such attacks can be launched over the network, they were regularly used as an infection vector by many computer worms [2, 3, 4, 5, 6]. More recently, they have been outweighed by other types of attacks, such as SQL injection and Cross Site Scripting (XSS). However, the recent Conficker [7] and Stuxnet [8] worm outbreaks, and the

Network Security Lab, Columbia University, New York, NY 10027, USA
e-mail: \{porto, angelos\}@cs.columbia.edu

multiple vulnerabilities discovered in Adobe's omnipresent software [9, 10], serve as a reminder that CI attacks still pose a significant threat to a large number of systems.

Code-injection attacks are frequently enabled by vulnerabilities such as buffer overflows [11, 12, 13], and other memory corruption vulnerabilities like dangling pointers [14, 15] and format string attacks [16], which allow attackers to first inject code in the vulnerable program, and then redirect its execution to the injected code. In their simplest form, they follow the overflow of a buffer in the stack, which overwrites the function's return address to transfer control to the code placed in the buffer as part of the overflow.

The techniques used to perform CI attacks can vary significantly. As such, one could assume that to stop these attacks, we would need to concurrently prevent all the types of exploits that make them possible. However, while the specific techniques used in each attack differ, they all result in attackers executing their code. This capability implies that attackers know what "type" of code (*e.g.*, x86) is understood by the system.

This observation led us [17] (and concurrently others [18, 19]) to introduce a general approach for preventing code-injection attacks, *instruction-set randomization (ISR)*. Inspired by biology where genetic variation protects organisms from environmental threats, ISR proposes the randomization of the underlying system's instructions, so that "foreign" code introduced within a running process by an attack would fail to execute correctly, regardless of the injection approach. ISR is a general approach that defeats *all types* of remote code injection, regardless of the way it was injected into a process, by providing an ever-shifting target to the attacker.

ISR protects running processes against all types of CI attacks, but it cannot protect against the most basic type of attack. Consider the case where the attacker manages to get his own malicious binary on the victim's file system, and then finds some way to launch that binary. ISR, as defined in previous work, would either randomize and then execute this binary, or would simply run it as-is since it is not randomized. In both cases the attacker can completely bypass ISR. However, the same holds for almost all other protection techniques aimed at the same class of vulnerabilities, such as address space layout randomization (ASLR). Comprehensive techniques such as Taint Tracking suffer from low performance and complexity, due to the requirement for continuous and complete monitoring of all that occurs within a system.

The means by which the attacker gets his malicious program (frequently called malware) on the target's system is secondary. Sophisticated attackers exploit other vulnerabilities to copy the malware on the victim's file system and then execute it, or overwrite already existing binaries, so that the next time the user launches the application the attacker's code executes instead. For instance, consider the Stuxnet [8] worm, which is considered one of the most sophisticated ever encountered, and for this reason it has received a lot of attention both from researchers and the media. Its main goal has been identified as being the infection of industrial control systems (ICS), but to propagate and reach its target, it uses many elaborately constructed infection vectors. One of its propagation methods involves a code-injection attack that follows the exploitation of a buffer overflow vulnerability in the Windows Server Service. ISR would avert the exploitation of this vulnerability, effectively disabling this infection vector. Unfortunately, Stuxnet can evade ISR by exploiting other vulnerabilities to place a binary in the target's file system (both remotely, and locally through removable storage), and then execute it.

*We propose the whole-sale adoption of ISR across all system layers, as a way to enforce non-von Neumann semantics. Doing so will prevent the execution of unauthorized code, and will protect systems from complex threats such as Stuxnet.* Our approach requires that all binaries in the system are pre-randomized. Our approach requires that all binaries in the system are pre-randomized. New binaries being installed will require user authorization before being copied to the filesystem, which will also randomize them in the process. As a result an unauthorized binary being dropped on the filesystem will not be able to execute, as it will be in the wrong "language". The benefits we obtain with this approach are twofold. First, we ensure the integrity of existing system binaries, and at the same time we ensure that new binaries that have not been installed through the proper channels (*e.g.,* an installer tool with proper rights) will fail to execute successfully. Thus, ISR simultaneously provides the benefits of program signing/whitelisting and runtime integrity.

Employing ISR in this fashion would thwart the propagation of worms like Stuxnet. Future worms would likely then resort in injecting interpreted code, if an interpreter for a language like Perl or Python is available. Injecting interpreted code would enable the attacker to bypass binary ISR and execute code, but it could be also used to extract information from the system that would enable him to "break" the randomization used (*e.g.,* by guessing the key used for randomizing authorized binaries). Fortunately, ISR is flexible enough that it can be also applied on interpreted languages like Perl and SQL, as we demonstrate in Sections 3.5 and 3.6.

In the remainder of this chapter, we discuss the principles behind ISR, our early work, and the open challenges in adopting it across the whole software stack.

## 3.2 Instruction-Set Randomization

ISR is based on the observation that code-injection attacks need to position executable code within the address space of the exploited application and then redirect control to it. The injected code needs to be compatible with the execution environment for these attacks to succeed. This means that the code needs to be compatible with the processor and software running at the target. For instance, injecting x86 code into a process running on an ARM system will most probably cause it to crash, either because of an illegal instruction being executed, or due to an illegal memory access. Note that for this particular example, it may be possible to construct somewhat limited code that will run without errors on both architectures.

We build on this observation to prevent attackers from executing injected code. We introduce a randomly mutating execution environment, whose "language" is not known to attackers, while legitimate binaries are "translated" to this language during installation. In this way, both injected code and binaries installed without authorization will fail to execute. Attempts to guess the language of the execution environment can be hindered by frequently mutating it, and by allowing for different parts of a program to "speak" different languages. For instance, every time an application crashes, which could be due to a failed attack, we re-randomize it, while various components of the application (*i.e.,* libraries or even functions) can be randomized in a different way. Attempts to execute the code injected into a randomized process will still crash it causing a denial of service (DoS), but attackers will no longer be able to perform any useful actions such as installing rootkits.

The strength of ISR lies in the fact that the attacker does not know the instruction set used by an application, and the high complexity of guessing it. As such, if an attacker has access to the original code, and he can gain access to the randomized code, he can launch an attack against the applied transformation to attempt to learn the new instruction set. This requires that the attacker has local access to the target host. In general, ISR is primarily focused on protecting against remote attacks that originate from the network, where the attacker does not have access to the target system or the randomized binaries. Consequently, we assume that attackers do not have local access.

Finally, the security of the scheme depends on the assumption that the attacker's code will raise an exception (*e.g.,* by accessing an illegal address or using an invalid opcode), similarly to the example where x86 code is injected into an application for ARM. While this will be generally true, there are a few permutations of injected code that will result in working code that performs the attacker's task. We argue that this number will be statistically insignificant [19], and it is comparable with the probability of creating a valid buffer-overflow exploit using the output of a random number generator as code.

### 3.2.1 ISR Operation

CPU instructions for common architectures, like x86 and ARM, consist of two parts: the *opcode* and *operands*. The opcode defines the action to be performed, while the operands are the arguments. For example, in the x86 architecture a software interrupt instruction (*INT*) comprises of the opcode *0xCD*, followed by a one-byte operand that specifies the type of interrupt. We can create new instruction sets by randomly creating new mappings between opcodes and actions. We can further randomize the instruction set by also including the operands in the transformation.

For ISR to be effective and efficient, the number of possible instruction sets must be large, and the mapping between the new opcodes and instructions should be efficient (*i.e.,* not completely arbitrary). We can achieve both these properties by employing cryptographic algorithms and a randomly generated secret key. As an example, consider a generic RISC processor with fixed-length 32-bit instructions. We can effectively generate random instruction sets by encoding instructions with XOR and a secret 32-bit key. In this example, an attacker would have to try at most

$2^{32}$ combinations to guess the key. Architectures with larger instructions (*i.e.,* 64 bits) can use longer keys to be even more resistant to brute-force attacks.

In the case of XOR, using a key size larger than the instruction size does not necessarily improve security, since the attacker may be able to attack it in a piece-meal fashion (*i.e.,* guess the bits corresponding to one instruction, and then proceed with guessing the bits for a second instruction in a sequence, and so forth). The situation is even more complicated on architectures with variable sized instructions like the x86. Many instructions in the x86 architecture are 1 or 2 bytes long. This effectively splits a 32-bit key in four or two sub-keys of 8 and 16 bits respectively. Thus, it is possible that a remote attacker attempts to guess each of the sub-keys independently [20]. A failed attempt to guess the key will cause the application to crash, which could be potentially detected by the attacker.

The deficiencies of XOR randomization on architectures like the x86 can be overcome using other ciphers that cannot be attacked in a piece-meal fashion. For example, using bit-transposition with a 32-bit instruction requires an 160-bit key. Although not all possible permutations are valid (the effective key size is $log_2(32!)$), the work factor for the attacker is high, as he would have to try at most 32! combinations to guess the key (notice that $32! >> 2^{32}$). Increasing the block size (*i.e.,* transposing bits between adjacent instructions) can further increase the work factor for an attacker. The drawback of using larger blocks is that we must have simultaneous access to the whole block of instructions during execution. This increases complexity, specially when implementing ISR in hardware. If the block size is not an issue, such as in software-only implementations of ISR, we could also use AES encryption with 128-bit blocks of code.

We adopt a different approach to protect against key guessing attacks. First, we re-randomize an application every time it crashes using a new randomly generated key. Thus, an attacker trying to remotely guess the key being used, will cause it to change with each failed attempt. Additionally, we use different keys to randomize different parts of an application, where the execution environment allows it. For instance, we can randomize every library or even function used by an application with a different key.

## 3.2.2 Randomization of Binaries

ELF (the executable and linking format) is a very common and standard file format used for executables and shared libraries in many Unix-type systems like Linux, BSD, Solaris, *etc.* Despite the fact that it is most commonly found on Unix systems, it is very flexible, and it is not bound to any particular architecture or OS. Additionally, the ELF format completely separates code and data, including control data such as the procedure linkage table (PLT), making binary randomization straightforward.

We modified the *objcopy* utility, which is part of the GNU binutils package to add support for randomizing ELF executables and libraries. *objcopy* can be used to perform certain transformations (*e.g.,* strip debugging symbols) on an object file, or simply copy it to another. Thus, it is able to parse the ELF headers of an executable or library and access its code. We modified *objcopy* to randomize a file's code using XOR and one or more 16-bit keys. Using a 16-bit key is sufficient as an attacker has an $1/2^{16}$ chance to correctly guess the key in one attempt, while failed guess attempts will cause the application to crash, and consequently trigger the re-randomization of the binary with a different key. Multiple keys can be used to randomize a single binary, in the case of software-only ISR. When using multiple keys, each function within the binary is encoded using a different key. As this will greatly affect the number of keys being used in the system, we expect such a setup to be only used with highly critical applications.

The keys for every binary in the system are stored in a database (DB), using the *sqlite* database system. *Sqlite* is a software library that implements a self-contained, serverless SQL database engine. The entire DB is stored in a single file, and can be accessed directly by the loader (using the *sqlite* library) without the need to run additional servers. Keys are indexed using a binary's full path on disk, and the operation of retrieving them from the DB is fast. Since it is an operation that is only performed when a binary is loaded to memory (*e.g.*, when an application is launched or a dynamic library is loaded), its performance is not critical for the system. New binaries can be installed using an installation script, which uses our modified version of *objcopy* to randomize the binaries being installed to the file system. Authorization is requested before completing the installation to copy the files, and insert the randomization keys in the DB.

Note that randomizing using XOR does not require that the target binary is aligned, so it does not increase its size or modify its layout. Moreover, while our implementation is currently only able to randomize ELF binaries, support for other binaries can be easily added. For instance, we plan to extend *objcopy* to also randomize *Portable Executable (PE)* binaries for Windows operating systems [21].

### 3.2.3 Execution Environment

A randomized process requires the appropriate execution environment to obtain the keys used by an applications and its libraries, and to de-randomize its instructions before executing them. Such an execution environment can be implemented both in hardware (Section 3.3) and software (Section 3.4).

Additionally, when an application is using multiple keys to randomize its various parts, the execution environment needs to be able to detect when execution switches between parts of the code using different randomization keys. For instance, each library being used by an application may be randomized with a different key, and even different functions within the application and libraries can be randomized with varying keys. Detecting such context switches can be complex in hardware, and as we discuss below, the proposed hardware-based implementation of ISR only handles statically linked executables (sacrificing flexibility for performance). In Section 3.4, we describe a software-only ISR solution that handles dynamically linked applications, and supports multiple instruction sets per process (*i.e.*, instructions randomized with different keys), albeit with higher overhead for the randomized applications.

## 3.3 Hardware-based ISR

Implementing ISR in hardware requires a programmable processor [22] or small modifications to current processor architectures like the IA-32 to perform the de-randomization of instructions before execution. Let us consider such a system running on top of such a CPU. Typically, software is separated between kernel and user space, where tasks such as virtual memory management and device drivers are running in *kernel space*, and user processes in *user space*. ISR aims to protect applications, and as such we currently ignore kernel space, which also simplifies our design because we do not have to consider the interactions between ISR and the various low-level processor events (*e.g.*, interrupts). However, a comprehensive solution would also apply ISR within the kernel.

When a new randomized process is launched (*e.g.*, as a result of an *exec()* system call), the processor needs to know the key being used before executing any of its instructions. The key used to randomize the binary is stored in the *sqlite* DB, which is stored in a file (as described in Section 3.2.2). We query the DB for the binary's key through a user space component, and then store it in the process' process control block (PCB) structure. When the process is actually scheduled for execution, the OS loads the key in the PCB on the processor. For this purpose, we provide for a special processor register where the decoding key is stored, and a special privileged instruction (called *GAVL*) that allows write-only access to this register when running in privileged mode (*i.e.*, in kernel space). To accommodate code that is not randomized (*e.g.*, the kernel and *init*), we provide a special key that, when loaded via the *GAVL* instruction, disables the decoding process. Since the key is always brought in from the PCB, there is no need to save its value during context switches. There is, thus, no instruction to read the value of the decoding register.

When a program is executed by the processor, instructions are first fetched from memory, decoded (this refers to the CPU's decoding and not ISR's), and then executed. Our design introduces a de-randomizing element, which lies between the fetching of the instruction, and its decoding. This element is responsible for de-randomizing the code fetched from memory, before delivering it to the CPU for decoding and execution. Such a scheme can be very efficiently implemented in the interface between the L2 cache and main memory, as shown by Rogers *et al.* [23]. When XOR randomization is used, this element simply applies XOR on the bytes received from memory using the key stored in *GAVL*.

Normally, applications use various libraries, which can be linked statically, or dynamically during loading, or even at runtime. But the ISR key is associated with an entire process, making it difficult to accommodate dynamically linked libraries. We could require that all shared libraries used by an application are randomized with its key, but then the memory occupied by each library will not be actually shared with other processes, as they may use a different key. To keep the hardware design simple and efficient, our early prototypes required that applications running under ISR are statically linked. Moreover, modern Linux systems frequently include a read-only *virtual shared object (VDSO)* in every running process. This object is used to export certain kernel functions to user space. For instance, it is used to perform system calls, replacing the older software interrupt mechanism (*INT 0x80*). If the use of a VDSO is required, we need to make small modifications to the kernel, so that a unique non-shared object is mapped to each process, and to randomize it using the process' key.

Finally, there are cases where the kernel injects a few non-randomized instructions in processes. For instance, some systems inject code within the stack of a process when a signal is delivered. These *signal trampolines* are used to set and clean up the context of signal handlers. They are a type of legitimate code-injection (approximately 5-7 instructions long) performed by the system itself. Fortunately, since the kernel performs this code-injection, we can modify it to randomize these instructions before injecting them in a process.

### 3.3.1 x86 Prototype Using Bochs

To determine the feasibility of a hardware-based ISR implementation, we built a prototype for the most widely used processor architecture, the x86, using the Bochs emulator [24]. As we discussed in Section 3.2, randomization on the x86 is more complicated than with RISC-type processors, because of its variable-sized instructions. So, by implementing our prototype for x86, we also test the feasibility of ISR in a worst-case scenario.

Bochs is an open-source emulator of the x86 architecture, which operates by interpreting every machine instruction in software. Bochs, in many ways, operates similarly to real hardware. For instance, in its core we find the CPU execution loop, which calls the function *fetchDecode()* that fetches an instruction from the emulator's virtual RAM, and decodes it. This behavior closely simulates the i486 and Pentium processors, with their instruction *prefetch streaming buffer*, which keeps the next 16 bytes of instructions (32 bytes on later processors). We implemented the de-randomization element in the beginning of *fetchDecode()*, after the fetching of an instruction byte, and before the decoding, as we would do in the real hardware. The decoding is driven by the contents of the *GAVL* register, which if empty indicates that instructions are not randomized, while otherwise contains the decoding key.

To simplify the creation and evaluation of our prototype, we adopted the techniques we used to construct embedded systems for VPN gateways [25]. We use automated scripts to produce compact (2-4MB) bootable single-system images that contain a system kernel and applications. We achieve this by linking the code of all the executables that we wish to be available at runtime in a single executable using the *crunchgen* utility. The single executable alters its behavior depending on the

|         | ftp   | sendmail | fibonacci |
|---------|-------|----------|-----------|
| **Bochs** | 39.0s | ≈ 28s    | ≈ 93s     |
| **Native** | 29.2s | ≈ 1.35s  | 0.322s    |

**Table 3.1** Average execution times (in seconds) for identical binaries under Bochs, and native execution (on the same host). The performance numbers of individual runs were within 10% of the listed averages.

name under which it is run (*argv[0]*). By associating this executable with the names of the individual utilities (via file system hard-links), we can create a fully functional */bin* directory where all the system commands are accessible as apparently distinct files. This aggregation of the system executables in a single image greatly simplifies the randomization process, as we do not need to support multiple executables or dynamic libraries.

Although this greatly limits the real-world applicability of our prototype, we feel it is an acceptable compromise for evaluating hardware-based ISR. Section 3.4 describes in detail a more practical software-only implementation of ISR.

The root of the runtime file system, together with the executable and associated links, are placed in a RAM-disk that is stored within the kernel binary. The kernel is then compressed (using *gzip*) and placed on a bootable medium (*i.e.,* a file that Bochs treats as a virtual hard drive). This file system image also contains the */etc* directory of the running system in uncompressed form, which allows us to easily reconfigure the runtime parameters. At boot time, the kernel is expanded from the boot image to Bochs' main memory, and executed. The */etc* directory is then copied from the bootable medium to the RAM-disk, so that the entire system is running entirely off it. This organization allows multiple applications to be combined with a single kernel, while leaving the configuration files in the */etc* directory on the boot medium.

### 3.3.2 Performance

Our Bochs prototype only serves the purpose of demonstrating the feasibility of an ISR implementation in hardware. Generally, interpreting emulators (as opposed to virtual machine emulators, such as VMWare and VirtualBox) impose a considerable performance penalty that ranges from a slow-down of one to several orders of magnitude. This makes the direct application of ISR using such an emulator impractical for production software, although it may be suitable for certain high-availability environments.

Table 3.1 compares the time taken by the respective server applications to handle some fairly involved client activity. The times recorded for the *ftp* server were for a client carrying out a sequence of common file and directory operations, like the repeated upload and download of a ≈200KB file, creation, deletion and renaming of directories, and generating directory listings by means of an automated script.

We repeated the same sequence of operations 10 times, and list the average. The results indicate that a network I/O-intensive process does not suffer execution time slowdown proportional to the reduction in processor speed. Next, the second column in the table shows the overall time needed by *sendmail* to receive 100 short e-mails of ≈1KB each from a remote host.

In contrast, the third column demonstrates the significant slowdown incurred by the emulator when running a CPU-intensive application (as opposed to the I/O-bound jobs represented in the first two examples), such as computation of the *fibonacci* numbers.

## 3.4 Software-only ISR

A fast implementation of ISR, built entirely in software, is currently the only way to apply ISR on production systems, since the idea of ISR-enabled hardware has had little allure with hardware vendors. Software-only implementations of ISR have been proposed before [26], but have seen little use in practice as they cannot be directly applied to commodity systems. For instance, they do not support shared libraries or dynamically loaded libraries (*i.e.*, they require that the application is statically linked), and increase the code size of encoded applications.

Our approach, much like previous solutions, uses dynamic binary translation to apply ISR on unmodified binaries, but it supports processes randomized with multiple keys (*e.g.*, shared libraries or even functions can use different keys), and incurs low overhead. Our tool builds on Intel's dynamic instrumentation tool called PIN [27], which provides the runtime environment. Similarly to hardware-based ISR, application code is randomized using the XOR function and a 16-bit key, and the application is re-randomized with a new key every time it crashes to make it resistant to remote key guessing attacks [20].

Supporting multiple keys per process means that every shared library used by a process can be randomized using a different key, and applications no longer need to be statically linked. When an application crashes, we do not need to re-randomize all the shared libraries used by it. Instead, we examine the key being used at the time of the crash, and re-randomize only the part of the process that was using that key, since the crash could not have revealed information about other keys to an attacker. Otherwise, we need to dynamically re-randomize the relevant libraries, and propagate the key to other processes that are concurrently using that library.

## 3.4.1 ISR Using PIN

We implemented the de-randomizing execution environment for x86 software run-ning on Linux[1], using Intel's dynamic binary instrumentation tool PIN [27]. PIN is an extremely versatile tool that operates entirely in user space, and supports multiple architectures (x86, 64-bit x86, ARM) and operating systems (Linux, Windows, Ma-cOS). It operates by just-in-time (JIT) compiling the target's instructions combined with any instrumentation into new code, which is placed into a code cache, and ex-ecuted from there. It also offers a rich API to inspect and modify an application's original instructions.

We make use of the supplied API to implement our ISR-enabled runtime. First, we install a callback that intercepts the loading of all file images. This provides us with the names of all the shared libraries being used, and the memory ranges where they have been loaded in the address space. We use the path and name of a library to query the DB for the key or keys used by the library. We save the returned keys, along with the memory address ranges that they correspond to, in a hash table-like data structure that allows us to quickly look up a key using a memory address.

The actual de-randomization is performed by installing a callback that replaces PIN's default function for fetching code from the target process. This second call-back reads instructions from memory, and uses the memory address to look up the key to use for decoding. To avoid performing a look up for every instruction fetched, we cache the last used key. During our evaluation this simple single entry cache achieved high hit ratios, so we did not explore other caching mechanisms. All instructions fetched from memory that have not been associated with a key are considered to be part of the executable, and are decoded using its key.

### 3.4.1.1 Memory Protection (MP)

When executing an application within PIN, they both operate on the same address space. This means that in theory an application can access and modify the data used by PIN and consequently ISR. Such illegal accesses may occur due to a program error, and could potentially be exploited by an attacker. For instance, an attacker could attempt to overwrite a function pointer or return address in PIN, so that control is diverted directly into the attacker's code in the application. Such a control transfer would circumvent ISR enabling the attacker to successfully execute his code. To defend against such attacks we need to protect PIN's memory from being written by the application.

When PIN loads and before the target application and its libraries gets loaded, we mark the entire address space as being "owned" by PIN, by asserting a flag in an array (*page-map*) that holds one byte for every addressable page. For instance, in a 32-bit Linux system, processes can typically access 3 out of the 4 GBytes that are

---

[1] While the current implementation only works on Linux, it can be easily ported to other platforms also supported by the runtime

directly addressable. For a page size of 4 KBytes, this corresponds to 786432 pages, so we allocate 768 KBytes to store the flags for the entire address space. As the target application gets loaded, and starts allocating additional memory, we update the flags for the application-owned pages. Memory protection is actually enforced by instrumenting all memory write operations performed by the application, and checking that the page being accessed is valid according to the page-map. If the application attempts to write to a page owned by PIN, the instrumentation causes a page-fault that will terminate it.

*Memory protection further hardens the system against code-injection attacks, but incurs a substantial overhead.* However, forcing an attacker to exploit a vulnerability in this fashion is already hardening the system considerably, as he would have to somehow discover one of the few memory locations that can be used to divert PIN's control flow. Alternatively, we can use address space layout randomization to decrease the probability of an attacker successfully guessing the location of PIN's control data.

### 3.4.1.2 Exceptions

As we previously mentioned in Section 3.3, there are cases where certain external non-randomized instructions need to be executed in the context of the process, like in the case of signal trampolines. When a signal is delivered to a process, we scan the code being executed to identify *trampolines*, and execute them without applying the decoding function. In the case of a shared object like the VDSO, we assign its memory range a null key, which does not require it to be randomized. Since it is a read-only object, we can safely do so.

### 3.4.1.3 Multiple Instruction Sets

Most executables in modern OSs are dynamically linked to one or more shared libraries. Shared libraries are preferred because they accommodate code reuse and minimize memory consumption, as their code can be concurrently mapped and used by multiple applications. As a result, mixing shared libraries with ISR has proved to be problematic in past work. Our implementation of ISR in software supports multiple instruction sets (*i.e.,* multiple randomization keys) for the same process, enabling us to support truly shared and randomized libraries.

We create a randomized copy of all libraries that are needed, and store them in a shadow folder (*e.g.,* "/usr/rand_lib"). Each library is encoded using a different key, and for extended randomization we can use a different key for each function within the library. To use these libraries, we modify the runtime environment, so that when an application is loaded, it first looks for shared libraries in the shadow folder. This way we can keep the original libraries in the usual system locations (*e.g.,* "/usr/lib" and "/lib" on Linux, and "c:\windows\system32" for Windows).

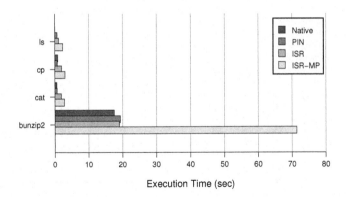

**Fig. 3.1** Execution time of basic Linux utilities. The figure draws the mean execution time and standard deviation when running four commonly used Linux utilities.

#### 3.4.1.4 Protection from Unauthorized Binaries

Implementing our extension to ISR in software-only is less attractive, mainly because of the performance overhead (discussed in Section 3.4.2). Because of this overhead, it will be probably applied only on selected applications, like network services. Nonetheless, if we desire to run all the processes in the system under ISR using PIN, we can modify the *init* process to launch all processes using PIN. This would cause all processes started later on (*e.g.*, via *exec()*) to also run under PIN and ISR.

### 3.4.2 Performance

Dynamic instrumentation tools usually incur significant slowdowns on target applications. While this is also true for PIN, we show that the overhead is not prohibitive. We conducted the measurements presented here on a DELL Precision T5500 workstation with a dual 4-core Xeon CPU and 24GB of RAM running Linux.

Figure 3.1 shows the mean execution time and standard deviation when running several commonly used Linux utilities. We draw the execution time for running *ls* on a directory with approximately 3400 files, and running *cp*, *cat*, and *bunzip2* with a 64MB file. We tested four execution scenarios: native execution, execution with PIN and no instrumentation (PIN's minimal overhead), our implementation of ISR without memory protection (MP), and lastly with MP enabled (ISR-MP). The figure shows that short-lived tasks suffer more, because the time needed to initialize PIN is relatively large when compared with the task's lifetime. In opposition, *when executing a longer-lived task, such as bunzip2, execution under ISR only takes about 10% more time to complete.*

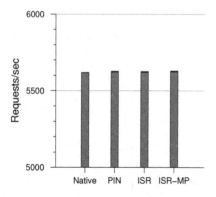

**Fig. 3.2** Apache web server throughput. The figure draws the mean reqs/sec and standard deviation as measured by Apache's benchmark utility *ab*.

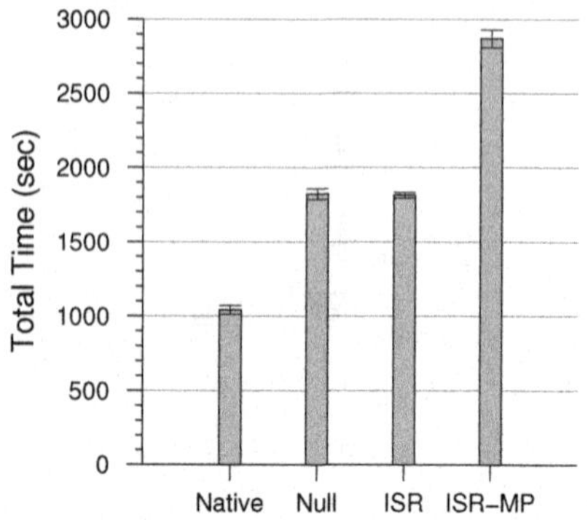

**Fig. 3.3** The MySQL *test-insert* benchmark measures various SQL operations. The figure draws total execution time as reported by the benchmark utility.

For all four utilities, when employing memory protection to protect PIN's memory from interference, execution takes significantly longer, with bunzip2 being the worst case requiring *almost 4 times* more time to complete. That is because memory protection introduces additional instructions at runtime to check the validity of all memory write operations. Another interesting observation is that running bunzip2 under ISR is slightly faster from just using PIN. We attribute this to the various optimizations that PIN introduces when actual instrumentation is introduced.

We also evaluate our implementation using two of the most popular open-source servers: the *Apache* web server, and the *MySQL* database server. For Apache, we measure the effect that PIN and ISR have on the maximum throughput of a static web page, using Apache's own benchmarking tool *ab* over a dedicated 1Gb/s network link. To avoid high fluctuations in performance due to Apache forking extra processes to handle the incoming requests in the beginning of the experiment, we configured it to pre-fork all worker processes (pre-forking is a standard multiprocessing Apache module), and left all other options to their default setting.

Figure 3.2 shows the mean throughput and standard deviation of Apache for the same four scenarios used in our first experiment. The graph shows that Apache's throughput is more limited by available network bandwidth than CPU power. Running the server over PIN has no effect on the attainable throughput, while applying ISR, even with memory protection enabled, does not affect server throughput either.

Finally, we benchmarked a MySQL database server using its own *test-insert* benchmark, which creates a table, fills it with data, and selects the data. Figure 3.3 shows the time needed to complete this benchmark for the same four scenarios. PIN introduces a 75% overhead compared with native execution, while our ISR implementation incurs no observable slowdown. Unlike Apache, enabling memory protection for MySQL is 57.5% slower that just using ISR (175% from native). As with Apache, the benchmark was run at a remote client over an 1Gb/s network link to avoid interference with the server.

## 3.5 Perl Randomization

We showed that using ISR with binaries can protect us from code-injection attacks, and malicious binaries being executed without authorization. Most probably, attackers would adopt new attack vectors that would allow them to bypass ISR-enabled systems. For example, they may attempt to exploit input sanitization errors in interpreted scripts to inject and execute script code. Fortunately, the concept of ISR is particularly versatile, and can be applied to also protect such languages from command injection. We demonstrate its applicability by implementing ISR for the Perl language.

We randomize all of Perl's keywords, operators, and function calls, by appending a random 9-digit number ("tag") suffix to each of them. For example,

```
foreach $k (sort keys %$tre) {
  $v = $tre->{$k};
  die ``duplicate key $k\n''
      if defined $list{$k};
  push @list, @{ $list{$k} };
}
```

by using "123456789" as the tag, becomes

```
foreach123456789 $k (sort123456789 keys %$tre)
{
  $v =1234567889 $tre->{$k};
  die123456789 ``duplicate key $k\n''
    if123456789 defined123456789 $list{$k};
  push123456789 @list, @{ $list{$k} };
}
```

Consequently, Perl code injected by an attacker will fail to execute, since the parser will not recognize a plain-text (not randomized) keyword, function, *etc.*

We implemented the randomization by modifying the Perl interpreter's lexical analyzer to recognize keywords followed by the correct tag. The key is provided to the interpreter via a command-line argument, thus allowing us to embed it inside the randomized script itself (*e.g.*, by using "#!/usr/bin/perl -r123456789" as the first line of the script). Upon reading the tag, the interpreter zeroes it out so that it is not available to the script itself via the ARGV array. These modifications were fairly straightforward, and took less than a day to implement. We automated the process of generating randomized code using Perltidy [28], which was originally used to indent and reformat Perl scripts to make them easier to read. This allowed us to easily parse valid Perl scripts and emit the randomized tags as needed.

This randomization scheme presents us with two problems. First, Perl's external modules that play the role of code libraries, and are frequently shared by many scripts and users. Second, the randomization key is provided in the command line, meaning that an attacker could drop his malicious randomized Perl script in the file system, and execute it.

To address these two issues, we define a system-wide key known only to the Perl interpreter. Using this scheme, the administrator can periodically randomize the system modules, without requiring any action from the user, while an attacker will have to successfully guess the "tag" used by the system to successfully run his malicious Perl script. For a 9- digit "tag" that would require at most $10^9 attempts$, but unlike before we can use an (almost) arbitrarily long "tag". Finally, although the size of the scripts increases considerably due to the randomization process, some preliminary measurements indicate that performance is unaffected.

*Shell scripts* can be randomized in a similar way to defend against shell injection attacks [29]. For instance,

```
#!/bin/sh
if987654 [ x$1 ==987654 x"" ]; then987654
    echo987654 "Must provide directory name."
    exit987654 1
fi987654
```

In all cases, we must hide low-level (*e.g.,* parsing) errors from the remote user, as these could reveal the tag and thus compromise the security of the scheme. Other interpreted languages that could benefit from ISR include VBS, Python, and others.

## 3.6 SQL Randomization

SQL-injection attacks have serious security and privacy implications [30], specially because they require little effort on the behalf of the attacker. Most frequently, they are used against web applications that accept user input, and use it to compose SQL queries. When these applications do not properly sanitize user inputs, an attacker can carefully craft inputs to inject SQL statements that can potentially allow him to access or corrupt database (DB) data, modify DB structures, *etc.*

For example, consider a log-in page of a CGI application that expects a user-name and the corresponding password. When the credentials are submitted, they are inserted within a query template such as the following:

```
"select * from mysql.user
    where username=' " . $uid . " ' and
        password=password(' ". $pwd . " ');"
```

Instead of a valid user-name, the malicious user sets the *$uid* variable to the string:

```
' or 1=1; --'
```

causing the CGI script to issue the following SQL query to the database:

```
"select * from mysql.user
    where username='' or 1=1; --'' and
        password=password('_any_text_');"
```

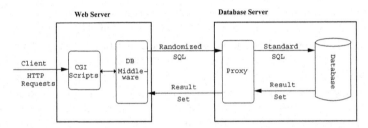

**Fig. 3.4** SQLrand System Architecture

The first single quotes balance the opening quote after *username*, and the remainder of the attacker's input is evaluated as an SQL script by the DB. In this case, *or 1=1* will result in the query returning all the records in *mysql.user*, since the *where* clause evaluates to true. The double hyphen comments out the rest of the SQL query to ensure that no error occurs. If an application uses the above query to determine whether a user's credentials are valid, an attacker supplying the above input would bypass the security check, resulting in a successful log in.

SQL-injection attacks are frequently used to gain unauthorized access to web sites, and then extract sensitive information. For instance, an attacker could read a randomized binary from the file system to launch a brute-force attack against its key, and (after discovering it) launch a successful code-injection attack. *We extend ISR to the SQL language to protect against such information leaking attacks.* We randomize SQL's standard operators (including keywords, mathematical operators, and other invariant language tokens) by appending a random integer (like the 9-digit "tag" used for Perl randomization). All SQL injection attacks are then prevented, because the user input inserted into the "randomized" query is classified as a set of non-operators, resulting in an invalid expression.

Essentially, we introduce a new set of keywords to SQL that will not be recognized by the DB's SQL interpreter. Unlike Perl randomization in Section 3.5, modifying the DB's interpreter to accept the new set of keywords is complicated. Furthermore, a modified DB engine would require that all applications using it conform to its new language. Although running a dedicated DB server for the web applications that we want to protect may be feasible, they would still be forced to all use the same random key.

Our design allows for a single DB server that can be used with multiple web applications employing multiple randomization keys, while at the same time it can be used by non-randomized applications. It consists of a proxy that sits between the client and database server as shown in Figure 3.4. By moving the de-randomization process outside the database management system (DBMS), we gain flexibility, simplicity, and security. Multiple proxies using different random keys can be listening for connections on behalf of the same database. Each proxy deciphers the randomized SQL query received, and then forwards it to the DB. It is also responsible for concealing DB errors which may reveal the key used by the application to the attacker. For example, the attacker could perform a simple SQL-injection to cause a parse error that would return an error message. This message could disclose a sub-set of the query or table information, which may be used to deduce hidden database properties. By stripping the randomization tags in the proxy, we need not worry about the DBMS inadvertently exposing such information through error messages; the DBMS itself never sees the randomization tags. Thus, to ensure the security of the scheme, we only need to ensure that no messages generated by the proxy itself are ever sent to the DBMS or the front-end server. Given that the proxy itself is fairly simple, it seems possible to secure it against attacks. If the proxy is compromised, the database remains safe, assuming that other security measures are in place.

We assist the developer to randomize his SQL statements, by providing a tool that reads a SQL statements and rewrites all keywords with the random key appended. For example, an SQL query, which takes user input, may look like the following:

```
select gender, avg(age)
   from cs101.students
      where dept = %d
   group by gender
```

The utility will identify the six keywords in the example query and append the key to each one (*e.g.*, when the key is "123"):

```
select123 gender, avg123 (age)
   from123 cs101.students
      where123 dept = %d
   group123 by123 gender
```

The generated SQL query can be inserted into the developer's web application. The proxy receives the randomized SQL, translates and validates it, before forwarding it to the database. Note that the proxy performs simple syntactic validation, but is otherwise unaware of the semantics of the query itself.

### 3.6.1 SQLrand Implementation

We built a proof-of-concept proxy server that implements ISR for the SQL language. The proxy detects SQL-injection attacks, and rejects the malicious queries, so they never reach the DB server. It consists of two components, the de-randomization (or decoding) element, and the communication component that implements the communi-cation protocol between the DB client and server. Our implementation focuses on CGI scripts being the query generators and DB clients, but our approach can be also applied to other environments like Java, and the Java database access framework (JDBC).

The decoding component is essentially an SQL parser that can "understand" the randomized SQL language. To create the parser, we utilized two popular tools fre-quently used in the development of compilers: flex and yacc. First, we used flex and regular expressions to match SQL keywords followed by zero or more digits, so we can capture the encoded SQL queries. (Technically, it did not require a key; practi-cally, it needs one.) The lexical analyzer uses these expressions to strip the random extension, and return the keyword for grammar processing and query reassembly by yacc. Tokens that did not match are labeled as identifiers. During parsing, any syntax error indicates that either the query was not properly randomized with the preselected key, or that an SQL-injection attack is taking place. In both cases, when an error occurs the parser returns NULL, while successfully parsing the query returns the de-randomized SQL string.

For the database server, we used MySQL, one of the most popular open-source DB systems. Our communication component implements MySQL's protocol between the proxy and the client, as well as between the proxy and the server. To communicate with the server, we used MySQL's C client library, which was sufficient. On the other hand, a server-side library implementing MySQL's protocol was not available. Therefore, we resorted to manually analyzing the MySQL protocol to obtain a rough sketch of the basics of the protocol: querying, error reporting, and disconnecting. The query message, as the name implies, carries the actual requests to the server. The disconnect message is necessary in cases where the client abruptly disconnects from the proxy, or sends the proxy an invalid query. In both cases, the proxy is responsible for disconnecting from the database by issuing the disconnect command on behalf of the client. Finally, the error message is sent to the client when an query generates a syntax error, indicating a possible injection attack.

Configuring a client application to use the proxy is straightforward. Assuming that the proxy is running on the same host as the server, it is adequate to modify the client to use the port of the proxy instead of the server's. After receiving a connection, the proxy establishes a connection with the database, where it forwards the messages it receives from the client. Messages that contain queries, and are successfully parsed by the proxy, are forwarded to the server. If parsing of a query fails, the proxy returns a generic syntax error to the client (so as not to reveal the randomization key), and disconnects from the server.

### 3.6.2 Limitations

Stored procedures

Stored procedures are SQL statements that are stored in the DB itself, and are invoked by the client as a function (*e.g., select new_employee(id, name, department)*). They are also susceptible to SQL-injection attacks, but cannot be protected using the current SQLrand design. In particular, it is impossible to de-randomize them without changing the SQL parsing logic in the database. Additionally, using a variable randomization key may also be problematic, depending on the DB's implementation. A potential solution could involve storing the queries in an external data source (*e.g.,* an XML file) that the application reads during execution. These queries can be randomized during runtime under a different key.

Problematic library calls

The client library may define some API methods, which use fixed queries. For instance, MySQL's *mysql_list_dbs()* call issues the query string "SHOW databases LIKE <wild-card-input>", which is hard coded. We could workaround this issue without modifying the client library, by manually constructing the query string with the proper randomized key, and executing it using the *mysql_query()* method. Moreover, pre-compiled binary SQL statements cannot be currently processed by the proxy, therefore *mysql_real_query()* must be avoided.

### 3.6.3 *Evaluation*

We created a small database with tables containing various numbers of records, ranging from twenty to a little more than a thousand, to evaluate the effectiveness and performance of SQLrand.

First, we wrote a sample CGI application that suffers from an SQL-injection vulnerability, which allows an attacker to inject SQL into the *where* clause of the query. An attacker could easily exploit this fault to retrieve all the records in the table, even though he should not be allowed to. When using the SQLrand proxy, the SQL-injection was identified and an error message was returned instead of the table data.

Then, we tested SQLrand with existing software like the phpBB v2.0.5 web bulletin board system (BBS). The script *viewtopic.php* of the BBS is vulnerable to an SQL-injection attack that can reveal critical information like user passwords. We first performed the SQL-injection attack without using randomization, and after ensuring it succeeded, we randomized the SQL queries in the script, and configured the BBS to use the SQLrand proxy. As expected, when we relaunched the attacked, the proxy recognized it, and dropped the query without forwarding it to the DB. While the phpBB application did not succumb to the SQL-injection attack, we observed that it displayed the SQL query when zero records are returned, revealing the encoding being used. So, while ISR stops SQL-injection attacks, it can be of little benefit, when bad coding practices result in critical information about the application being divulged to potential attackers.

We also tested another content management system (CMS) that is prone to SQL injection attacks. The PHP-Nuke CMS, depends on PHP's *magic_quotes_gpc* option being enabled, or otherwise several modules are open to attack. Interestingly, even with this option set, injections using unchecked numeric fields are still possible. For example, PHP-Nuke uses the numeric variable *lid*, which is passed through the URL when downloading content. An attacker can perform SQL-injection using this variable, to retrieve all user passwords (*e.g.*, by appending *select pass from users_table* to an invalid *lid* value). However, when using SQLrand this attack was averted.

| Users | Min | Max | Mean | Std |
|-------|-----|------|-------|-------|
| 10 | 74 | 1300 | 183.5 | 126.9 |
| 25 | 73 | 2782 | 223.8 | 268.1 |
| 50 | 73 | 6533 | 316.6 | 548.8 |

**Table 3.2** Proxy Overhead (in microseconds)

Next, we measured the overhead imposed by SQLrand. We designed an experiment to measure the additional processing time required, when multiple users (*i.e.,* 10, 25, and 50 respectively) perform queries concurrently. The users executed, in a round-robin fashion, a set of five queries over 100 trials. The average length of the queries was 639 bytes, and the random key length was 32 bytes. For this experiment, the DB, proxy, and client were all running on different hosts running RedHat Linux, within the same network. Table 3.2 lists the results of our experiments. We see that the overhead ranges from 183 to 316 microseconds, and in the worst-case scenario the proxy adds approximately 6.5 milliseconds to the processing time of each query. Since acceptable response times for most web applications usually fall between a few seconds to tens of seconds, depending on the purpose of the application, we believe that the additional delay introduced by the proxy is acceptable for the majority of applications.

## 3.7 Security Considerations

Performing code injection in a few vulnerable applications running under ISR, caused the targets to terminate with a segmentation violation or illegal opcode exception. Barrantes *et al.* [19] performed a study on the faults exhibited by a compromised process running under ISR, and show that such a process executes 5 or less x86 instructions before causing a fatal exception. The instructions that get actually executed are essentially random bytes produced by the de-randomization of the attacker's injected code.

The rest of this section discusses the methods that might be employed by an attacker to bypass instruction-set randomization.

### 3.7.1 Key Guessing Attacks

The most obvious way to attack ISR is by attempting to guess the key, or one of the keys used by a process. As we re-randomize a process with a new key every time it crashes, such brute-force attacks become purely a game of chance. For instance, when using a 16-bit key the attacker has an $1/2^{16}$ probability to guess the key correctly in the first attempt. An incorrect attempt to guess the key, will cause the process to fail and re-randomize. Even if the attacker manages to attack part of the key (the 8 bits corresponding to a single-byte instruction), as shown in [20], he would still have only an $1/2^8$ probability to guess the key correctly. Furthermore, Cox *et al.* [31] showed that a quorum architecture, where each replica is randomized differently (with a different key), would defeat all key guessing attacks.

Some server processes use *fork()* to create a copy of the parent process every time a new request is received to handle that request. An attacker can then attempt multiple guesses against the same key. In such cases, the *fork()* system call can be itself modified, so that if the process is employing instruction-set randomization, the text segment is actually copied (rather than just copying the page table entries of the parent) and re-randomized. It is worth noting that such failures can be used to perform near-real-time forensic analysis to identify the vulnerability the attacker is exploiting and to generate a signature [32, 33, 34, 35]. Alternatively, the parent process can be restarted every time a child process crashes. This would ensure that the parent process itself and new children processes will use a new key, while processes already serving clients will keep operating normally.

### 3.7.2 Known Ciphertext Attacks

Since binary code is highly structured, an attacker with access to the randomized code of a process can easily determine the randomization key, and create valid attack payloads. An attacker may easily gain access to randomized code, if he already has local access to the system (*e.g.*, through the */proc* interface on Linux). Since local access is already available to him, he would then target processes running with higher privileges than his own (a privilege escalation attack). We could mitigate this problem by using a stronger encryption algorithm such as AES or bit transposition for the randomization, possibly taking a performance hit. As we mentioned earlier, our technique is primarily focused on deterring remote attackers from gaining local access through code injection. For this task XOR encryption remains sufficient.

However, even for remote attackers, it is imperative that the system does not expose information that could be used by the attacker to increase his chances to brute-force attack ISR. For instance, SQL-injection could be used by an attacker to gain partial access on the system, and obtain a randomized binary. He can then launch a brute-force attack against its key, and later perform a successful code-injection attack. In Section 3.6, we discussed how we can apply ISR on SQL to defeat such attacks.

### 3.7.3 Attacks Using Interpreters

With the application of our approach, attackers will no longer be able to execute binary code on the system. As a result, they may resort to attacking applications written in an interpreted or scripting language, or to simply drop and execute such a script on the targeted system. In Section 3.5, we described how ISR can be applied on an interpreted language like Perl, and argued that it can be applied with little effort on other languages as well. As many such interpreters are frequently present on a system concurrently, the process of identifying and securing all of them using ISR becomes problematic. For instance, in Linux we find multiple shell binaries that implement various scripting languages (*e.g.,* bash, tcsh, ksh, *etc.*), and interpreted programming environments like Perl, Python, Tcl, *etc.* An attacker would need only one of them to be running without ISR to subvert our defenses.

We can prevent such attacks by identifying the interpreters present on a system, and requiring that they are ISR-enabled, or disallowing their execution. Frequently, scripts written in such languages begin by specifying a "magic number" (*i.e.,* '#!') followed by the location and name of the interpreter required for execution (*e.g.,* *#!/usr/bin/perl*). When such scripts execute, we can modify the kernel to look for this string, and check if the executed interpreter uses randomization, or whether it is allowed to execute. Unfortunately, scripts can be also run by directly invoking the interpreter binary, even if they do not contain such a magic number (*e.g.,* */usr/bin/perl myscript.pl*).

Alternatively, we can scan the file system for files beginning with '#!' to statically identify existing interpreters. While not all script files contain this magic number, it is more likely that at least one script for each installed interpreter will exist that contains it. For example, even if all Perl scripts observed running do not begin with the magic number, there will be other Perl scripts in the file system (*e.g.,* Perl modules) that begin with it. More elaborate solutions, could even employ static and dynamic analysis to detect interpreter binaries based on their features and behavior (*e.g.,* detect their lexical analyzer).

## 3.8 Related Work

Instruction-set randomization was initially proposed as a general approach against code-injection attacks by Gaurav *et al.* [17]. They propose a low-overhead implementation of ISR in hardware, and evaluate it using the Bochs x86 emulator. They also demonstrate the applicability of the approach on interpreted languages such as Perl, and later SQL [36]. Concurrently, Barrantes *et al.* [18] proposed a similar randomization technique for binaries (RISE), which builds on the Valgrind x86 emulator. RISE provides limited support for shared libraries by creating randomized copies of the libraries for each process. As such, the libraries are not actually shared, and consume additional memory each time they are loaded. Furthermore, Valgrind incurs a minimum performance overhead of 400% [37], which makes its use impractical.

Hu *et al.* [26] implemented ISR using a virtual execution environment based on a dynamic binary translation framework named STRATA. Their implementation uses AES encryption with a 128-bit key, which requires that code segments are aligned at 128-bit blocks. Unlike our implementation over PIN, they do not support self-modifying code, and they produce randomized binaries that are significantly larger from the originals (*e.g.,* the randomized version of Apache was 77% larger than the original). Also, to the best of our knowledge previous work on ISR does not address the implications introduced by signal trampolines and VDSO, nor does it investigate the costs involved with protecting the execution environment from the hosted process (STRATA protects only a part of its data).

Address obfuscation is another approach based on randomizing the execution environment (*i.e.,* the locations of code and data) to harden software against attacks [38, 39]. It can be performed at runtime by randomizing the layout of a process (ASLR) including the stack, heap, dynamically linked libraries, static data, and the process's base address. Additionally, it can be performed at compile time to also randomize the location of program routines and variables. Shacham *et al.* [40] show that ASLR may not be very effective on 32-bit systems, as they do not allow for sufficient entropy. In contrast, Bhatkar *et al.* [41] argue that it is possible to introduce enough entropy for ASLR to be effective. Meanwhile, attackers have successfully exploited ASLR enabled systems by predicting process layout, exploiting applications to expose layout information [42], or using techniques like heap spraying [43].

Hardware extensions such as the NoExecute (NX) bit in modern processors [44, 39] can stop code-injection attacks all together without impacting performance. This is accomplished by disallowing the execution of code from memory pages that are marked with the NX bit. Unfortunately, its effectiveness is dependent on its proper use by software. For instance, many applications like browsers do not set it on all data segments. This can be due to backward compatibility constraints (*e.g.,* systems using signal trampolines), or even just bad developing practice. More importantly, NX does not protect from unauthorized code execution.

PointGuard [45] uses encryption to protect pointers from buffer overflows. It encrypts pointers in memory, and decrypts them only when they are loaded to a register. It is implemented as a compiler extension, so it requires that source code is available for recompilation. Also, while it is able to deter buffer overflow attacks, it can be defeated by format string attacks that frequently employ code-injection later on. Other solutions implemented as compiler extensions include Stackguard [46] and ProPolice [47]. They operate by introducing special secret values in the stack to identify and prevent stack overflow attacks, but can be subverted [48]. Write integrity testing [49] uses static analysis and "guard" values between variables to prevent memory corruption errors, but static analysis alone cannot correctly classify all program writes. CCured [50] is a source code transformation system that adds type safety to C programs, but it incurs a significant performance overhead and is unable to statically handle some data types. Generally, solutions that require recompilation of software are less practical, as source code or parts of it (*e.g.,* third-party libraries) are not always available.

Dynamic binary instrumentation is used by many other solutions to retrofit unmodified binaries with defenses against remote attacks. For instance, dynamic taint analysis (DTA) is used by many projects [51, 52, 32, 53], and is a able to detect control hijacking and code-injection attacks, but incurs large slowdowns (*e.g.,* frequently 20x or more). Due to their large overhead, dynamic solutions are mostly used for the analysis of attacks and malware [54], and in honeypots [55].

## 3.9 Conclusions

Instruction-set randomization (ISR) is a powerful scheme that can protect binaries from code-injection attacks regardless of how code is injected within a process, by presenting a moving target to an attacker that is attempting to inject malicious code to the system. The original ISR scheme, despite its versatility, could not protect against the most rudimentary type of attack, such as the execution of a malicious and unauthorized binaries. We propose the whole-sale adoption of ISR across all layers of the software stack to protect against such attacks. By pre-randomizing all of a system's binaries with different and most importantly secret keys, the execution of binaries placed on the target by an attacker or worm like Stuxnet will fail to execute in the ISR-enabled environment. At the same time, new binaries can be installed using an installation script that requires user authorization, and that automatically randomizes the installed binary. We also describe in detail how ISR can be implemented in hardware, as well as entirely in software. Finally, we show how ISR can be applied on interpreted languages like Perl and SQL, which may be targeted next by attackers that wish to circumvent ISR. In both cases, we demonstrate that ISR is extremely versatile and can be applied on both Perl and SQL with success and low overhead.

ISR does not address the core issue of software vulnerabilities, which derive from programming errors, and bad coding practices. Nevertheless, given the apparent resistance to the wide adoption of safe languages, and the recent rise of extremely elaborate worms like Conficker and Stuxnet, we believe that ISR can play an important role in hardening systems.

## Acknowledgements

This work was supported by the NSF through Grant CNS-09-14845, and by the Air Force through Contracts AFOSR-FA9550-07-1-0527 and AFRL-FA8650-10-C-7024. Any opinions, findings, conclusions or recommendations expressed herein are those of the authors, and do not necessarily reflect those of the US Government, the Air Force, or the NSF.

# References

1. Wagner, D., Foster, J.S., Brewer, E.A., Aiken, A.: A first step towards automated detection of buffer overrun vulnerabilities. In: Proceedings of the Symposium on Network and Distributed System Security (NDSS). (2000) 3–17
2. Spafford, E.H.: The Internet worm program: An analysis. Technical Report CSD-TR-823, Purdue University (1988)
3. CERT: Advisory CA-2001-19: "Code Red" worm exploiting buffer overflow in IIS indexing service DLL. http://www.cert.org/advisories/CA-2001-19.html (2001)
4. CERT: Advisory CA-2003-04: MS-SQL Server Worm. http://www.cert.org/advisories/CA-2003-04.html (2003)
5. Moore, D., Shanning, C., Claffy, K.: Code-Red: a case study on the spread and victims of an Internet worm. In: Proceedings of the $2^{nd}$ Internet Measurement Workshop (IMW). (2002) 273–284
6. Zou, C.C., Gong, W., Towsley, D.: Code Red worm propagation modeling and analysis. In: Proceedings of the $9^{th}$ ACM Conference on Computer and Communications Security (CCS). (2002) 138–147
7. Porras, P., Saidi, H., Yegneswaran, V.: Conficker C analysis. Technical report, SRI International (2009)
8. Falliere, N., Murchu, L.O., Chien, E.: W32.Stuxnet Dossier version 1.2. White paper (2010)
9. Adobe: Security advisory for flash player, adobe reader and acrobat. http://www.adobe.com/support/security/advisories/apsa10-01.html (2010)
10. Symantec: Analysis of a zero-day exploit for adobe flash and reader. Symantec Threat Research (2010)
11. Pincus, J., Baker, B.: Beyond stack smashing: Recent advances in exploiting buffer overflows. IEEE Security & Privacy Magazine 2 (2004) 20–27
12. Aleph One: Smashing the stack for fun and profit. Phrack 7 (1996)
13. M. Conover and w00w00 Security Team: w00w00 on heap overflows. http://www.w00w00.org/files/articles/heaptut.txt (2010)
14. Enumeration, C.W.: CWE-416: use after free. http://cwe.mitre.org/data/definitions/416.html (2010)
15. PCWorld: Dangling pointers could be dangerous. http://www.pcworld.com/article/134982/dangling\_pointers\_could\_be\_dangerous.html (2007)
16. Shankar, U., Talwar, K., Foster, J.S., Wagner, D.: Detecting format string vulnerabilities with type qualifiers. In: Proceedings of the $10^{th}$ USENIX Security Symposium. (2001) 201–216
17. Kc, G.S., Keromytis, A.D., Prevelakis, V.: Countering code-injection attacks with instruction-set randomization. In: Proceedings of the $10^{th}$ ACM Conference on Computer and Communications Security (CCS). (2003)
18. Barrantes, E.G., Ackley, D.H., Forrest, S., Palmer, T.S., Stefanovic, D., Zovi, D.D.: Randomized instruction set emulation to disrupt binary code injection attacks. In: Proceedings of the ACM Conference on Computer and Communications Security. (2003) 281–289
19. Barrantes, E.G., Ackley, D.H., Forrest, S., Stefanović, D.: Randomized instruction set emulation. ACM Transactions on Information System Security 8 (2005) 3–40
20. Sovarel, A.N., Evans, D., Paul, N.: Where's the FEEB? the effectiveness of instruction set randomization. In: Proceedings of the $14^{th}$ USENIX Security Symposium. (2005) 145–160
21. Microsoft: Microsoft Portable Executable and Common Object File Format Specification. http://www.microsoft.com/whdc/system/platform/firmware/PECOFF.mspx (2010)
22. Raghuram, S., Chakrabarti, C.: A programmable processor for cryptography. In: Proceedings of the 2000 IEEE International Symposium on Circuits and Systems (ISCAS). Volume 5. (2000) 685–688

23. Rogers, B., Solihin, Y., Prvulovic, M.: Memory Predecryption: Hiding the Latency Over-head of Memory Encryption. In: Proceedings of the Workshop on Architectural Support for Security and Anti-virus (WASSA). (2004) 22–28

24. The Bochs Project: The cross platform IA-32 emulator. http://bochs.sourceforge.net/ (2010)

25. Prevelakis, V., Keromytis, A.D.: Drop-in Security for Distributed and Portable Computing Elements. Internet Research: Electronic Networking, Applications and Policy **13** (2003)

26. Hu, W., Hiser, J., Williams, D., Filipi, A., Davidson, J.W., Evans, D., Knight, J.C., Nguyen-Tuong, A., Rowanhill, J.: Secure and practical defense against code-injection attacks using software dynamic translation. In: Proceedings of the $2^{nd}$ International Conference on Virtual Execution Environments (VEE). (2006) 2–12

27. Luk, C.K., Cohn, R., Muth, R., Patil, H., Klauser, A., Lowney, G., Wallace, S., Reddi, V.J., Hazelwood, K.: Pin: Building customized program analysis tools with dynamic instrumenta-tion. In: Proceedings of Programming Language Design and Implementation (PLDI). (2005) 190–200

28. Hancock, S.: The Perltidy Home Page. http://perltidy.sourceforge.net/ (2009)

29. CERT: Vulnerability Note VU#496064. http://www.kb.cert.org/vuls/id/496064 (2002)

30. CERT: Vulnerability Note VU#282403. http://www.kb.cert.org/vuls/id/282403 (2002)

31. Cox, B., Evans, D., Filipi, A., Rowanhill, J., Hu, W., Davidson, J., Knight, J., Nguyen-Tuong, A., Hiser, J.: N-Variant Systems: A Secretless Framework for Security through Diversity. In: Proceedings of the $15^{th}$ USENIX Security Symposium. (2005) 105–120

32. Costa, M., Crowcroft, J., Castro, M., Rowstron, A.: Vigilante: End-to-end containment of internet worms. In: Proceedings of the ACM Symposium on Systems and Operating Systems Principles (SOSP). (2005)

33. Xu, J., Ning, P., Kil, C., Zhai, Y., Bookholt, C.: Automatic Diagnosis and Response to Memory Corruption Vulnerabilities. In: Proceedings of the $12^{th}$ ACM Conference on Computer and Communications Security (CCS). (2005) 222–234

34. Locasto, M., Wang, K., Keromytis, A., Stolfo, S.: FLIPS: Hybrid Adaptive Intrusion Preven-tion. In: Proceedings of the Symposium on Recent Advances in Intrusion Detection. (2005) 82–101

35. Liang, Z., Sekar, R.: Fast and Automated Generation of Attack Signatures: A Basis for Build-ing Self-Protecting Servers. In: Proceedings of the $12^{th}$ ACM Conference on Computer and Communications Security (CCS). (2005) 213–222

36. Boyd, S.W., Kc, G.S., Locasto, M.E., Keromytis, A.D., Prevelakis, V.: On the general ap-plicability of instruction-set randomization. IEEE Transactions on Dependable and Secure Computing **99** (2008)

37. Developers, V.: Valgrind user manual – callgrind. http://valgrind.org/docs/manual/cl-manual.html (2010)

38. Bhatkar, S., DuVarney, D.C., Sekar, R.: Address obfuscation: an efficient approach to com-bat a broad range of memory error exploits. In: Proceedings of the $12^{th}$ USENIX Security Symposium. (2003) 105–120

39. The PaX Team: Homepage of The Pax Team. http://pax.grsecurity.net/ (2010)

40. Shacham, H., Page, M., Pfaff, B., Goh, E., Modadugu, N., Boneh, D.: On the effectiveness of address-space randomization. In: Proceedings of the $11^{th}$ ACM Conference on Computer and Communications Security (CCS). (2004) 298–307

41. Bhatkar, S., Sekar, R., DuVarney, D.C.: Efficient techniques for comprehensive protection from memory error exploits. In: Proceedings of the $14^{th}$ USENIX Security Symposium. (2005) 255–270

42. Durden, T.: Bypassing PaX ASLR protection. Phrack **0x0b** (2002)

43. DarkReading: Heap spraying: Attackers' latest weapon of choice. `http://www.darkreading.com/security/vulnerabilities/showArticle.jhtml?articleID=221901428` (2009)
44. Hardware, E.: CPU-based security: The NX bit. `http://hardware.earthweb.com/chips/article.php/3358421` (2004)
45. Cowan, C., Beattie, S., Johansen, J., Wagle, P.: PointGuard: Protecting pointers from buffer overflow vulnerabilities. In: Proceedings of the 12$^{th}$ USENIX Security Symposium. (2003) 91–104
46. Cowan, C., Pu, C., Maier, D., Hinton, H., Walpole, J., Bakke, P., Beattie, S., Grier, A., Wagle, P., Zhang, Q.: StackGuard: Automatic adaptive detection and prevention of buffer-overflow attacks. In: Proceedings of the 7$^{th}$ USENIX Security Symposium. (1998)
47. Etoh, J.: GCC extension for protecting applications from stack-smashing attacks. `http://www.trl.ibm.com/projects/security/ssp/` (2000)
48. Bulba, Kil3r: Bypassing StackGuard and StackShield. Phrack **5** (2000)
49. Akritidis, P., Cadar, C., Raiciu, C., Costa, M., Castro, M.: Preventing memory error exploits with WIT. In: Proceedings of the 2008 IEEE Symposium on Security and Privacy. (2008) 263–277
50. Necula, G.C., Condit, J., Harren, M., McPeak, S., Weimer, W.: CCured: type-safe retrofitting of legacy software. ACM Trans. Program. Lang. Syst. **27** (2005) 477–526
51. Newsome, J., Song, D.: Dynamic taint analysis for automatic detection, analysis, and signature generation of exploits on commodity software. In: Proceedings of the 12$^{th}$ Annual Symposium on Network and Distributed System Security (NDSS). (2005)
52. Denning, D.E.: A lattice model of secure information flow. Commun. ACM **19** (1976) 236–243
53. Ho, A., Fetterman, M., Clark, C., Warfield, A., Hand, S.: Practical taint-based protection using demand emulation. In: Proceedings of the 1$^{st}$ ACM EuroSys Conference. (2006) 29–41
54. Bayer, U., Kruegel, C., Kirda, E.: TTAnalyze: A tool for analyzing malware. In: Proceedings of the 15$^{th}$ European Institute for Computer Antivirus Research (EICAR) Annual Conference. (2006)
55. Portokalidis, G., Slowinska, A., Bos, H.: Argos: an emulator for fingerprinting zero-day attacks. In: Proceedings of the 1$^{st}$ ACM EuroSys Conference. (2006)

# Chapter 4
# Compiler-Generated Software Diversity

Todd Jackson, Babak Salamat, Andrei Homescu, Karthikeyan Manivannan, Gregor Wagner, Andreas Gal, Stefan Brunthaler, Christian Wimmer, Michael Franz

**Abstract** Present approaches to software security are to a large extent *reactive*: when vulnerabilities are discovered, developers scramble to fix the underlying error. The advantage is on the side of the attackers because they only have to find a single vulnerability to exploit all vulnerable systems, while defenders have to prevent the exploitation of all vulnerabilities. We argue that the compiler is at the heart of the solution for this problem: when the compiler is translating high-level source code to low-level machine code, it is able to automatically diversify the machine code, thus creating multiple functionally equivalent, but internally different variants of a program. We present two orthogonal compiler-based techniques. With multi-variant execution, a monitoring layer executes several diversified variants in lockstep while examining their behavior for differences that indicate attacks. With massive-scale software diversity, every user gets its own diversified variant, so that the attacker has no knowledge about the internal structure of that variant and therefore cannot construct an attack. Both techniques make it harder for an attacker to run a successful attack. We discuss variation techniques that the compiler can utilize to diversify software, and evaluate their effectiveness for our two execution models.

## 4.1 Introduction and Motivation

Networked computers are under constant attack from a variety of adversaries. Software vulnerabilities, such as errors in operating systems, device drivers, shared libraries, and application programs enable most of these attacks. Attackers exploit these errors to perform unauthorized operations on the vulnerable computers. While substantial and impressive results have been and continue to be reported on finding and eliminating various vulnerabilities, the complexity of modern software makes

This research was performed while all of the authors were affiliated with the Department of Computer Science, University of California, Irvine. Please direct questions to the first author at tmjackso@uci.edu.

it nearly impossible to eliminate all errors leading to security vulnerabilities. The incidence of such errors tends to be proportional to the overall code size and decreases over time. The existence of such residual software errors becomes a significant threat when large numbers of computers are simultaneously affected by identical vulnerabilities. Unfortunately, this is the situation today. We currently live in a *software monoculture*—for some widely used software, identical binary code runs on millions, sometimes hundreds of millions, of computers. This makes widespread exploitation easy and attractive for an attacker, because the same attack vector is likely to succeed on a large number of targets.

Compilers are central to software development processes, particularly those that translate high-level source code of the programmer to machine-level executable code. The prevalent design paradigm of compilers is deterministic: the same source code always translates to the same executable. However, during the compilation process, compilers make many optimization decisions that are based on heuristics and best guesses of the compilers' developers. In addition, the compilers may make assumptions or decisions based on legacy behavior of previous compilers or assumed conventions. We claim that the compiler is the ideal place to bring diversity—the key to solving the previously described inherent problems of our present software monoculture—to software, because the compiler can easily produce large amounts of *functionally equivalent*, but *internally different* variants of any input program. These variants have the same *in-specification behavior*, but different *out-of-specification behavior*, i.e., they behave differently when attackers try to exploit out-of-specification behavior (which is then usually called a "vulnerability").

Our work focuses on basic scientific research with the aim of harnessing compiler-generated software diversity for defense purposes. We present two approaches that support all users. Common home/office users who use standalone computers and do not need high security guarantees download software from an App Store such as Apple's App Store or the Android Marketplace. This App Store contains a diversification engine (a "multicompiler") that automatically generates a unique, but functionally identical, variant of the desired application per download request (Figure 4.1). Alternatively, for users who have higher security requirements, a multi-variant execution environment (MVEE) provides significantly higher security guarantees. Because this MVEE system runs multiple variants at the same time in lockstep and verifies input and output, it is well suited for network-facing applications. In both cases, however, all variants of the same application behave in exactly the same way from the perspective of the end user. The differences are due to subtle changes in their implementation. As a result, any specific attack affects only a small fraction of variants.

By combining a set of variation methods in different ways, we can create many different variants. When the number of variants is sufficiently large, targeted attacks become uneconomical, since an attacker would have to develop a large number of different attacks in order to exploit the variants that the attacker believes are in use. However, the attacker has no way of knowing *a priori* which specific attack succeeds on a specific target, and therefore needs to resort to guessing. Consequently, this

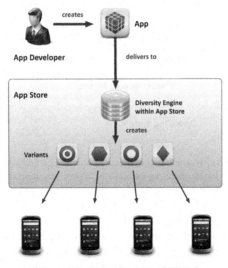

**Fig. 4.1** Architecture of massive-scale software diversity. Our system does not need changes on the side of the developer or the user of an application, but only in the software distribution system.

increases the costs for attackers and the chances of detection. The distribution of diversified binaries also has the effect that adversaries can no longer simply analyze their own copies of any given piece of software to develop exploits. Hence, even directed attacks against specific targets running a particular variant of some software become much more difficult, as long as the attacker has no way of determining which specific binary is present on a particular target.

Equally important, these approaches make it significantly more difficult for an attacker to generate attack vectors by way of reverse engineering of security patches. An attacker requires two pieces of information to extract the vital information about a vulnerability from a bug fix: the version of the software that is vulnerable and the specific patch that fixes the vulnerability. In a diversified software environment, where every instance of every piece of software is unique, we can set things up so that it is highly unlikely that an attacker obtains a matching pair of vulnerable software and its corresponding bug fix that could be used to identify the vulnerability.

In summary, we can make computing safer for all users by replacing the prevalent software monoculture by a more sophisticated *polyculture*. This article describes two orthogonal implementation approaches:

- Multiple variants are run simultaneously, thus making it much more difficult to exploit a known vulnerability (Section 4.2), and
- Distributing individualized variants for all users, thus making it much more difficult to reuse a vulnerability against multiple targets (Section 4.3).

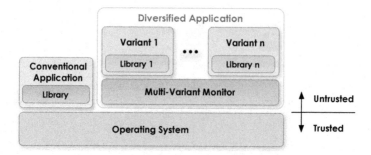

**Fig. 4.2** Architecture of a multi-variant execution environment. Our architecture does not increase the amount of trusted code in the operating system and allows execution of conventional applications without utilizing the MVEE.

Since both approaches are orthogonal, we can combine them to increase the level of security even further. Furthermore, we also present a variety of diversification techniques (Section 4.4), which can be applied in one or both of the two approaches.

## 4.2 Multi-Variant Execution

Multi-variant code execution (Figure 4.2) is a technique that prevents malicious code execution at run time [8, 19]. We execute multiple semantically equivalent instances, or *variants*, of one program and compare their behavior at *synchronization points*. Whenever we detect diverging behavior, we notify users and system administrators so they can take appropriate action.

A *Multi-Variant Execution Environment* (MVEE) duplicates the proper behavior of an unmodified program, while leveraging protections that the variants provide against specific classes of vulnerabilities. This characteristic allows effective monitoring systems that can detect exploitation of vulnerabilities at run time before the attacker has the opportunity to compromise the system. In an MVEE, input to the system is simultaneously fed to all variants. This design makes it nearly impossible for an attacker to send individual malicious input to different variants and compromise them one at a time. If the variants are chosen properly, a malicious input to one variant leads to collateral damage in at least one of the other variants, causing a divergence. A monitoring agent detects such situations.

Multi-variant execution imposes extra computational overhead, since at least two variants of the same program must be executed in lockstep to provide the benefits mentioned above. Although performance is always important, some private and government organizations require higher levels of security for their sensitive applications, and these organizations are likely to trade off performance for additional security. The method we propose here primarily targets these kinds of applications, however, the existence of multi-core processors enables the technique for a wider range of applications while minimizing overhead.

One example of a multi-variant execution environment is the N-variant Systems Framework by Cox et al. [8]. Their environment requires kernel modification as the monitoring agent runs in kernel space. Our framework [19] takes a user-space approach using the monitoring agent described in Section 4.2.1.

### 4.2.1 The Monitor

Multi-variant execution is a monitoring mechanism that controls the states of the executed variants and verifies that they comply to pre-defined rules. A monitoring agent, or *monitor*, is responsible for performing these checks and ensuring that no program instance has been corrupted. Monitoring happens at varying granularities, ranging from a coarse-grained approach that only checks that the final output of each variant is identical, all the way down to a checkpointing mechanism that compares each executed instruction. While the granularity of monitoring does not impact what can be detected, it determines how soon an attack can be caught.

We use a monitoring technique that allows synchronization of program instances at varying granularities as coarse as system calls [19] and as fine as instructions. Our rationale for starting at system call granularity and subsequently choosing finer granularities is that the semantics of modern operating systems prevent processes from having any outside effect unless they invoke a system call. Thus, injected malicious code cannot damage the system without invoking a system call. Our chosen granularities detects malicious attempts at invoking system calls either at the time of invocation or some time earlier. Moreover, coarse-grained monitoring has lower overhead compared to fine-grained monitoring, since it reduces the number of comparisons and synchronization operations.

Our monitor runs completely in user space. First, the user launches the monitor process and specifies the paths of the executables that it should execute as variants. Next, the monitor allows the variants to run without interruption as long as they do not require data or resources outside of their process spaces. Whenever a variant issues a system call, the monitor intercepts the request and suspends variant execution. The monitor then attempts to synchronize the system call with the other variants. All variants need to make the exact same system call with equivalent arguments within a small time window. The invocation of a system call is a *synchronization point* in our technique. Finer grained synchronization levels may require additional synchronization points.

Note that argument equivalence does not necessarily imply that argument values are identical. For example, when an argument is a pointer to a buffer, the monitor compares the buffers' contents and expects them to be identical, whereas the pointers themselves can be different. Non-pointer arguments are considered equivalent only when they are identical.

Formally, the monitor determines whether the variants are in complying states based on the following rules. If $p_1$ to $p_n$ are the variants of the same program $p$, they are in conforming states if, and only if, at every system call synchronization point, the following conditions hold:

1. $\forall s_i, s_j \in S : s_i = s_j$
   where $S = \{s_1, s_2, \ldots, s_n\}$ is the set of all invoked system calls at the synchronization point and $s_i$ is the system call invoked by variant $p_i$.

2. $\forall a_{ij}, a_{ik} \in A : a_{ij} \equiv a_{ik}$
   where $A = \{a_{11}, a_{12}, \ldots, a_{mn}\}$ is the set of all the system call arguments encountered at the synchronization point, $a_{ij}$ is the $i^{th}$ argument of the system call invoked by $p_j$ and $m$ is the number of arguments used by the encountered system call. $A$ is empty for system calls that do not take arguments. Formally, the argument equivalence operator is defined as:

$$a \equiv b \Leftrightarrow \begin{cases} \text{if type} \neq \text{buffer} : a = b \\ \text{else} : \text{content}(a) = \text{content}(b) \end{cases}$$

with *type* being the argument type expected for this argument of the system call. The content of a buffer is the set of all bytes contained within:

$$\text{content}(a) := \{a[0]\ldots a[\text{size}(a) - 1]\}$$

with the *size* function returning the first occurrence of a zero byte in the buffer in case of a zero-terminated buffer, or the value of a system call argument used to indicate the size of the buffer in case of buffers with explicit size specification.

3. $\forall t_i \in T : t_i - t_s \leq \omega$
   where $T = \{t_1, t_2, \ldots, t_n\}$ is the set of times when the monitor intercepts system calls, $t_i$ is the time that system call $s_i$ is intercepted by the monitor, and $t_s$ is the time that the synchronization point is triggered. This is the time of the first system call encountered at this synchronization point. $\omega$ is the maximum amount of wall-clock time that the monitor waits for a variant. $\omega$ is specified in the policy given to the monitor and depends on the application and hardware.

Failure to comply to these conditions triggers an alarm, and the monitor takes an appropriate action based on a configurable policy. By default, our monitor terminates and restarts all variants, but other policies such as terminating only the non-conforming ones based on majority voting are possible.

### 4.2.2 Granularity

**System Call Granularity.** Our most coarse-grained approach to synchronize variants is at the granularity of system calls. As mentioned earlier, this granularity was chosen because modern operating systems do not permit damage to the system without first invoking a system call. Consequently, we allow all variants to run without interruption until they attempt to examine the environment outside of their process space. At that point, the monitor intercepts the system call (Figure 4.3) and compares

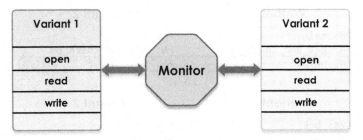

**Fig. 4.3** Synchronizing an MVEE with system call granularity.

the variants' states as described in Section 4.2.1. Because the monitor suspends variants that have made a system call and waits for the remaining variants, specifying a limit for the amount of time that the monitor may wait for a variant is important. Otherwise, a compromised variant might try to run long traces of instructions without invoking any system call to halt the system. In our monitoring mechanism, once the time limit has elapsed, the monitor considers variants that have not invoked any system call as non-complying and treats them in a manner specified by a configurable policy.

After making sure that the system call is legitimate, the monitor decides whether to execute the system call on behalf of the variants or permit the variants to execute the system call themselves. We have examined the system calls of the host operating system (Linux) and considered the range of possible arguments that can be passed to them. Depending on the effects of these system calls and their results, we specify which ones are executed by the variants or the monitor.

The monitor executes system calls that change the state of the system (e.g., socket). This is because the multi-variant execution environment must impersonate one single program that would be executed normally on the system. In addition, system calls that return non-immutable results must also be executed by the monitor. In this case, the variants receive identical results of the system call (e.g., gettimeofday) in order to ensure that code depending on the results produces identical output. Otherwise, all variants execute the system call directly (e.g., chdir). This is necessary since subsequent system calls may depend on the result of the current system call.

**Function Call Granularity.** System call granularity is effective at stopping injected code from causing damage to the target system. When we require more fine-grained control, we lower the monitor granularity. Multi-variant execution that also synchronizes on function calls is possible with minor modifications to a system call-based MVEE. Function call synchronization requires introspection into the variants so that the monitor is aware of the inner workings of each variant process. To implement this, the MVEE needs to include a dynamic binary instrumentor that detects when a variant enters a new function. The instrumentor needs to be sophisticated enough to support C setjmp/longjmp jumps as well as execution of dynamically generated code.

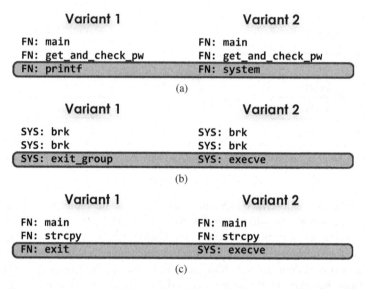

**Fig. 4.4** Divergence in a system and function call monitoring MVEE is detected if the functions called differ (a), the system calls are not equivalent (b), or a mixture of function and system calls are invoked at the same time (c). Function calls are prefixed with "FN" and system calls are prefixed with "SYS".

This level of granularity is effective at preventing attacks because it enforces stricter constraints on the behavior of the variants. By synchronizing on function entries, the monitor detects changes in program flow before execution of injected code. We use this information to create execution traces that demonstrate divergence in execution. When combined with system call granularity, the execution trace can be combined with a system call trace that indicates the kind of input that caused the divergence and the path the variants took before diverging [12]. It also allows for detecting other classes of divergences, such as mismatches between system calls and function calls (Figure 4.4).

Function call synchronization has limits in the types of code optimizations and diversifications it allows. Function inlining, for example, is not permissible in variants intended for monitoring at this level unless all variants have identical function inlining decisions. Similarly, transformations that insert wrapper functions are not allowed without corresponding wrappers in other variants.

**Instruction Granularity.** An even more fine-grained approach that is appropriate for high-security applications is monitoring at instruction level (Figure 4.5). We are generating variants in such a way that the instruction stream is equivalent among all variants. This does not come without overhead: we have to insert some instructions that are only necessary in one variant, but have to be present in the instruction stream of all variants, since we check that all variants execute the same instructions.

As mentioned before, the system call granularity is usually enough to protect a system. At this granularity level, however, we are able to detect programming errors

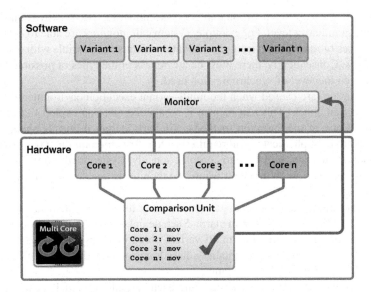

**Fig. 4.5** Several variants that have the same instruction sequence, but behave differently internally, are executed within a monitor. Small hardware changes allow us to execute all variants at full speed.

that lead to control flow divergence that may not be harmful to a system. Moreover, we detect cases where an attacker was able to inject code that failed. This reduces the risk of compromising a system by trial and error.

### 4.2.3 Discussion

Multi-variant execution has the benefit of having highly localized changes done to the binary. Consequently, all of the variants can be tested extensively and independently for compatibility with the variation method used. This makes it easier for administrators to identify sources of alarms raised by the multi-variant execution environment.

Multi-variant execution environments are inherently scalable. The most basic multi-variant execution environment configuration involves three processes: a monitor and two variants. If the user requires extra security and processing power is available, then additional variants can be added to the MVEE seamlessly. Moreover, we have found that while a two-variant MVEE is enough to stop attacks, a three-variant MVEE is sufficient to begin localizing vulnerabilities within a program. Use of four or more variants significantly increases the resilience of the MVEE [11]. This property makes multi-variant execution environments quite suitable for production use.

Multi-variant execution environments are susceptible to false positives that depend on the granularity level. For example, system call monitors are able to abstract certain sources of randomness from the variants, which is not possible with instruction monitors. Consequently, there must be awareness of the types of possible false positives given the level of synchronization used.

False negatives are caused when the multi-variant execution environment is unable to detect an attack. This can happen if an attacker uses an exploit that is not mitigated by one of the variation methods. Similarly, targeted attacks against an MVEE need to be sophisticated and require inside information on the types of variations. Such an attack would have to combine sensitive system call mimicry while maintaining control flow to the point where the monitor is unable to determine that the variants diverged.

An attacker that does not wish to gain control over the target system can deliberately attack an MVEE and trigger an alarm. Such denial of service attacks are nearly impossible to prevent. In addition, multi-variant execution does not protect against small injected code chunks that contain endless loops or slow down the MVEE by making the monitor wait for the variants.

Maintaining an MVEE requires managing each variant individually. For example, in order to apply a source code patch or upgrade the software used in an MVEE, the variants need to be rebuilt. This is especially true if the change modifies the variants' behavior that the monitor would detect. Our MVEE does not support dynamically reloading a variant, so the user needs to restart the MVEE when this is required.

## 4.3 Massive-Scale Software Diversity

Our second approach to combat attackers recognizes the current software monoculture as enabling attackers [9]. When all users of a particular product use identical copies of the same software package, attackers can first "practice" on their local copy. Once the attacker finishes creating an exploit, the attacker can release it and be confident of a high success rate. This is widely believed to have led to several worm outbreaks on the Internet.

Creation of a diverse software ecosystem—a *polyculture*—for the same software package has the benefit of making it more expensive for an attacker to develop exploits. When users are running two variations of the same package, the attacker must either create one attack for each variation, or create an attack that is sophisticated enough to exploit both variations simultaneously. Therefore, the attacker must spend more time and effort to get the same return on investment for an attack. The aim of *massive-scale software diversity* (MSSD) is to make it feasible for developers to seamlessly create such a diverse software ecosystem by providing tools to make the process easier (Figure 4.6), but also provide enough variation within a package to make exploitation economically unreasonable. In an era where unpatched and undisclosed Windows vulnerabilities are bought and sold in underground market-

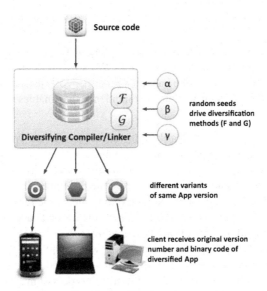

**Fig. 4.6** Illustration of massive-scale software diversity

places [16], massive-scale software diversity renders the markets for exploits useless because the ability to get large amounts of targets is diminished.

By creating many variants of the same application, we intend to create a kind of *herd immunity* for applications. The notion of herd immunity comes from immunology, where if a sizable amount of the population is immune to a particular pathogen, there are no outbreaks, but isolated cases of infection still occur. Massive-scale diversity aims to create a similar situation for computer systems. Our approach diversifies programs statically at compile time—this implies limited diversification potential at run time. However, if the diversification engine is able to create an environment where the vast majority of systems are immune to a particular attack, then serious worm outbreaks become unlikely. Similarly, attackers find that creating such attacks is too expensive and aim for easier targets.

Massive-scale software diversity removes another major problem of current software monoculture: the fact that releasing a patch for a discovered vulnerability alerts adversaries about its existence. It is current best practice to fix software vulnerabilities as soon as possible after their discovery. With massive-scale software diversity, this can be achieved by sending a patch to the vulnerable host, or by simply replacing the whole application with a new, diversified, already patched variant.

A bug fix (in the form of either a patch or a replacement program) gives a potential adversary information that can be used to precisely identify the vulnerability being fixed in the new version. A significant proportion of software exploits today come from reverse engineering of error fixes. Consequently, it is imperative that updates are applied as soon as they are available. The elapsed time between availability of an update and its installation on a vulnerable target is often a good predictor for overall vulnerability. Massive-scale software diversity makes it much more difficult for an attacker to generate attack vectors by way of reverse engineering of security patches.

Massive-scale software diversity is also a technique that is practical for everyday users in average desktop and mobile systems. We argue that this is due to several paradigm shifts that occurred in the last few years [9]. While each of these is remarkable in its own right, it is their fortuitous coincidence that enables the new defensive technique.

1. *Online Software Delivery*: Until quite recently, software was predominantly shipped in a shrinkwrapped box that contained some kind of disk media. This made it impractical to give every user a different variant. Today, many software packages are downloaded by the user from the developer. In a download-based delivery model, the physical packaging requirements are removed. The lack of packaging and physical media makes it possible to send each user a subtly different variant with the exact same functionality.

2. *Ultra-Reliable Compilers*: Compilation is now a predictable process. While almost all other types of software have grown in size and complexity, sometimes by orders of magnitude, compilers today are not orders of magnitude more complex than they were 20 years ago. Instead of testing and certifying a software binary, it should be sufficient to certify and test a representative binary or a set of representative binaries coming out of a diversifying compiler. It is our position that statistical methods can then be used to ensure that the compiler is not introducing bugs into the binary.

3. *Cloud Computing*: In the past, it would have been prohibitively expensive to set up an infrastructure that generates a unique variant of each program for each user. Today's cloud computing offerings solve that problem. The cost per variant of a program is essentially constant, regardless of whether we are generating 1000 or 10 million variants per day. Developers can react to changing demand almost instantaneously by scaling up and down their cloud computing needs as necessary.

4. *"Good Enough" Performance*: Because software performance is now mostly "good enough," users are likely to accept a small performance penalty if it gives them added security. Therefore, even if a diversifying compiler were to create program variants that are less efficient by a few percent, this no longer automatically dooms the prospect of massive-scale software diversity becoming a success.

### 4.3.1 Discussion

The primary difference between multi-variant code execution and massive-scale software diversity is that the latter is a static technique. This prevents any notion of run-time checks or intrusion detection that can detect attacks at run time except that diversified software may behave in an unusual manner when attacked. Thus, the security guarantees of diversified software are lower than that of multi-variant execution. Also, there is no concept of a false positive or a false negative to use in order to compare diversification methods.

Use of diversified software also requires planning in order to properly utilize a cloud infrastructure. Large software developers projecting a major release may have to utilize a cloud service before the release in order to build many copies of the software ahead of time. Hence, the planning needs to include projections on how many copies are required at release time and how much time is required to build a diversified variant. This prevents users from having to wait for long periods of time in a download queue. Open source software users can compile their software locally, lessening the burden on developers.

Similarly, there are issues related to support and troubleshooting with respect to diversified software. Developers need methods to reproduce bugs that occur in diversified software. Since some diversification techniques take parameters such as a maximum size, the parameters may need to be recorded. Privacy issues represent another problem for users if each copy of a software package is unique and can be identified per instance on the Internet.

Software validation is another issue when each copy of software is different. Instead of depending on cryptographic hashes and checksums, concerned users need other methods of verifying that a binary is genuine. However, since the source code is identical in all diversified software, users who compile from source can use existing methods to verify a source code package.

One of the major advantages of diversified software it that it helps create a form of herd immunity. Today's worms and botnets depend on the fact that identical code is ubiquitous. With massive-scale software diversity, there is a large enough installed base of diversified software, so major worm outbreaks become unlikely and actual worm infections become scattered. Systems and network administrators can then have a much easier time identifying and isolating infected hosts.

## 4.4 Diversification Techniques

In this section we discuss several behavioral variations that are applicable to modify an executable. All variants can be generated at compile time, and some of them (like system call randomization or register randomization) by manipulating binary executables. In addition to some well understood variation techniques, the list introduces new variations that are simple and seem to be ineffective when used alone, but are powerful in the context of a multi-variant execution environment. We describe only approaches that do not change the internal behavior of an executable in such a way that run-time comparison with other variants becomes impossible.

**Reverse Stack.** Most processor architectures are asymmetrically designed for one stack growth direction. In the Intel x86 instruction set, for example, all the predefined stack manipulation operations like push and pop are only suitable for a downward growing stack [10]. By augmenting the stack manipulation instructions with additions and subtractions of the stack pointer, it is possible to generate a vari-

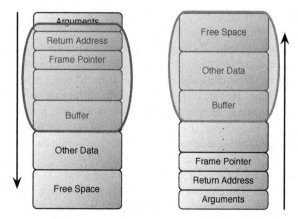

**Fig. 4.7** The return address and frame pointer of the current function cannot be overwritten by exploiting buffer overflow vulnerabilities when the stack grows upward.

ant with an upward growing stack [18]. This defends against the historic buffer overflows and classic stack smashing attacks [1] that rely on a downward growing stack because the stack layout, including buffers and variables allocated on the stack, is completely different. By changing the stack growth direction, the affected stack area that is overwritten by buffer overflows contains completely different data and control values. Figure 4.7 shows a buffer overflow that changes the return value in a downward growing stack cannot be harmful at the same time to a variant where the stack grows upwards. The overwritten area is stack space that is not used.

**Instruction Set Randomization.** Machine instructions usually consist of an opcode followed by zero or more arguments. Randomizing the encoding of the opcode leads to a completely new instruction set, and programs modified in such a way behave differently when executed on a normal CPU. A simple randomization technique is to apply the `xor` function, with a random key, on the instruction stream (Figure 4.8). Immediately before execution on the CPU, opcodes have to be decoded using the randomization key. This can be done in software, or in hardware by an extended CPU to eliminate the overhead. If an attacker injects code that is not properly encoded, it still goes through the decoding process just before execution. This leads to illegal code and most probably raises a CPU exception after a few instructions, or at least does not perform as intended. Kc et al. [14] discuss this variant and show that this technique on its own does not protect against attacks that only modify stack or heap variables and change the control flow of the program. Sovarel et al. [22] show that under certain circumstances where the program under attack is observable, Instruction Set Randomization can be defeated by guessing the randomization key.

**Heap Layout Randomization.** Heap overflow attacks can be rendered ineffective by heap layout randomization. Dynamically allocated memory on the heap is placed randomly, making it difficult to to predict where the next allocated memory

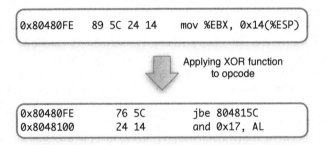

**Fig. 4.8** Example of instruction set randomization, where a xor was applied.

block is located. Tools like DieHard [2] show how to prevent heap overflows with heap layout randomization.

**Stack Base Randomization.** A protection mechanism already added to several operating systems is stack base randomization. At every startup of an application, the stack starts at a different base address. It is harder for attackers to hijack a system since stack-based addresses are not fixed any more. However, widespread use of NOP sleds limits the effectiveness of randomizing the stack base. The PaX [17] patch for the Linux kernel implements this diversification technique.

**Canaries.** One of the first stack smashing protection mechanism was inserting a "canary" value between a buffer and the activation records (return address and frame pointer) of a stack frame. Whenever the activation record of a stack frame is modified by exploiting a buffer overflow, the canary value is also overwritten. Before returning from a function, the canary value is checked and program execution is aborted if the canary is changed. StackGuard [7] uses canaries to detect return address overwrites. This technique protects against the standard stack smashing attacks, but does not protect against buffer overflows in the heap and function pointer overwrites. Moreover, existence of certain conditions in a program enables an attacker to overwrite the activation records without modifying the canary [4].

**Variable Reordering.** This technique increases the effectiveness of the previously explained canaries protection. Even with canaries, an attacker can overwrite local variables that are placed between a buffer and the canary value on the stack. To prevent this, buffers are placed immediately after the canary value and other variables, and copies of the arguments of a function are placed after all buffers. This technique in combination with the canaries is more powerful against attacks that take over the control of the execution before the canary value is checked. Sotirov et al. [21] even claim that this is not possible at all.

**System Call Number Randomization.** This variation technique is related to instruction set randomization. All exploits that use directly encoded system calls have to know the correct system call numbers. By changing the numbers of the system call, the injected code executes a random system call that leads to a completely different behavior or even an error. However, brute force attacks to get the new system call numbers are possible since their number is limited. Another disadvantage is that either the kernel has to understand the new system call number, or a rewriting tool has to restore the system call numbers before execution. This method was first envisioned by Chew and Song [6] and the RandSys [13] system uses this technique to protect Linux and Windows based systems.

**Register Randomization.** Register randomization exchanges the meaning of two registers. For example, the stack pointer register of the Intel x86 architecture, esp, can be exchanged with a random other register like eax. Most attacks rely on fixed contents in registers. For example, attacks that put a system call number in eax and execute the system call fail because the system takes the value that is stored in esp. Since there is no hardware architecture that supports randomized registers, it is necessary to exchange the registers before execution of instructions that implicitly rely on the values in esp or eax, like stack manipulation instructions or system calls. Extensions to existing architectures, or an instruction set where all registers are completely interchangeable, would simplify this variation technique considerably. A more portable and light-weight approach would only change the registers allocated to variables and temporaries where their values are not used by instructions that need the value in a specific register. For example, an **addl %eax , %ebx** instruction can be replaced easily with **addl %esi , %ecx** . However, **shl %cl , %eax** requires that the first value (the number of bits to shift by) be stored in the cl register.

**Library Entry Point Randomization.** Another possibility to gain control over a system is to call directly into a library instead of using hard coded system calls. For this approach, an attacker has to know the exact addresses of the library functions. Guessing the addresses of the library functions is fairly easy since similar operating systems tend to map shared libraries to the same virtual address. Randomized library entry points is an effective way to defend such attacks. This can be done either by rewriting the function names in the binary or during load time. Rewriting has the advantage that it only has to be done once. This technique does not protect against buffer overflows in the traditional sense, but defends the system by making the injected code ineffective. The PaX [17] Linux patch performs Library Entry Point Randomization by changing the base address of the mmap() function call, which is used to load dynamic libraries.

**Stack Frame Padding.** A method that is used to prevent stack based buffer overflows is to extend the length of the stack frame. By extending the stack frame, stack based buffer overflows are unable to successfully exploit the target because the payload is not large enough to overwrite the return address in the vulnerable stack frame. Adding dummy stack objects, or pads, is a straightforward method of implementing this kind of randomization. This can be done in two ways: with a large space at the top of the stack frame and with spacing placed in between stack objects. While there are no theoretical limits to the size of the pads that can be applied to stack frames, code in highly recursive programs or programs that naturally make extremely large stack allocations is not able to use large pads. Figure 4.9 illustrates the effectiveness of combining both stack frame padding and stack layout randomization.

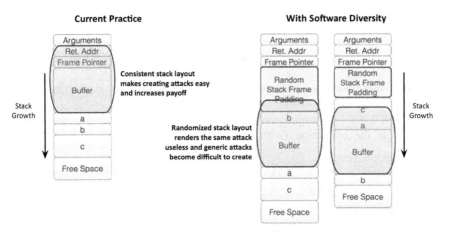

**Fig. 4.9** Applying stack frame padding and stack layout randomization to a stack frame.

**Code Sequence Randomization.** Use of instruction scheduling, call inlining, code hoisting, loop distribution, partial redundancy elimination, and many other compiler transformations change the generated machine code. These transformations can be changed further to create randomized output. Diversified applications are no longer vulnerable to return oriented programming [20, 5] attacks and similar attacks that rely on the knowledge that a certain instruction is present at a certain location.

**NOP Insertion.** Another approach that is useful in preventing return oriented programming [20, 5] that makes it much harder for attackers to use knowledge they possess on the layout of the targeted executable is similar to stack frame padding and stack layout randomization, except that the operations are done at the binary code level instead of the data level. There are short code sequences that have no practical effect when executed; these sequences can be used as padding in the code in order to "push" the following instructions forward by a small number of bytes. The offsets introduced by these *no-operations*, or *NOP*s, accumulate over the length of the binary and can significantly displace some of the later code sequences. This prevents attacks that rely on the existence of some known bytes at fixed locations. Some examples of such NOPs are: **movl %eax , %eax , xchgl %esi , %esi** , and **leal (%edi) , %edi** . The PittSFIeld [15] Software Fault Isolation system uses NOP Insertion to enforce alignment of jump targets, so the attacker cannot exploit an existing jump instruction to jump into the middle of a proper instruction, turning it into a gadget. Figure 4.10 provides examples of the effects of NOP insertion and code sequence randomization.

**Equivalent Instructions.** Many instruction set architectures offer different instructions that in some particular cases have identical effects and can be substituted for each other. We can often replace any such instruction with an equivalent one without any loss in performance, but changing the binary sequence significantly.

**Fig. 4.10** Example of effects of NOP insertion and code sequence randomization on binary code.

For example, the instructions (with byte encodings):

| | |
|---|---|
| movl %edx , %eax | 89 D0 |
| xchgl %edx , %eax | 92 |

can be replaced with:

| | |
|---|---|
| leal (%edx) , %eax | 8D 02 |
| xchgl %eax , %edx | 87 D0 |

The leal in the transformed stream combines the "load address of" instruction that loads the address of a memory operand into a register with the register-based addressing mode, transforming into a simple register-to-register move; the other examples uses the commutativity of the "exchange" operation or of the x86 operands in the encoding. Although the transformed instructions are equivalent to the ones before, their binary encoding can be significantly different, as seen in the second column of the table.

Switching between the different forms of instructions such as these should have no impact on performance, while changing the statistical properties and contents of the code in different ways. Similar changes can also be done on arithmetic instructions, e.g., changing mul into shl and back, but such changes are already done by the compiler as the well-known technique of strength reduction, which sometimes has a significant impact on performance. One well-known optimization done either manually by the programmers or automatically by the compilers is changing all multiplications by power of 2 into bit-shifts; multiplication is much slower on most processors than shifting. However, doing this in reverse can improve the security of the application.

**Program Base Address Randomization.** Address space layout randomization (ASLR) is a recent security technique that has been implemented in most major operating systems that relies on run-time randomization to improve security. Its effectiveness has been empirically demonstrated many times, and it has turned out as an efficient technique to prevent attacks. However, since current binary formats were designed before this technique was implemented, many existing programs are built with the assumption that they are loaded at a specific, fixed address in memory. For these programs, ASLR can only be enabled for the dynamic libraries used by the program, not by the program itself. However, one way to simulate this randomization is to randomize the loading address of the program at link time, so that each individual program is loaded at a different address that the attacker cannot predict.

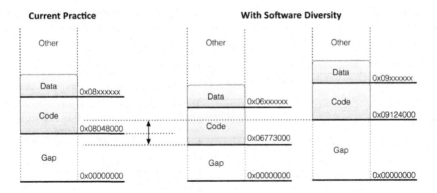

**Fig. 4.11** Example of program base address randomization with 2 different random base addresses

For example, programs built for the Linux operating system have a default base address of $0x08048000$, which is 128 megabytes in the address space. The space before that is never used by the program, so it is effectively wasted. By shrinking or enlarging this gap we can add randomness into the layout of the program in memory, sacrificing only the amount of available memory that can be used by the program. Figure 4.11 shows examples of this technique. One implementation of base address randomization uses a binary rewriter that diversifies binaries by changing the program code after compilation [3].

**Program Section and Function Reordering.** Modern programs are built by putting together many modules, each module often corresponding to an individual source file. Each module is grouped into sections of different types, such as data sections and code sections. The modules themselves are usually organized into functions, which call each other. Some attacks rely on knowledge of the particular location of certain global functions, so one way to make the programs more vulnerable is to reorder the functions themselves at the local level and then reorder the code sections at the linking stage. Another approach is to apply a link-time optimizer to the program and simply reorder all functions in the program globally. This technique can be applied to the data sections and variables, an idea presented previously as Heap Layout Randomization, and to any other sections from the binary.

## 4.4.1 Suitability and Applicability

Table 4.1 summarizes the applicability and suitability of the various diversification techniques for use in a multi-variant execution environment or a software ecosystem created with massive-scale software diversity. The table can be used as a guide for those wishing to utilize either diversity approach to implement increased security.

**Table 4.1** Table summarizing the diversification techniques and their applicability to multi-variant execution environments (MVEEs) and massive-scale software diversity (MSSD) diversity approaches.

| Applicability | Target | Technique | Implementation |
|---|---|---|---|
| MVEE and MSSD | Code | Library Entry Point Randomization | The load address of libraries are randomized |
| | | Register Randomization | The role of registers are changed |
| | | NOP insertion | Instructions that have a NOP-like effect are inserted into the instruction stream |
| | Data | Variable Reordering | Non-buffer locals are placed before buffer locals |
| | | Stack Frame Padding | Random padding is added between locals and the return address |
| | | Heap Layout Randomization | Dynamically allocated memory is placed randomly in the heap |
| MVEE | Code | Instruction Set Randomization | The instruction stream is randomized with a randomly selected key |
| | | System Call Number Randomization | The numbers assigned to system calls are randomly changed |
| | Data | Canaries | A random value is placed on the stack, before the return address of the function frame, and is checked in the epilogue |
| | | Reverse Stack | Stack is grown in reverse of native architecture order |
| MSSD | Code | Code Sequence Randomization | Compiler transformations are selectively used to randomize the instruction stream |
| | | Equivalent Instructions | Instructions are replaced with functionally equivalent alternatives |
| | Code / Data | Program Base Address Randomization | The load address of the program is randomly changed |
| | | Program Section and Function Reordering | Functions and sections are placed in random locations in the address space |
| | Data | Stack Base Randomization | The stack is placed at a random location in the address space |

## 4.5 Conclusions

Adopting compiler-generated software diversity will have a dramatic impact on the way software is distributed and is likely to change many of the assumptions and models underlying current threats to deployed software. It becomes much less likely that a single attack will affect large numbers of targets simultaneously. Hence, the impact of phenomena such as viruses and worms will be greatly reduced. It also has the effect that adversaries can no longer simply analyze their own copies of any given piece of software to find exploitable vulnerabilities, because any vulnerabilities they may find will no longer automatically translate to all other instances of the same software. Hence, even directed attacks against specific targets running some variant of some software will become much more difficult, as long as the attacker has no way of determining which and how many specific binaries are present on what target. Without doubt, the new paradigm of compiler-generated software diversity will change many of the existing approaches to software security and make the digital domain safer.

**Acknowledgements** Parts of this effort have been sponsored by the Defense Advanced Research Projects Agency (DARPA) under agreement number D11PC20024, by the Air Force Research Laboratory (AFRL) under agreement number FA8750-05-2-0216, and by the National Science Foundation (NSF) under grants CNS-0905684 and CNS-0627747.

The U.S. Government is authorized to reproduce and distribute reprints for Governmental purposes notwithstanding any copyright annotation thereon. Any opinions, findings, and conclusions or recommendations expressed here are those of the authors and should not be interpreted as necessarily representing the official views, policies, or endorsements, either expressed or implied, of DARPA, AFRL, NSF, or any other agency of the U.S. Government.

# References

1. Aleph One. Smashing the stack for fun and profit. *Phrack Magazine*, Issue 49, 1996.
2. E.D. Berger and B.G. Zorn. DieHard: Probabilistic Memory Safety for Unsafe Languages. In *Proceedings of the ACM SIGPLAN Conference on Programming Language Design and Implementation*, pages 158–168. ACM Press, 2006.
3. S. Bhatkar, D.C. DuVarney, and R. Sekar. Address Obfuscation: An Efficient Approach to Combat a Broad Range of Memory Error Exploits. In *Proceedings of the 12th USENIX Security Symposium*, pages 105–120. USENIX Association, 2003.
4. Bulba and Kil3r. Bypassing StackGuard and StackShield. *Phrack Magazine*, Issue 56, 2000.
5. S. Checkoway, L. Davi, A. Dmitrienko, A. Sadeghi, H. Shacham, and M. Winandy. Return-Oriented Programming without Returns. In *Proceedings of the 17th ACM Conference on Computer and Communications Security*, pages 559–72. ACM Press, October 2010.
6. M. Chew and D. Song. Mitigating Buffer Overflows by Operating System Randomization. Technical Report CMU-CS-02-197, Department of Computer Science, Carnegie Mellon University, 2002.
7. C. Cowan, C. Pu, D. Maier, J. Walpole, P. Bakke, D. Beattie, A. Grier, P. Wagle, Q. Zhang, and H. Hinton. StackGuard: Automatic Adaptive Detection and Prevention of Buffer-Overflow Attacks. In *Proceedings of the 7th USENIX Security Symposium*, pages 63–78. USENIX Association, 1998.
8. B. Cox, D. Evans, A. Filipi, J. Rowanhill, W. Hu, J. Davidson, J. Knight, A. Nguyen-Tuong, and J. Hiser. N-variant systems: A Secretless Framework for Security through Diversity. In *Proceedings of the 15th USENIX Security Symposium*, pages 105–120. USENIX Association, 2006.
9. M. Franz. E unibus pluram: Massive-Scale Software Diversity as a Defense Mechanism. In *Proceedings of the 2010 Workshop on New Security Paradigms*, NSPW '10, pages 7–16, New York, NY, USA, 2010. ACM.
10. Intel. *Intel 64 and IA-32 Architectures Software Developer's Manual*, March 2009.
11. T. Jackson, B. Salamat, G. Wagner, C. Wimmer, and M. Franz. On the Effectiveness of Multi-Variant Program Execution for Vulnerability Detection and Prevention. In *Proceedings of the 6th International Workshop on Security Measurements and Metrics*, MetriSec '10, pages 7:1–8, New York, NY, USA, 2010. ACM.

12. T. Jackson, C. Wimmer, and M. Franz. Multi-Variant Program Execution for Vulnerability Detection and Analysis. In *Proceedings of the Sixth Annual Workshop on Cyber Security and Information Intelligence Research*, CSIIRW '10, pages 38:1–4, New York, NY, USA, 2010. ACM.

13. X. Jiang, H.J. Wang, D. Xu, and Y. Wang. RandSys: Thwarting Code Injection Attacks with System Service Interface Randomization. In *Proceedings of the 26th IEEE International Symposium on Reliable Distributed Systems*, SRDS '07, pages 209–218, Washington, DC, USA, 2007. IEEE Computer Society.

14. G.S. Kc, A.D. Keromytis, and V. Prevelakis. Countering Code-Injection Attacks with Instruction-Set Randomization. In *Proceedings of the 10th ACM Conference on Computer and Communications Security*, pages 272–280. ACM Press, 2003.

15. S. McCamant and G. Morrisett. Evaluating SFI for a CISC architecture. In *Proceedings of the 15th USENIX Security Symposium*, Berkeley, CA, USA, 2006. USENIX Association.

16. C. Miller. The legitimate vulnerability market: Inside the secretive world of 0-day exploit sales. In *In Sixth Workshop on the Economics of Information Security*, 2007.

17. PaX. *Homepage of The PaX Team*, 2009. http://pax.grsecurity.net (April 2011).

18. B. Salamat, A. Gal, and M. Franz. Reverse Stack Execution in a Multi-Variant Execution Environment. In *Workshop on Compiler and Architectural Techniques for Application Reliability and Security*, 2008.

19. B. Salamat, T. Jackson, G. Wagner, C. Wimmer, and M. Franz. Run-Time Defense against Code Injection Attacks using Replicated Execution. *IEEE Transactions on Dependable and Secure Computing*, 2011.

20. H. Shacham. The Geometry of Innocent Flesh on the Bone: Return-into-libc without Function Calls (on the x86). In *Proceedings of the 14th ACM Conference on Computer and Communications Security*, pages 552–61. ACM Press, October 2007.

21. A. Sotirov and M. Dowd. Bypassing Browser Memory Protections. In *Black Hat*, 2008.

22. A.N. Sovarel, D. Evans, and N. Paul. Where's the FEEB?: The Effectiveness of Instruction Set Randomization. In *Proceedings of the 14th USENIX Security Symposium*, pages 145–160. USENIX Association, 2005.

# Chapter 5
# Symbiotes and defensive Mutualism: Moving Target Defense

Ang Cui and Salvatore J. Stolfo

**Abstract** If we wish to break the continual cycle of patching and replacing our core monoculture systems to defend against attacker evasion tactics, we must re-design the way systems are deployed so that the attacker can no longer glean the information about one system that allows attacking any other like system. Hence, a new poly-culture architecture that provides complete uniqueness for each distinct device would thwart many remote attacks (except perhaps for insider attacks). We believe a new security paradigm based on perpetual mutation and diversity, driven by symbiotic defensive mutualism can fundamentally change the 'cat and mouse' dynamic which has impeded the development of truly effective security mechanism to date. We propose this new 'clean slate design' principle and conjecture that this defensive strategy can also be applied to legacy systems widely deployed today. Fundamentally, the technique diversifies the defensive system of the protected host system thwarting attacks against defenses commonly executed by modern malware.

## 5.1 Introduction

We propose a host-based defense mechanism that we call Symbiotic Embedded Machines (SEM). SEM, or simply the Symbiote, is a code structure inspired by a natural phenomenon known as Symbiotic Defensive Mutualism. This phenomenon generally refers to any short- or long-term association between populations of different species where the survival or 'evolutionary fitness' of one or more population partners is enhanced by the association. Mutual benefits are often the result of some emergent behavior between two or more vastly different biological systems. This synergistic dynamic is observed across the spectrum of living things, from microbes

Ang Cui
Columbia University, e-mail: ang@cs.columbia.edu

Salvatore J. Stolfo
Columbia University e-mail: sal@cs.columbia.edu

like viruses and bacteria to fungi and to flora and fauna. When considered within the digital realm, Symbiotic Embedded Machines can be thought of as digital 'life forms' which tightly co-exist with arbitrary executables in a mutually defensive arrangement, extracting computational resources (CPU cycles) from it's host while simultaneously protecting the host from attack and exploitation. Furthermore, the diverse nature of symbiotes provide inherent protection against direct attack by adversaries that directly target host defenses. Hence, defenses are defended by the principle of defensive mutualism.

We envision a general-purpose computing architecture consisting of two mutual defensive systems whereby a self-contained, distinct and unique Symbiote machine is embedded in each instance of a host program. The Symbiote can reside within any arbitrary body of software, regardless of its place within the system stack. The Symbiote can be injected into an arbitrary host in many different ways, while the code of the Symbiote can be 'randomized' by advanced polymorphic code engines. Thus, a distinct defensive Symbiote can be used to protect device drivers, the kernel, as well as userland applications. The combination of Symbiote with host program creates a unique executable different from any other instance, and thus breaks the mono-culture by creating a plethora of 'moved targets'.

Once the Symbiote injection process is complete, it will execute along-side it's host program. Since the Symbiote is a self-contained entity, it is not installed onto the host program in the traditional sense. Current anti-virus and host-based defenses must be installed onto or into an operating system, which places a heavy dependence on the features and integrity of the operating system. In general, this arrangement requires a strong trust relationship with the very software (often of unknown integrity) it tries to protect.

In contrast, the Symbiote treats it's entire host program as an external and untrusted entity, and therefore eliminates this unsound trust relationship. Much like how certain ants reside within the Bullhorn Acacia tree and acts as a natural defense mechanism against harmful insects, Symbiotic Embedded Machines reside within its host executable, protecting it against exploitation and unauthorized modification. Just as the ants are unfamiliar with the inner workings of the Acacia tree, and as the Acacia tree is unaware of the existence of the ants, SEM's reside within the target binary in a similar arrangement. At runtime, the host program requires the Symbiote to successfully execute in order to operate. The Symbiote monitors the behavior of its host to ensure it operates correctly, and if not, stops the host from doing harm. Removal, or attempted removal, of the Symbiote renders the host inoperable.

## 5.2 Related Work

Symbiotic Embedded Machines can be thought of as a generic way of injecting host-based defenses into arbitrary host programs. Traditional host-based defenses are typically installed into well-known operating systems to fortify the entire OS from various types of exploitation. For example, numerous rootkit and malware detection and mitigation mechanisms have been proposed in the past but largely target general purpose computers. Commercial products from vendors like Symantec, Norton, Kapersky and Microsoft [1] all advertise some form of protection against kernel level rootkits. Kernel integrity validation and security posture assessment capability has been integrated into several Network Admission Control (NAC) systems. These commercial products largely depend on signature-based detection methods and can be subverted by well known methods [11, 12, 13]. Sophisticated detection and prevention strategies have been proposed by the research community. Virtualization-based strategies using hypervisors, VMM's and memory shadowing [10] have been applied to kernel-level rootkit detection. Others have proposed detection strategies using binary analysis [5], function hook monitoring [15] and hardware-assisted solutions to kernel integrity validation [14].

The above strategies may perform well within general purpose computers and well known operating systems but have not been adapted to operate within the unique characteristics and constraints of embedded device firmware. Effective prevention of binary exploitation of embedded devices requires a rethinking of detection strategies and deployment vehicles.

The Symbiotic Embedded Machine provide a means of enforcing the integrity of system code and control flow within embedded devices. SEM's platform agnostic code injection methodology can be used to extend the use of run-time program monitors [4] for embedded devices. The vast majority of these devices are built on standard CPU architectures (MIPS, PPC, ARM etc). Therefore, compilation of executable code for these devices using languages like C is trivial. The SEM structure exploits this homogeneity and represents a general method of installing compiled code into firmware of existing network embedded devices, regardless of the underlying operating system, by finding "unused" portions of the firmware that allows stealthy embedded code.

SEM can also be thought of as a novel type of embedded device rootkit. Unlike prior works [9, 6, 8], which are adaptations of existing methods onto embedded operating systems, SEM contains a payload delivery mechanism designed specifically to operate within unfamiliar and heterogeneous proprietary operating systems. SEM can **automatically** inject the same types of rootkit payloads to execute across many different firmware versions and physical device types without requiring deep knowledge of each firmware instance.

## 5.2.1 Related Work: Software Guards

Guards, originally proposed by Chang and Atallah [2], is a promising technology which uses mechanisms of action similar to Symbiotes. Originally proposed as an anti-tampering mechanism for x86 software, the guard mechanism have been used in both security research [3] as well as commercial products[1]. A Guard is a simple

---

[1] www.arxan.com

piece of security code which is injected into the protected software using binary rewriting techniques similar to our Symbiote system. Once injected, a guard will perform tamper-resistance functionality like self-checksumming and software repair. To further improve the resilience of the protection scheme, a large number of Guards can be deployed in intricate networks as a graph of mutually defensive security units.

While promising, the Guard approach does have several draw backs and limitations which Symbiotes overcome. For example, since the Guard has no mechanism to pause and resume its computation, the entire guard routine must complete execution each time it is invoked. This limits the amount of computation each Guard can realistically perform without affecting functionality, specially when Guards are used in time sensitive software and real-time embedded devices. In contrast, the Symbiote Manager allows its payload to be arbitrarily complex. Instead of executing the entire payload each time a randomly intercepted function invokes the Symbiote, the Symbiote Manager executes a small portion of the payload before pausing it, saving its execution context and returning control back to the intercepted function. This way, Symbiote payloads can implement arbitrarily complex defensive mechanisms, even in time sensitive software.

Removing the limitation on the complexity of Symbiote payloads allows us to further address several draw backs of the Guard framework. Because each guard can only compute for a very short amount of time, they generally performed simple checksums on small patches of software. In order for guards to checksum over the entire protected binary, an intricate network of guards must be injected. Furthermore, guards must be individually instantiated and hooked into the control flow of its protected binary in a specific way in order for the entire guard network to be mutually defensive. This heavy dependence on the execution flow information of the protected program makes the guard injection process complex and error prone. For example, static analysis of the target binary can not always reveal its runtime control flow behavior, specially when computed control-flow transfers are used. In contrast, a single Symbiote payload can compute the checksum of the entire protected host program, and does not require detailed knowledge of control-flow transfers within the host program. Therefore, the Symbiote injection process is greatly simplified and less error prone.

## 5.3 The Symbiote / Host Relationship

The Defensive Mutualistic relationship between the Symbiote and host program can be broadly described as follows:

1. Each entity in the symbiotic relationship must have their own innate defenses. In the case of our proposed system, adaptation, randomization and polymorphic mutation will be applied to both the protected software system as well as the injected SEM's.

2. Both the Symbiote and the protected software host will be genetically diverse and functionally autonomous. Specifically, the Symbiote will not be a standard piece of software that depends on and operates within the software system it is protecting. Instead, the Symbiote can be thought of as a fortified and self-contained execution environment that is infused into the host software.

3. The Symbiote will reside within the host software, extracting computational resources (CPU cycles) to execute it's own SEM payloads. In return, the SEM payloads will constantly monitor the execution and integrity of the host software, fortifying the entire system against exploitation.

4. SEM's are injected into the host software rather then 'installed' in the traditional sense. Once injected, the code of the SEM is pseudorandomly dispersed across the body of the host. Special mechanisms provided by the SEM injection process will assure that the SEM is executed along-side the host software.

5. The Symbiote and host program must operate correctly in tandem. The Symbiote monitors the behavior of the protected host program, and can alert on and react to exploitation and incorrect behavior. The Symbiote is also self-fortified with anti-tampering mechanisms. If an unauthorized party attempts to disable, interfere with or modify the Symbiote, the protected host program will become inoperable if the attempt is successful.

6. Symbiotes are moving targets. No two instantiations of the same Symbiote is ever the same. Each time a Symbiote is created and prepared for injection into a host program, its code is randomized and mutated, resulting in a vastly genetically dissimilar variant of itself. When observed at the macro level, the collective Symbiote population is highly diverse.

### 5.3.1 Software Symbiotes and Possible Hardware Extensions

Figure 5.1 illustrates the process of fortifying an arbitrary executable with a Symbiote. In our prior work we have demonstrated the feasibility of the software-only Symbiote, a Symbiote which is completely implemented in software and can execute on existing commodity systems without any need for specialized hardware. While the software-only Symbiote is capable of delivering the three fundamental security properties described in this section, additional hardware can greatly improve the efficiency and monitoring/mitigative capabilities of the Symbiote, as well as provide even tighter security guarantees in certain situations. Section 2.1 discusses several of such hardware extensions.

Symbiote Creation: The Symbiote is prepared for injection into the host program. A set of policies and defensive payloads are combined with a generic stub Symbiote binary. This process produces a completely self-contained executable loaded with a Symbiote execution manager, Symbiote monitoring engine, as well as the chosen set of defensive payloads and policies.

Mutation and Randomization: Both the host program and Symbiote binaries are analyzed, randomized and mutated into an unique instantiation of their original pro-

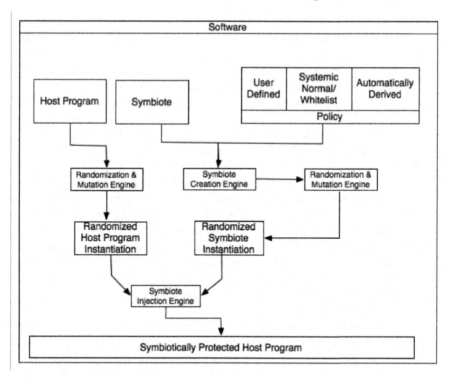

**Fig. 5.1** Symbiotic Embedded Machine

gram. These new binaries are functionally equivalent to the original code. However, techniques like ISR, ASR and polymorphic mutation are used to greatly increase the randomness and diversity of both the host program as well as its defense Symbiote.

Symbiote Injection: The Symbiote Injection Engine analyzes both executables and injects the Symbiote into the randomized host program, producing a single fortified program. One or more Symbiotic Monitoring Engines (SEM) can be injected into a piece of arbitrary executable code to augment the target code with sophisticated defensive capabilities. Unlike existing host-based defense and anti-virus mechanisms, SEM's do not operate on top of or as a part of the protected application or operating system. Instead, Symbiotes are essentially infused into the protected executable, providing the following four fundamental properties:

1. The Symbiote executes alongside the host software. In order for the host to function as before, it's injected SEM's must execute, and vice versa.
2. The Symbiote's code cannot be modified or disabled by unauthorized parties through either online or offline attacks.
3. The Symbiote has full visibility into the code and execution state of its host program, and can either passively monitor or actively react to the observed events

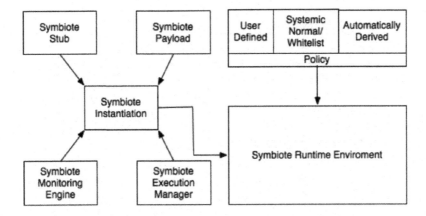

**Fig. 5.2** Symbiotic Embedded Machine

at runtime. Hence, malware that attempts to hijack the host's execution environment cannot see the Symbiote, but the Symbiote can see the malware.

4. No two instantiations of the same Symbiote is the same. Each time a Symbiote is created, its code is randomized and mutated, rendering signature based detection methods and attacks requiring predictable memory and code structures within the Symbiote ineffective. Each instantiation of a Symbiote is polymorphically mutated and randomized during the injection process. Therefore, studying and reverse engineering one instance of a particular Symbiote provides the attacker with little to no useful information about the specifics of any other instantiation of the same Symbiote.

The Symbiote code structure, displayed in Figure 5.2, is modular and configurable through a standard interface. At instantiation time, a Symbiote is created by simply mixing and matching code that delivers the desired functionality from each of the following five principal components:

Symbiote Stub: The stub is the base platform of the Symbiote. It dictates how the Symbiote's code will be embedded into the host program, and how tandem execution with the host is accomplished.

Symbiote Payload: The payload is the actual defensive mechanism that is executed in tandem with the host program. Payloads are arbitrarily complex standalone executables. For example, code integrity checkers, proof carrying codes and anomaly detectors can all be implemented as a Symbiote Payload.

Symbiote Monitoring Engine: The Monitoring Engine acquires and organizes static and runtime information about the host program. It enables the Symbiote payload to fully inspect the host program, and provides an event-driven interface, allowing the payload to alert and react to runtime events within the host program.

Symbiote Execution Manager: The Execution Manager is the resource manager for the Symbiote. It controls the tandem execution behavior of the host program / Symbiote pairing. Specifically, the execution manager controls how and when

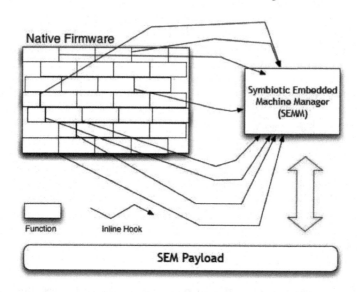

the Symbiote and the host program is executed on the CPU. Execution managers can implement different static or dynamic CPU allocation algorithms, leverage single/multi-core hardware architectures, as well as utilize specialized hardware.

Policy: The Policy is a collection of rules which the Symbiote will enforce.

The manner in which Symbiotes are injected into (legacy) host programs in a novel fashion using inline hooking. Inline hooking is a well known technique for function interception. However, the Symbiote injection process uses function interception in a very different way. Instead of targeting specific functions for interception which requires precise a priori knowledge of the code layout of the target device, the Symbiote injection randomly intercepts a large number of automatically detected function entry points. The inline hooks inserted provide as a means to redivert periodically and consistently a small portion of the device's CPU cycles to execute the SEM payload. This approach allows SEMs to remain agnostic to operating system specifics while executing its payload alongside the original OS. The SEM payload has full access to the internals of the original OS but is not constrained by it. This allows the SEM payload to carry out powerful functionality which are not possible under the original OS.

Figure 5.3.1 provides an overview of this injection process whereby Symbiote control code (the SEM Manager) and its executed SEM payload are dispersed throughout a binary using gaps of unused memory created by block allocation assignment.

## 5.3.2 Applications of Symbiotes and Further Research

The Symbiote is a self-contained code entity that does not depend on features within its host program to function. Instead, the Symbiote treats the host program as an external untrusted entity, and uses its own internal monitoring and analysis facilities to protect the host program. Since no assumptions are made about the functionality of the host program, a Symbiote can reside within any level of the software stack. Further, multiple Symbiotes can reside within the same software system as well as within the same piece of individual executable. This software defense strategy fundamentally rearranges the trust relationship and dependencies between the defense mechanism and the protected program.

The Symbiote treats all external code as untrusted software, thereby drastically reducing the amount of trust and dependence it places on the system in which it resides. The Symbiote and the Defensive mutualistic protection strategy can subsume the functionality of current security mechanisms under a new paradigm where the security software co-exist with, but completely distrusts the host program which it is protecting.

Proof Carrying Code: Proof-Carrying Code is a technique which can validate the integrity of untrusted code. Since the Symbiote is directly injected into the host program, a Symbiote payload implementing PCC can be trivially injected into arbitrary untrusted code.

Host-based IDS: The Symbiote Monitoring Engine collects and organizes the runtime information about the system in which it resides. By injecting an IDS payload into the host operating system or individual host programs, complex IDS and Anomaly Detection mechanisms can be directly injected into the host system with extremely fine granularity. Note that deploying a host-based IDS in this manner is extremely attractive because the monitoring system does not depend on the functionality provided by the operating system. Should the OS be compromised, the Symbiote's visibility into host system will remain unaffected.

Rootkit Detection: Rootkit detection using software-only Symbiotes have already been demonstrated to be feasible and effective on proprietary embedded systems like Cisco IOS and Android devices.

# References

1. Microsoft Corporation, Kernel Patch Protection: Frequently Asked Questions. http://tinyurl.com/y7pss5y, 2006.
2. Hoi Chang and Mikhail J. Atallah. Protecting software code by guards. In Tomas Sander, editor, *Digital Rights Management Workshop*, volume 2320 of *Lecture Notes in Computer Science*, pages 160–175. Springer, 2001.
3. Úlfar Erlingsson, Martín Abadi, Michael Vrable, Mihai Budiu, and George C. Necula. Xfi: Software guards for system address spaces. In *OSDI*, pages 75–88. USENIX Association, 2006.

4. Ligati et al. Enforcing security policies with run-time program monitors. Princeton University, 2005.
5. Christopher Krügel, William K. Robertson, and Giovanni Vigna. Detecting kernel-level rootkits through binary analysis. In *ACSAC*, pages 91–100. IEEE Computer Society, 2004.
6. Felix "FX" Linder. Cisco IOS Router Exploitation. In *In BlackHat USA*, 2009.
7. Richard Lippmann, Engin Kirda, and Ari Trachtenberg, editors. *Recent Advances in Intrusion Detection, 11th International Symposium, RAID 2008, Cambridge, MA, USA, September 15-17, 2008. Proceedings*, volume 5230 of *Lecture Notes in Computer Science*. Springer, 2008.
8. Michael Lynn. Cisco IOS Shellcode, 2005. In BlackHat USA.
9. Sebastian Muniz. Killing the myth of Cisco IOS rootkits: DIK, 2008. In EUSecWest.
10. Ryan Riley, Xuxian Jiang, and Dongyan Xu. Guest-transparent prevention of kernel rootkits with vmm-based memory shadowing. In Lippmann et al. [7], pages 1–20.
11. Dror-John Roecher and Michael Thumann. NAC Attack. In *In BlackHat USA*, 2007.
12. Skywing. Subverting PatchGuard Version 2, 2008. Uninformed,Volume 6.
13. Yingbo Song, Pratap V. Prahbu, and Salvatore J. Stolfo. Smashing the stack with hydra: The many heads of advanced shellcode polymorphism. In *Defcon 17*, 2009.
14. Vikas R. Vasisht and Hsien-Hsin S. Lee. Shark: Architectural support for autonomic protection against stealth by rootkit exploits. In *MICRO*, pages 106–116. IEEE Computer Society, 2008.
15. Zhi Wang, Xuxian Jiang, Weidong Cui, and Xinyuan Wang. Countering persistent kernel rootkits through systematic hook discovery. In Lippmann et al. [7], pages 21–38.

# Chapter 6
# Manipulating Program Functionality to Eliminate Security Vulnerabilities

Martin Rinard

**Abstract** Security vulnerabilities can be seen as excess undesirable functionality present in a software system. We present several mechanisms that can either excise or change system functionality in ways that may 1) eliminate security vulnerabilities while 2) enabling the system to continue to deliver acceptable service.

## 6.1 Introduction

We discuss several automatic techniques for changing program behavior in ways that may eliminate security vulnerabilities. We take the perspective that vulnerabilities are undesirable functionality and therefore focus on techniques that change or even eliminate some of the functionality that the system offers to users.

One of the observations motivating our approach is that many software systems provide substantially more functionality than users require, desire, or are even aware of. There are several reasons for this phenomenon:

- **General-Purpose Software:** Because of the high cost of developing software systems and the consequent need to amortize this cost over many users, many software systems are designed to contain functionality for a wide range of users. Because users have such varying needs, each user winds up using only a small fraction of the total functionality.
- **Feature Accretion:** As software systems go through their life cycle, developers almost always preserve existing features (to ensure backwards compatibility) while adding new features. Over time the software accumulates more and more functionality, much of it obsolete and designed for operating contexts that have changed since the introduction of much of the functionality.

Martin Rinard
EECS Department, MIT CSAIL, Massachusetts Institute of Technology, e-mail: `rinard@mit.edu`

- **Subsystem Reuse:** It is often quicker to build systems by incorporating existing subsystems than by building the desired functionality from scratch. But good building blocks are often more general and contain more functionality than necessary for the specific usage scenario at hand.
- **Development Errors:** Developers have been known to produce software systems that contain errors. These errors can be the result of simple coding errors, specification misunderstandings, incorrect specifications, or misunderstandings of language features, library interfaces, or other aspects of the software development environment, to name a few possibilities.
- **Vulnerability Insertion:** Malicious attackers may insert vulnerabilities into widely used subsystems so that they can successfully attack systems that incorporate the subsystems. One can view the vulnerability as simply additional undesirable functionality.

A disadvantage of this kind of functionality oversupply is that (from the perspective of any given user) it produces systems with large attack surfaces (each additional piece of functionality typically increases the attack surface) in which most of the attack surface comes from functionality that the user does not need and may not even be aware of. So automatic techniques that remove superfluous functionality can significantly reduce the size of the attack surface and eliminate the corresponding vulnerabilities all without substantially impairing the utility of the system for the current user.

We also consider techniques that may affect desired functionality. The observation here is that users may be willing to accept different variants of a given piece of desired functionality. If this functionality contains a vulnerability, it may be possible change the functionality to eliminate the vulnerability while still providing acceptable service to users.

We next discuss several techniques that we have used successfully to change desired functionality or eliminate undesirable functionality.

## 6.2 Input Rectification

Most errors are exposed only by a few inputs — errors that occur on most inputs are usually detected and eliminated during testing. The goal of input rectification is to automatically convert inputs that expose errors into inputs that the system can process without error [14, 19, 16].

One approach is to identify a set of constraints that characterize the *comfort zone* of the software system — a set of inputs that are similar to those the system has seen before and for which it is almost certain to deliver expected and acceptable behavior [16]. The rectifier then automatically converts each input into an input that is within the comfort zone, typically by discarding pieces of the input that violate the constraints. The goal is to enable the system to process a safe input that is close as possible to the original input (and therefore should deliver most of the benefit to the user) while ensuring that the input is within the comfort zone of the program.

We have demonstrated that this approach can successfully eliminate vulnerabilities in the Pine email client [16]. The presented results use handcrafted rectifiers. We anticipate that it should be possible to build rectifiers automatically using the following approach:

- **Fault Attribution:** Given an input that exposes an error, use taint tracing [8] to identify the input regions involved in the computation that contains the error.
- **Constraint Synthesis:** Synthesize a constraint that the error-exposing input regions fail to satisfy.
- **Constraint Enforcement:**  Perhaps using techniques similar to data structure repair [2, 6, 5, 4, 3, 3], deploy a constraint enforcement technique to automatically convert the input to an input that does not contain the error.

If successful, this approach would make it possible for a system to automatically analyze an attack to produce a rectifier that eliminates the attack from all future inputs.

## 6.3 Functionality Excision

It is often possible to view a computation as a collection of tasks [20]. It is possible to empirically partition the tasks in a program into *critical* and *forgiving* tasks [17, 1, 15]. Eliminating a critical task usually causes the computation to fail. Eliminating a forgiving task may introduce some noise into the result that the computation produces, but typically does not cause the program to fail [17, 15]. It is possible to generate behavioral variation by eliminating forgiving tasks, ideally under the direction of a blame assignment mechanism that analyzes a successful attack to find the task that it exploited. It is possible to view this mechanism as eliminating the functionality of the eliminated task. Once again, this mechanism may make it possible to vary the behavior of the system (in a directed way) to automatically avoid vulnerabilities.

It is also possible to apply this mechanism (at a potentially finer granularity) to less structured programs by excising code at the granularity of statements, basic blocks, procedures, modules, or other program units [14]. The basic idea is to find and eliminate parts of the system that contain counterproductive or undesirable functionality. Examples of potentially dangerous functionality that may be suitable targets for this mechanism include interpreters for embedded scripting languages and vestigial pieces of functionality left over from early versions of the system.

## 6.4 Functionality Replacement

It is often possible to find multiple implementations of the same functionality. Switching in different implementations can deliver combinatorially generated system variation that may change the system enough to neutralize an attack. We also envision the use of machine learning techniques to automatically synthesize alternate implementations of different pieces of functionality. Even in situations in which it is difficult to automatically synthesize a complete version of the desired functionality, these automatically synthesized alternate implementations may enable the system to deliver acceptable service to its users while eliminating the vulnerability present in the original implementation.

## 6.5 Loop Perforation

Many programs contain loops. For many of these loops, reducing the number of executed loop iterations reduces the amount of time required to execute the computation. This transformation typically changes the result that the system produces. But it is often possible to find time-consuming loops which still produce acceptable results after this transformation [11, 9]. This mechanism can produce, automatically, a range of computations with different implementations that all provide acceptable results. If the current implementation of the loop has a vulnerability, it may be possible to eliminate the vulnerability by changing the number of iterations the loop performs. Consider, for example, a loop that copies data from one buffer to another. If the second buffer is too small to hold the data, eliminating a block of the last loop iterations may eliminate a buffer overflow vulnerability.

## 6.6 Dynamic Reconfiguration via Dynamic Knobs

Many systems come with static configuration parameters. Changing the parameter settings can often either expose or eliminate vulnerabilities — for example, misconfigured systems often exhibit vulnerabilities.

We have recently developed a technique that can automatically convert static configuration parameters into dynamic configuration patterns that can be changed without requiring the system to restart [10]. This mechanism should make it possible to automatically eliminate misconfiguration vulnerabilities without disrupting the execution of the system. It can also make it possible to dynamically change the configuration so that the system continually presents a different configuration to potential attackers.

## 6.7 Observed Invariant Enforcement

It is possible to observe normal executions of the system to build a model (in the form of a set of invariants) that characterizes that normal execution [13]. Because normal executions do not usually exhibit vulnerability exploitations, such exploitations may fall outside the model. It is often possible to force the system back within its normal operating mode by changing the state to satisfy any violated invariants [13]. This invariant enforcement can eliminate otherwise exploitable security vulnerabilities [13].

## 6.8 Cyclic Memory Allocation

Memory leaks can cause a system to fail by exhausting its address space. It is possible to eliminate memory leaks via the simple expedient of statically allocating a buffer, then cyclically allocating items out of that buffer (instead of allocating a new element each time) [12]. While this allocation strategy may wind up allocating multiple live elements in the same buffer slot, the experimental results indicate that it can enable systems to survive otherwise fatal memory leaks while degrading gracefully in the presence of overlaid live elements.

## 6.9 Failure-Oblivious Computing

Memory addressing errors such as null pointer dereferences or out of bounds memory accesses can cause programs to fail and open up vulnerabilities for attackers to exploit. Failure-oblivious computing dynamically checks for memory errors, discarding out of bounds or otherwise illegal writes and manufacturing values for illegal reads. For the tested set of benchmark programs, this technique closes memory vulnerabilities and enables programs to provide service to legitimate users [18].

## 6.10 Conclusion

Security vulnerabilities can be seen as undesirable functionality present in a system. One way to eliminate such vulnerabilities is to change the functionality in a way that eliminates the vulnerability. We have identified and experimentally evaluated several mechanisms that can change the functionality of the program in ways that may eliminate security vulnerabilities while still leaving the program able to provide acceptable functionality.

# References

1. Michael Carbin and Martin C. Rinard. Automatically identifying critical input regions and code in applications. In Paolo Tonella and Alessandro Orso, editors, *ISSTA*, pages 37–48. ACM, 2010.
2. Brian Demsky, Michael D. Ernst, Philip J. Guo, Stephen McCamant, Jeff H. Perkins, and Martin C. Rinard. Inference and enforcement of data structure consistency specifications. In Lori L. Pollock and Mauro Pezzè, editors, *ISSTA*, pages 233–244. ACM, 2006.
3. Brian Demsky and Martin C. Rinard. Automatic detection and repair of errors in data structures. In Ron Crocker and Guy L. Steele Jr., editors, *OOPSLA*, pages 78–95. ACM, 2003.
4. Brian Demsky and Martin C. Rinard. Static specification analysis for termination of specification-based data structure repair. In *ISSRE*, pages 71–84. IEEE Computer Society, 2003.
5. Brian Demsky and Martin C. Rinard. Data structure repair using goal-directed reasoning. In Gruia-Catalin Roman, William G. Griswold, and Bashar Nuseibeh, editors, *ICSE*, pages 176–185. ACM, 2005.
6. Brian Demsky and Martin C. Rinard. Goal-directed reasoning for specification-based data structure repair. *IEEE Trans. Software Eng.*, 32(12):931–951, 2006.
7. Richard P. Gabriel, David F. Bacon, Cristina Videira Lopes, and Guy L. Steele Jr., editors. *Proceedings of the 22nd Annual ACM SIGPLAN Conference on Object-Oriented Programming, Systems, Languages, and Applications, OOPSLA 2007, October 21-25, 2007, Montreal, Quebec, Canada.* ACM, 2007.
8. Vijay Ganesh, Tim Leek, and Martin C. Rinard. Taint-based directed whitebox fuzzing. In *ICSE*, pages 474–484. IEEE, 2009.
9. Henry Hoffman, Sasa Misailovic, Stelios Sidiroglou, Anant Agarwal, and Martin Rinard. Using Code Perforation to Improve Performance, Reduce Energy Consumption, and Respond to Failures. Technical Report TR-2009-042, Computer Science and Artificial Intelligence Laboratory, MIT, September 2009.
10. Henry Hoffmann, Stelios Sidiroglou, Michael Carbin, Sasa Misailovic, Anant Agarwal, and Martin Rinard. Power-Aware Computing with Dynamic Knobs. Technical Report TR-2010-027, Computer Science and Artificial Intelligence Laboratory, MIT, May 2010.
11. Sasa Misailovic, Stelios Sidiroglou, Henry Hoffmann, and Martin C. Rinard. Quality of service profiling. In Jeff Kramer, Judith Bishop, Premkumar T. Devanbu, and Sebastián Uchitel, editors, *ICSE (1)*, pages 25–34. ACM, 2010.
12. Huu Hai Nguyen and Martin C. Rinard. Detecting and eliminating memory leaks using cyclic memory allocation. In Greg Morrisett and Mooly Sagiv, editors, *ISMM*, pages 15–30. ACM, 2007.
13. Jeff H. Perkins, Sunghun Kim, Samuel Larsen, Saman P. Amarasinghe, Jonathan Bachrach, Michael Carbin, Carlos Pacheco, Frank Sherwood, Stelios Sidiroglou, Greg Sullivan, Weng-Fai Wong, Yoav Zibin, Michael D. Ernst, and Martin C. Rinard. Automatically patching errors in deployed software. In Jeanna Neefe Matthews and Thomas E. Anderson, editors, *SOSP*, pages 87–102. ACM, 2009.
14. Martin C. Rinard. Acceptability-oriented computing. In Ron Crocker and Guy L. Steele Jr., editors, *OOPSLA Companion*, pages 221–239. ACM, 2003.
15. Martin C. Rinard. Probabilistic accuracy bounds for fault-tolerant computations that discard tasks. In Gregory K. Egan and Yoichi Muraoka, editors, *ICS*, pages 324–334. ACM, 2006.
16. Martin C. Rinard. Living in the comfort zone. In Gabriel et al. [7], pages 611–622.
17. Martin C. Rinard. Using early phase termination to eliminate load imbalances at barrier synchronization points. In Gabriel et al. [7], pages 369–386.
18. Martin C. Rinard, Cristian Cadar, Daniel Dumitran, Daniel M. Roy, Tudor Leu, and William S. Beebee. Enhancing server availability and security through failure-oblivious computing. In *OSDI*, pages 303–316, 2004.

19. Martin C. Rinard, Cristian Cadar, and Huu Hai Nguyen. Exploring the acceptability envelope. In Ralph E. Johnson and Richard P. Gabriel, editors, *OOPSLA Companion*, pages 21–30. ACM, 2005.
20. Martin C. Rinard and Monica S. Lam. The design, implementation, and evaluation of jade. *ACM Trans. Program. Lang. Syst.*, 20(3):483–545, 1998.

# Chapter 7
# End-to-End Software Diversification of Internet Services

Mihai Christodorescu, Matthew Fredrikson, Somesh Jha, and Jonathon Giffin

**Abstract** Software diversification has been approached as a tool to provide security guarantees for programs that lack type safety (e.g., programs written in C). In this setting, diversification operates by changing the memory layout of program code or data and by changing the syntax of program code. These techniques succeed as a defense against an attacker's use of type-safety vulnerabilities (e.g., buffer overflows) because they randomize the key elements necessary to a successful low-level intrusion (memory addresses and memory contents). This chapter proposes to extend software diversification from a point technique, applied to hand-picked aspects of a single program, to an comprehensive technique *applied by default to all components of an application*. Internet services is used as a focused example here.

Mihai Christodorescu
IBM T.J. Watson Research Center
19 Skyline Dr., Hawthorne, NY 10532
e-mail: mihai@us.ibm.com

Matthew Fredrikson
University of Wisconsin, Madison
1210 W. Dayton St., Madison, WI 53706-1685
e-mail: mfredik@cs.wisc.edu

Somesh Jha
University of Wisconsin, Madison
1210 W. Dayton St., Madison, WI 53706-1685
e-mail: jha@cs.wisc.edu

Jonathon Giffin
Georgia Institute of Technology
266 Ferst Dr., Atlanta, GA 30332-0765
e-mail: giffin@cc.gatech.edu

## 7.1 Introduction

Attackers that employ SQL injection, command injection, and cross-site scripting (XSS) rely on *a priori* knowledge of the back-end systems used by the vulnerable program. For almost all the forms of SQL injection, an attacker has to know (or be able to learn) the names of tables and the names and types of table columns. For command injection, an attacker has to know the names of executables available on the system. For XSS, the attacker has to know the structure of the HTML DOM and the DOM node identifiers of interest. But there is no reason for this type of information to be easily and predictably known to an attacker. Users of the program have no need to know the names of database tables as used by their program. Software diversification exploits this information asymmetry to render the impact of any attacks that abuse embedded subprograms (i.e., SQL query strings, shell commands, HTML text with JavaScript code). The key idea is to apply transformations to the subprogram (*e.g.*, the SQL query), coupled with similar transformations to the execution environment (*e.g.*, the database), such that each instance of the program uses syntactically and semantically distinct subprograms. Thus the attacker's success rate is diminished significantly when software is diversified.

We make the observation that an Internet-facing service is characterized by an externally visible interface, whose syntax and semantics are fixed, and an internal implementation that can change arbitrarily within the constraints of the interface. Thus diversification can be applied to any part of the implementation, to any extent necessary to achieve the desired security guarantees. In other words, as long as the interface presented to the users is preserved, the implementation can take any form and can change often during execution. In a typical multi-tier web application, many aspects are amenable to diversification: the HTML document presented to the client browser, its communication with the web server, the application running on the web server, its communication with the middleware, the middleware itself, and its communication with the database server. This ensures that the service is protected from different classes of attacks, not any just one particular class.

We make the following contributions:

- We propose the use of end-to-end diversification for all applications, in particular for Internet-facing application. Instead of targeting known attacks against known vulnerability classes in known runtime components, we believe end-to-end diversification can harden an application against all attacks that violate its functional specification.
- We outline the challenges involved in realizing end-to-end diversification and propose appropriate approaches. Since our proposal impacts both the application development phases and the deployment and operation phases, the technical challenges are numerous. Furthermore, users in each of these phases (e.g., developers, system administrators) have distinct needs and expectations that must be addressed.

**Fig. 7.1** The architecture of our example web application. Note that the functionality of the web application is fully defined, from the user's point of view, by the communication between the user and the web browser. The other communication protocols, from the browser to the web server and from the web server to the database server, are of no relevance to the user.

```
1  String userName = request.getQueryString();
2  String query = "SELECT * FROM profiles WHERE
      name = '" + userName + "'";
3
4  Statement stmt = conn.createStatement();
5  stmt.executeQuery(query);
```

**Fig. 7.2** SQL-injection vulnerability in Java program.

- We present a web-application use case to highlight the practicality of our framework. We describe a (hypothetical) implementation of a Facebook-like web application and show how two of its many aspects benefit from diversification.

## 7.2 Running Example

Consider a complex web service such as Facebook (sketched in Figure 7.1). The core functionality of this service involves persistent user input in many forms, third-party script interaction, and user-directed data retrieval. Needless to say, the implementation of this service is bound to be complex and error-prone [2], and matters are only made worse by the fact that nearly every one of its features gives attackers another way to push vulnerability-inducing data into the back-end. This application presents many fruitful opportunities for diversification, two of which we will illustrate in greater detail.

Consider a user who searches for profiles matching a given name. Assume that the back-end stores all of the data for a given user in a relational database, and answers search queries by constructing a suitable SQL statement. In this case, a portion of the back-end code may look something like the code in Figure 7.2. However, this code is vulnerable to SQL injection, due to a fairly common developer mistake wherein inputs provided by the user are not properly sanitized [1]. For example, by issuing a query for a user named "123'; DELETE * FROM profiles;", the attacker forces this program to issue the following SQL query to the database:

**SELECT** * **FROM** profiles **WHERE** name = '123';
   **DELETE** * **FROM** profiles;

This is clearly not the developer's intended effect, as the publicly-exposed search routine should not delete the profile database. Existing automated solutions to this problem, such as "magic quotes" [3], attempt to automatically place sanitizers on strings that might be used in an attack. However, they have not met with success, and SQL injection remains a problem [3].

This class of attack can be mitigated by randomizing the identifiers of various aspects of the database interface in such a way as not to affect the semantics of the program. In our example, the strategy reduces to creating a new database schema for the query:

| Old name | New name |
|---|---|
| table profiles $\longrightarrow$ | table fc11 |
| column name $\longrightarrow$ | column bbd6 |

We must also change the way that the program interfaces with the database to reflect this transformation. In the program above, this change could be reflected by changing the second line of Figure 7.2 to:

```
2  String query = "SELECT * FROM fc11 WHERE bbd6 =
       '" + userName + "'";
```

The attack above will request in the following query, which will be rejected by the database server as invalid because it refers to non-existent tables and columns:

```
SELECT * FROM fc11 WHERE bbd6 = '123'; DELETE *
    FROM profiles;
```

Effectively, the DELETE portion of the SQL query is rendered ineffective, thwarting the attack.

Of course changing the database schema just once might not provide enough security because an attacker could eventually learn the new names of the database objects. Thus, a different user accessing the same web application would use this database schema:

| Old name | New name |
|---|---|
| table profiles $\longrightarrow$ | table ae76e015705 |
| column name $\longrightarrow$ | column beb38f0f750 |

and the corresponding SQL query would be:

```
2  String query = "SELECT * FROM ae76e015705 WHERE
       beb38f0f750 = '" + userName +
3  "'";
```

Because the specific aspects of the database are now randomized, it becomes very difficult for the attacker to construct valid code to inject.

Another type of attack to which a user-driven website is vulnerable is cross-site scripting (XSS). There are dozens of ways that users submit content to our web

```
1   <input name="status">
2   <input type="submit" value="Share">
3
4   <!-- User-provided data starts here -->
5   <script>
6   // Find the status input box
7   statusBox = document.getElementById("input");
8   statusBox.innerHTML = "skipping work";
9   btns = document.getElementsByTagName("input");
10  // Submit the form
11  foreach(var btn in btns) {
12      if(btn.getAttribute("value") == "Share")
13          btn.onclick();
14  }
15  </script>
```

**Fig. 7.3** HTML page containing injected code (lines 5–15).

application that is subsequently rendered in the context of an HTML document. Currently, the best known methods for preventing users from submitting JavaScript content that is subsequently run in the context of web application boils down to correctly placing string santiziers at all code points that generate HTML from untrusted inputs. This is commonly understood to be an error-prone process, and automatic procedures for placing sanitizers must cope with understanding program-level information flows, as well as the subtle interactions between various HTML contexts and the semantics of string sanitizers [4]. These factors make string sanitization an insufficient solution to the problem.

In order for a cross-site scripting attack to do any damage, the injected code must be able to reference aspects of the browser execution environment that allow it to affect the state of the enclosing site. It follows that diversification of the browser's runtime environment, namely the Document Object Model (DOM) APIs, can subvert this assumption and stop most malicious cross-site scripting activities. Consider the JavaScript code in Figure 7.3, which is a relatively benign cross-site scripting payload for web application. Its functionality is straightforward: it finds the input box for the user's status, writes a fake status update, searches for the form submission button, and activates its click event handler. In order to interact and eventually interfere with the enclosing page, the script makes use of three DOM API's: getElementById, getElementsByTagName, and getAttribute. Diversifying the names of these methods in a manner unknown to the attacker subverts the attack.

Diversifying the JavaScript runtime environment to protect against this type of attack proceeds in a similar manner to SQL diversification. First, a plan is derived for mapping non-essential characteristics of the environment, in this case API method names, to random elements. Next, all JavaScript source files that are sent to the

```
1   <input name="status">
2   <input type="submit" value="Share">
3
4   <!-- Diversification code -->
5   <script>
6   document.getelbyid10239 = document.getElementById;
7   document.getElementById = null;
8   document.getatt90254 = document.getAttribute;
9   document.getAttribute = null;
10  // ...Additional diversification setup
11  </script>
12
13  <!-- User-provided data starts here -->
14  <script>
15  statusBox = document.getElementById("input");
16  statusBox.innerHTML = "skipping work";
17  btns = document.getElementsByTagName("input");
18  foreach(var btn in btns) {
19      if(btn.getAttribute("value") == "Share")
20          btn.onclick();
21  }
22  </script>
```

**Fig. 7.4** HTML page protected by diversification (lines 5–11) and containing injected code (lines 14–22).

client are analyzed for references to diversified API's, and rewritten to call the actual methods. Analyzing JavaScript is a non-trivial task; we can utilize our previous work to aid this task. Because the target JavaScript code is essentially re-generated every time a new HTTP connection is made to the server, there are many opportunities for generating new diversification plans, so selecting a frequency is a matter left for configuration on a case-by-case basis.

Figure 7.4 shows the result of applying environment diversification to the current example. At the top of the JavaScript code for the page, the new environment is created, and the default one erased. The loose nature of JavaScript in the browser allows us to do this without modifying the interpreter or browser implementation, simply by swapping references to the necessary DOM methods. Note that each DOM API that can possibly be used in an attack must be diversified, and every default reference to each API must be set to null; for space reasons, the code in Figure 7.4 does not exemplify this. Most importantly, observe that the XSS payload cannot successfully execute, as each of the DOM calls is to a null reference.

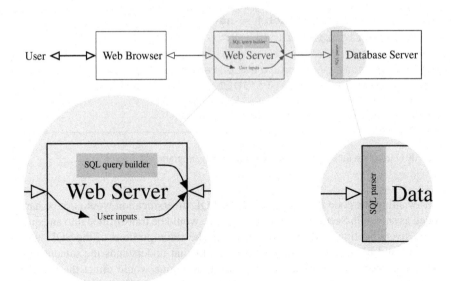

**Fig. 7.5** The architecture of our example web application after diversification of the SQL interface. The components highlighted in red are subjected to diversification, while all other data is untouched. In particular, notice that user inputs are not transformed by diversification.

## 7.3 End-to-End Diversification of a Software Stack

Our running example, presented above, illustrates two key characteristics of the diversification approach. First, diversification cannot be applied to only one or two hand-picked aspects of the program, but rather to all aspects of the program. In our example, we showed that both the Javascript component and the SQL DB component of the web application benefit from diversification. Second, diversification is not a one-time transformation of the program, but it consists of the repeated application of a set of transformations. The frequency of transformation is program dependent and would ideally be such that each user input is processed by a differently diversified instance of the program. Based on the key characteristics, we can now describe how the end-to-end approach to diversification works.

End-to-end diversification randomly changes the names (and, more generally, the static identifiers) that are used in a software system to communicate between the system components, as long as these names and identifiers do not impact the functionality exposed to the user. The changes are performed on a schedule that satisfies given security goals and performance constraints. We observe that the set of names that are candidates for diversification is fixed for a given software system, and thus need to be derived only once, while the diversification procedure itself can be applied repeatedly to those names. We thus distinguish between the transformation of a software system into a diversification-ready system and the actual diversification of such a system.

```
2  DiversificationPlan dobj = new
       DiversificationPlan(...);

3
4  Statement stmt = conn.createStatement();
5  String query = dobj.sql("SELECT * FROM profiles
       WHERE name = '") + userName +
6  dobj.sql("'");
```

**Fig. 7.6** One option for creating a diversification-ready program.

Revisiting the code from Figure 7.2, the SQL diversification would not be hard-coded as shown in Section 7.2. Instead the code would be transformed into an equivalent, diversification-ready version, in which the static portions of the SQL-query string would be passed to a diversification API that understands the semantics of SQL. Then during execution the diversification engine would effect the transformation. In this case, the code would resemble Figure 7.6. The new names for the diversification plan are generated randomly for each program instance, and possibly changed during execution, such that two distinct program instances would generate the two queries shown in Section 7.2.

Our approach consists components that must be applied both statically and at run-time. Before a potentially vulnerable application is run, the static component must infer three types of information:

- the entities referenced by all subprograms,
- the code locations at which subprograms are evaluated, and
- a semantics-preserving way to re-write the application to diversify entity references in subprograms.

Note that the static component requires specific knowledge of the subprogram semantics for each possible type of subprogram that is evaluated, e.g. SQL, JavaScript, or shell script. Once the static component completes, the re-written application calls into a run-time component which generates a unique diversification strategy, applies it to each subprogram encountered at run-time, and modifies the execution environment accordingly.

Moving from ad-hoc or piecemeal diversification, in which only selected aspects of the application are transformed using pre-computed diversification plans, to end-to-end diversification, in which the functional aspects of the application are preserved and everything else is transformed, requires a methodical approach to ensure completeness of coverage. Every software system has a multitude of aspects that are open to diversification. Table 7.1 lists some of the diversifiable aspects of the web-application system of Figure 7.1.

We sketch here the key elements necessary for achieving this methodical, end-to-end approach to diversification. We denote by *diversification strategy* a particular random program transformation to be applied to a particular application aspect.

| | |
|---|---|
| Javascript APIs | SQL keywords |
| Javascript variables | SQL syntax |
| HTML DOM structure | database table names |
| HTML DOM identifiers | database column names |
| HTTP protocol keywords | SQL response format |
| HTTP protocol syntax | database server IP and port numbers |
| HTTP protocol headers | database server ISA |
| HTTP protocol content encoding | local files used by web server |
| web server memory layout | local files used by database server |
| web server ISA | database server memory layout |

**Table 7.1** Aspects of our web-application system that are candidates for diversification. Not all diversifiable aspects are desirable to be diversified, since each incurs different costs at runtime.

Address-space layout randomization and SQL diversification (illustrated in Section 7.2) are examples of such strategies, with the first one designed to change the memory layout of binary programs, and the second to change the database schema and any corresponding SQL queries. Each diversification strategy is characterized by three attributes:

- the application aspect it transforms (e.g., SQL database schema),
- the security gains it brings (e.g., prevention of SQL-injection attacks), and
- the performance overhead it imposes.

It is important to note that all possible diversification strategies (or even the existing ones) are not disjoint along any of the above attribute axes. For example, instruction set randomization and address space layout randomization overlap in the application aspect they transform (i.e., representation of binary code in memory) and in the security gain they bring (i.e., protection against code-injection attacks). Of course, they differ in the overhead each one introduces.

A diversification strategy is applied according to a *diversification plan*, which defines the application points to be transformed (selected from the application aspect to which this strategy applies), the frequency of re-applying the transformation, and any other parameters specific to the diversification strategy at hand. The diversification plan can affect the attributes of a diversification strategy, in particular the security gains and the performance overhead. Separating the diversification strategies from their diversification plans allows us to cleanly split the effort between the application development/building phase and the application deployment/operation phase.

We now illustrate the basic procedure for end-to-end diversification (see Figure 7.7). At development and build time, the software developer uses all diversification strategies available and applicable to transform the application so as to support later diversification plans. At deployment time, the system administrator instantiates the application according to a chosen set of diversification plans, one per strategy. The diversified application instance then operates normally, while the runtime environment executes the diversification plan to re-apply each diversification strategy as specified.

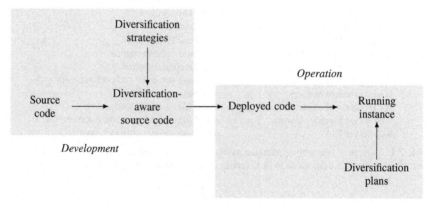

**Fig. 7.7** The modification of the software lifecycle to allow for diversification.

This procedure for end-to-end diversification creates a number of challenges, which we discuss in turn below.

## 7.4 First Technical Challenge: Impact on Security

The fundamental challenge in understanding the impact of diversification is in precisely characterizing the amount of protection offered by end-to-end diversification. Intuitively, software diversification as described in Section 7.3 protects the software system from attacks by ensuring that attackers cannot arbitrarily control the system even when vulnerabilities are present. Formalizing this intuition and proving its correctness are necessary to ensure that the end result is resilient to attack. In other words, since end-to-end diversification does not fix the vulnerabilities in the system, but makes it harder for the attacker to abuse the vulnerable system, we need a precise, computationally-meaningful way to measure the increase in difficulty for the attacker.

We note that diversification changes only the syntax of various interfaces between components of the software stack — it does not change algorithms, data structures, or other artifacts crucial to the functionality of the program. Thus, it cannot address security vulnerabilities or other logic errors that are inherently part of the design of the software and its algorithms. In spite of this limitation, end-to-end diversification targets a large class of vulnerabilities, from buffer overflows to SQL injection to cross-site scripting; essentially, any vulnerability not present in the logic of the program itself. Protection is achieved not by eliminating the bug, but by changing the environment on which the attack relies.

The security of diversified software relies fundamentally on making each diversified instance sufficiently different from the others. Then, under the assumption that the attacker cannot learn or predict the values from the diversification plan applied to a software instance, security is achieved. It is crucial that the parameters of a diversification plan are not easy to guess or otherwise learn by an attacker. This means that these parameters must satisfy several requirements:

- The current values of the diversification parameters must not leak to the attacker, even when the software system fails or encounters an error.
- Diversification parameters must have a wide range of valid values so as to make brute-force attacks infeasible.
- The sequence of values over time for any diversification parameter must be unpredictable so as to make guessing attacks infeasible, even if past values are leaked to the attacker.

We observe that these requirements are similar to those for cryptographic secrets, and that many cryptographic schemes for secure random number generation would be effective here.

Unfortunately, the amount of available randomness available to many targets of diversification is not as large as it may initially seem. Oftentimes, the semantics of the underlying system impose restrictions that make values easier to guess. For example, on a 32-bit system memory locations are necessarily expressed as 32-bit integers, and are further constrained by architectural and operating system-level requirements. This combination of factors effectively leads to a range much smaller than $2^{32}$ for diversifying memory locations, reducing the security benefits of diversification. Additionally, support for diversified parameters can incur performance costs, so in effect diversification plans provide a control point for system administrators to balance security with performance. This can lead to unfortunate incentives, for example if the system administrator chooses a diversification plans that is not aggressive enough to trade for increased performance. These difficulties point to the need for a threshold parameter on each diversification strategy, such that any chosen diversification plan must meet this threshold to guarantee an improvement in security.

Finally, the question of diversification completeness needs further research. End-to-end diversification relies on transforming all application aspects that do not affect functionality. Determining all such aspects and the corresponding diversification strategies is non-trivial. As Table 7.1 shows, even a simple system has many candidates for diversification. Identifying all candidate aspects is key for the end-to-end security argument, as any aspect left undiversified provides a potential avenue for attack.

## 7.5 Second Technical Challenge: Impact on Software Development

Perhaps the most important concern is the amount of automation available in an end-to-end diversification toolchain, as this impacts both the cost and security of an implementation. A large number of vulnerabilities are created by inattentive or unknowledgeable programmers, so we cannot rely on programmers to apply transformations for each diversification strategy in a reliable and consistent manner. Rather the diversification has to be applied automatically at the end of the development process, possibly as part of the build process. We note that it cannot be fully automated, as the developer has to provide information about the functional requirements that must be preserved for the application to be useful. This leads us to another challenge, namely that of minimizing the size and complexity of the functional specification needed by the toolchain.

Ideally, the programmer would just describe the interface needed to maintain functionality (e.g., the HTML structure for a web application), and the toolchain would automatically verify semantic preservation after diversification. In fact, straightforward programs with well-documented interfaces, can likely be dealt with in this fashion. However, many software components are designed and developed with only a partial understanding of their future integration into a complete system. Thus, it is challenging to determine the provenance of each data item that flows through the program, i.e. whether it is a user input or a predefined value generated by another component of the larger system. One solution is to construct a symbolic provenance diagram that ties inputs to outputs without taking into account whether an input is user-generated or not. This would allow a diversification-ready program to provide other components with the information needed to determine which data elements are good candidates for diversification, given an minimal set of user inputs that must not be diversified. At system-building time, when components are connected and input sources are well defined, a system architect or developer can identify the few inputs that come from the user, while the rest of the inputs and outputs are to be diversified as they are internal to the system.

A final item of concern for developers is the need for debugging and post-crash analysis support. This can be achieved by sending to the developer, as part of the feedback process, the diversification plan and its parameters so that the running instance can be replicated. A system administrator has to collect the fault information (such as the core dump and any error traces) together with the diversification plan in effect at the time of the fault. Debugging and post-mortem analyzers must be adapted to take into account the diversification parameters, in order to undo the diversification artifacts present in the fault-related information.

## 7.6 Third Technical Challenge: Impact on Runtime Performance

Diversification strategies have distinct, non-trivial performance implications. For example, randomizing the instruction set architecture, while effective against buffer-overflow attacks, incurs a huge runtime overhead because commercial hardware platforms lack built-in support for this feature. As a result, ISA diversification relies on a system emulator that translates diversified instructions at runtime into instructions for the real hardware. This sort of emulation is extremely expensive, making ISA diversification a costly technique of limited use. We do not foresee a generic approach to optimizing diversification strategies, but remain optimistic that the performance overhead of particular diversification strategies can be reduced and made insignificant in comparison to other performance bottlenecks in the system. As an example, diversification of database schemas is quite efficient thanks to existing support for database views, which can be created and changed on the fly. While there is a small overhead associated with querying a view instead of a database table, this overhead disappears when considering the cost of executing the query itself.

Beyond the obvious requirement that performance overhead introduced by diversification remain minimal, we also recognize the need to develop methods for predicting the overhead. This becomes particularly important if we expect system administrators to create diversification plans that inherently force them to make a choice between security and performance, lest the dangerous incentives mentioned above manifest themselves.

## 7.7 Fourth Technical Challenge: Impact on Deployment

Diversification introduces new failure modes, and end-to-end diversification multiplies the number of failure modes. In our web-application example from Section 7.2, the XSS diversification does not result in new failures in case of attack, as the attack simply does not succeed, and in fact has no side effects. But in the same example, an attack against the SQL-diversified application would result in the database returning a "No such table" error, which the application might not be prepared to handle. The challenge here is to include error handling for the diversified aspects when the application is transformed. This issue is closely related to the software development concerns discussed in Section 7.5.

## 7.8 Conclusion and Open Problems

In this chapter, we have outlined an attractive solution to a large class of software attacks that work by subverting the intended logic of a vulnerable program. Examples of this type of attack are buffer overflow, cross-site scripting, and SQL injection attacks. Our solution generalizes a small-but-effective set of defenses based on *diversifying* various non-essential features of an application's runtime state. We have argued that performing this diversification in a ubiquitous, principled way will stymie attackers by making it impossible for them to make well-founded assumptions about the environment of their victims. Finally, we outlined the key challenges posed by this solution, and discussed their implications for real systems.

To realize the end-to-end diversification concept proposed in this work, we identified four key research areas that require further development. Each point depends on a solution to at least one difficult open problem.

- We need to develop *a complete set of diversification strategies*. End-to-end diversification depends on matching diversification strategies with each application aspect, so a rich set of diversification strategies is a prerequisite.
- Since even the simplest application have many aspects amenable to diversification, we have to consider the *composition of diversification strategies*. Composition is not necessarily straightforward, as unexpected results (e.g., increased performance overhead) might result from combining two seemingly orthogonal strategies.
- Selecting an *optimal set of diversification strategies* for a given application is non trivial, as a number of factor come into play, including security, performance, and usability. It is not clear at this point how such selection should be performed or how to allow developers or system administrators to guide the selection process.
- *Tools for applying diversification strategies and instantiating them at runtime* are needed if a sizable impact on current practices is desired. In previous sections we hinted at how such tools could use static analysis and program transformation, but more work is needed to perfect them.

# References

1. Sql injections top attack statistics.   Dark Reading: `http://www.darkreading.com/database_security/security/app-security/showArticle.jhtml?articleID=223100129`, February 2010.
2. Multiple     facebook     vulnerabilities     reported     on     full-disclosure. Zero                Day:                `http://www.zdnet.com/blog/security/multiple-facebook-vulnerabilities-reported-on-full-disclosure/1414`, July 2008.
3. PHP    manual:    Magic    quotes.        `http://php.net/manual/en/security.magicquotes.php`, September 2010.
4. The web application security consortium: Web application security statistics.   `http://projects.webappsec.org/Web-Application-Security-Statistics`, September 2010.

# Chapter 8
# Introducing Diversity and Uncertainty to Create Moving Attack Surfaces for Web Services

Yih Huang and Anup K. Ghosh

**Abstract** Web servers are primary targets for cyber attack because of the documents they may contain, transactions they support, or the opportunity to cause brand damage or reputational embarrassment to the victim organization. Today most web services are implemented by employing a fixed software stack that includes a web server program, web application programs, an operating system, and a virtualization layer. This software mix as a whole constitutes the attack surface of the web service and a vulnerability in one of the components that make up the web service is a potential threat to the entire service.

This chapter presents an approach that employs a rotational scheme for substituting different software stacks for any given request in order to create a dynamic and uncertain attack surface area of the system. In particular, our approach automatically creates a set of diverse virtual servers (VSs), each configured with a unique software mix, producing diversified attack surfaces. Our approach includes a rotational scheme with a set of diversified offline servers rotating in to replace a set of diversified online servers on either a fixed rotation schedule or an event-driven basis. Assuming $N$ different VSs, $M < N$ of them will serve online at a time while off-line VSs are reverted to predefined pristine state. By constantly changing the set of $M$ online VSs and introducing randomness in their selections, attackers will face multiple, constantly changing, and unpredictable attack surfaces.

Yih Huang and Anup K. Ghosh
Center for Secure Information Systems
George Mason University
4400 University Drive, MS 5B5
Fairfax, VA 22030
e-mail: huangyih@cs.gmu.eduandaghosh@gmu.edu

## 8.1 Introduction

Web services have become attractive targets of cyber attacks because they aggregate valuable information such as customer personally identifiable information, corporate documents, and sensitive financial transactions [1]. Attractive attacks include stock exchanges, banks, retail online stores, online dating sites, and major corporations, all of which have significant value at risk if their web services get compromised.

In current web services, a fairly substantial amount of software forms the attack surface area for would-be cyber attackers, including the web server software, the web application logic, the operating systems these programs run on, and even the underlying hypervisor. In current architectures, it may takes only a single bug, such as a server buffer overflow, to gain full control of the web service for an unauthorized user.

Our approach addresses the single flaw vulnerability by incorporating unpredictable diversity with secure architectures for web services. Specifically, we employ two significant methods to defeat attacks against web services: (1) we diversify a set of software stacks that provide the objective web service and employ them in an architecture that will yield different instances for requests at different times, and (2) we rotate in pristine instances of diversified software stacks on a fixed time interval or event-driven basis, while rotating out and restoring software stacks that have been in production to their pristine states.

### 8.1.1 Attack Surface

Web services typically include a mix of operating systems, web server software, web application programs, and virtualization technologies. Shown in Fig. 8.1, this software mix is exposed to the public Internet and therefore constitutes the "attack surface" of the web service. A security-conscious IT administrator will follow standard best security practices, which entails hardening configuration of the server system itself (e.g., to prevent access to unnecessary programs, run a server program with minimal privilege, and apply current patches on a consistent basis). This reactive approach creates three major problems:

- The single attack surface is always reachable.
- The fixed attack surface can be probed and studied over long periods of time.
- Once identified, vulnerabilities in the attack surface remain exploitable for relatively long periods of time, measured in months typically.

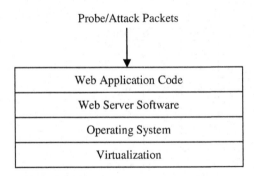

Probe/Attack Packets

| Web Application Code |
| Web Server Software |
| Operating System |
| Virtualization |

**Fig. 8.1** The Software Stack of Fixed Attack Surface

## 8.1.2 Moving Attack Surfaces

In this chapter, we describe a proactive approach where multiple attack surfaces are deployed in unpredictable fashion. Moreover these attack surfaces are constantly changing. This approach will be called Moving Attack Surfaces (MAS). The basic concept of MAS is shown in Fig. 8.2.

A standard, large-scale commercial web server architecture is assumed where web servers are virtualized in a pool of server resources behind a load balancing server with a single advertised IP address. In Fig. 8.2, $i$ versions of the web application implementations I, $w$ web server software W, $o$ different operation systems O, and $v$ different virtualization technologies V, are used to create $N$ different virtual servers (VSs). These VSs have different software stacks and therefore different attack surfaces. In Fig. 8.2(a), two VSs are used online at time $t_1$, resulting in two different attack surfaces. Fig. 8.2(b) shows that at a later time $t_2$, the VSs in Fig. 8.2(a) have been replaced by other VSs, causing the attack surfaces to change. In general, $M < N$ VSs will be deployed online at a time with $N - M$ servers held in reserve to replace expiring servers [2, 3]. In this way, every VS rotation presents a new online server stack that attackers will have to probe to find vulnerabilities. With a short enough time constant on automatic server rotations, the knowledge gained will not be usable on the next diverse server instance that services a request. We use randomness in the selection of VS instances to avoid predictability.

Uncertainty has traditionally been considered a liability in engineering, but in this approach it can be strength. In particular, MAS creates two types of uncertainty to increase the intrusion resilience of web services. The *composition* uncertainty refers to the random selection of $M$ online VSs/attack-surfaces at any given time. In Fig. 8.2, for instance, the attack surface composition at time $t_1 = \{VS_1, VS_2\}$ and the one at time $t_2 = \{VS_3, VS_4\}$. With MAS the composition of online attack surfaces constantly changes in unpredictable fashion. The *reachability* uncertainty refers to the fact that the adversary cannot determine which VS stack will be servicing a request at any given time. A load balancer, termed dispatcher in Fig. 3, makes that decision with some random algorithm. Consequently, even if an attacker figures

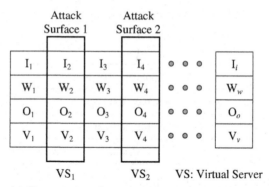

(a) Two attach surfaces at time $t_1$

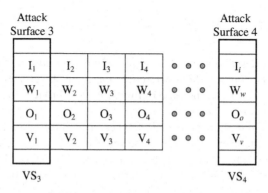

(b) The attach surfaces at time $t_2 > t_1$

**Fig. 8.2** Moving Attack Surfaces

out an attack path used against a particular VS, the attack will likely fail because consecutive steps of the attack from reconnaissance to exploitation will be directed to different VSs.

To further increase unpredictability, the MAS concept can be generalized to have $M' < N \times K$ VSs serving online at a time. That is, every VS software mix is replicated $K$ times to produce $K$ VSs of the same types. A larger pool of VSs allows the use of $M' > M$ online VSs, further increasing the level of composition unpredictability. In this way, the present composition of attack surfaces may have ones of the same types. However, the increased reachability uncertainty will make it even more unlikely that attack packets will be directed to the same VS.

### 8.1.3 MAS Web Service Architecture

As shown in Fig. 8.3, a MAS-based web service architecture runs a pool of diversified VSs on one or more physical hosts. The selection of the server from the VS pool is made randomly (only online VSs are shown in the figure). Each VS in the system runs through the cycles of three modes. In the online mode, the VS is part of the present composition of attack surfaces, serving client requests. When the Trustworthy Controller (TC) in Fig. 8.3 [3], decides to take the VS offline, the VS enters the graceful shutdown mode, wherein it finishes servicing existing requests but will not accept new requests. After completing all requests, the VS enters the offline mode and will be reverted back to its clean state. The cycle repeats itself when the VS is chosen by TC to serve online again.

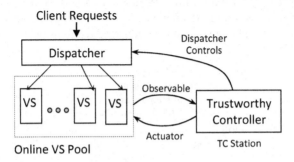

**Fig. 8.3** MAS Web Service Architecture

MAS uses a closed-loop feedback control to monitor and manage the virtual server pool through the Trustworthy Controller (TC) in Fig. 8.3 [3]. Intrusion and anomaly sensors in the network, server boxes, and in each VS report observable status and events, such as server CPU/memory usage, system call behavior and attack alarms. Based on preponderance of evidence in these data, the MAS TC will invoke actuators to address perceived threats and service deterioration. Examples of actuators include restarting services in a VS, killing suspicious processes, and reverting virtual servers back to a clean state.

### 8.1.4 Non-Persistent VS State

When a VS is online, there is a chance, however small with MAS, that it could be corrupted. The next time it is brought online, corruption may persist, allowing for instance an adversary to reuse a previously established foothold on the VS. For this reason, MAS imposes the non-persistence requirement: each MAS VS must start in pristine state in memory and file systems next time when it goes online.

Note that the common practice of rebooting does not satisfy the non-persistence requirement because reboots carry over file system corruption. With a corrupted file system, the memory state after a reboot cannot be guaranteed either. While some virtualization technologies offer off-the-shelf solutions to meet the non-persistence requirement, others do not. However, creative solutions could be developed for those virtualization technologies that do not provide direct supports. In the following discussion, we will use the term revert or reversion to refer to any mechanisms that enforce the non-persistence requirement. Actual implementations of the enforcement with various virtualization technologies will be discussed later in Section 8.3.5.

We show the state transition of MAS VSs in Fig. 8.4. For clarity, the grace mode is omitted for it is merely a transitional period from online to offline mode. As seen, when an online VS is to retire, it is simply "powered off" without going through the normal shutdown procedure. For a virtual machine, powering off is the same as gracefully eliminating it from memory. We use a dashed circle for the offline mode to emphasize that the powered-off VS imposes no processing and memory overhead. When the VS is selected to go online later, it is reverted to its pristine state.

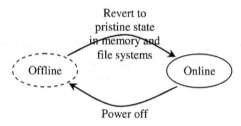

**Fig. 8.4** State transition methods for MAS VSs

It must be emphasized that mode switches of a VS is not based on fixed intervals. There are three types of "triggers" to bring an online VS to the offline mode (through the transitional grace mode).

**Event Driven** A VS can be taken offline because of the accumulation of anomalous events or other failed integrity checks received by the TC in Fig. 8.3 pertaining to the VS. A large number of $M$ online VSs will ease the performance penalty on the entire system when individual VSs are brought offline. This mitigates the problem of excessive false positives, characteristic of many intrusion detection systems.

**Random Selection** Even when there is no anomaly present, a VS can be randomly selected anytime to retire to the offline mode while an offline VS is selected as a substitute. This increases the unpredictability of MAS without affecting the availability of the service.

**Maximum Lifespan Expired** All VSs are subject to maximum online lifespan to limit its exposure to attacks. The maximum online lifespan of a VS helps contain the damages of undetected intrusion and zero-day attack to a limited time window, for the offline mode will restore the pristine state of the VS (the non-persistence requirement). MAS lifetimes are measured in minutes.

Finally, the advantages of the MAS concept are summarized as follows.

- First and most importantly, MAS presents constantly changing and unpredictable attack surfaces to potential cyber adversaries.
- MAS denies adversaries the certainty to reach a particular target surface, either because the surface is not presently online or the load balancer (i.e., the dispatcher) directs probe/attack packets to other surfaces. This makes it extremely difficult for adversaries to "lock on" an attack surface for probing and attacks.
- MAS limits the damages in VSs caused by zero-day exploits. When an attack is successful, its corruption is limited by the maximum lifespan. Since each VS is periodically reverted to a pristine state on corruption or on a clock, corruption in a VS will not be persistent. Admittedly, this is a stopgap solution until the VS software can be patched, but it will prevent exploits from being persistent.

In the rest of the chapter, we will discuss the best web programming practices to take advantage of MAS. Opportunities of attack surface diversification will be investigated in length. As discovered in this investigation, there are thousands of different attack surfaces that can be constructed with well-known web server software, operating systems and virtualization technologies. We will present our position on the management complexity issue. We will also weigh the merits of large diversified attack surfaces versus small and hardened ones and discuss the need for new metrics to assess the efficacy of these approaches.

## 8.2 Web Programming Practices with MAS

Because every MAS VS returns to its pristine state periodically or on event detection, one might intuitively deduce that the limit excludes MAS from stateful web services. A similar issue has been addressed in our previously published paper [2]. In the next paragraph, we reiterate our previous finding.

> The web service industry is generally moving away from stateful servers, lest crashes of individual servers affect user satisfaction. In particular, the Representational State Transfer (REST) framework for web application development [4] ensures that all web servers are stateless while still being able to provide stateful services. The REST framework enjoys wide support, including major server operating systems, such as Windows, Solaris, and Linux.

Consequently, REST is recommended as the best programming practices for MAS. In general, any web application that does not leave service state on servers or only keeps them for short, limited times can be ported to a MAS environment. With MAS, individual VSs routinely go through online and offline modes (not necessarily with fixed intervals). This causes problems for applications that require persistent TCP connections, such as downloading large files and media streaming. For these applications, a direct porting to a MAS environment will not work. Rather, large contents must be divided into blocks which are delivered individually. There already are file download protocols, such as BitTorrent, that follows this approach. We believe that similar protocols can be developed for media streaming

## 8.3 Opportunities for Diversification

This work advocates introducing diversification and uncertainty to increase intrusion resilience of web services. In this section, we explore the potential sources of diversification at every level of the software stack: application layer, web server layer, operating system layer, and virtualization layer.

As we discovered in this investigation, there are overwhelmingly large numbers of diversification sources at various layers. A complete enumeration is impossible. We will therefore set criteria for the candidates of consideration. Using virtualization layer as an example, we will consider only those technologies that are well known to be used in production environments. In other cases, the selection can be subjective and kept small to avoid exponential explosion of combinations. Exact criteria for each layer will be explained in respective discussions. The resultant estimation, though in thousands, should be considered (very) conservative.

### 8.3.1 Application Layer

The MAS architecture requires web applications to be REST conformant, or *Restful*. There are many Restful programming platforms based on Java, Perl, PHP, Python, and Ruby programming languages. As part of the .NET framework, Microsoft also provides a Restful platform called WCF Data Services [5]. (Though it is not clear from the name, web services are part of the framework.) According to Wikipedia.org, there are more than 20 Restful programming frameworks. However, Ruby on Rails, or simply Rails, is by far the most popular framework in the REST community. Therefore only Rails will be considered in this investigation. We acknowledge that the choice is somewhat subjective. Of course, by considering only one programming language, the result is very conservative.

While N-version programming has been well known for a long time, it is rarely employed in web applications, though it is not unusual for web application developers to *switch* to different implementations. More practical approaches to the diversification at the application level include using different versions of libraries, interpreters, among others. However, the various versions of the above factors are typically, but not always, tied to specific operating systems. For instance, Red Hat Enterprise Linux 5 supports Ruby interpreter version 1.8.5, while Ubuntu 8.04 supports 1.8.6. To be conservative in our assessment, we consider the version issues to be part of the operating system diversification, discussed later.

In the case of Rails, there are two *implementations* (not just versions) of the Ruby interpreter: the official implementation by its creator Yukihiro "Matz" Matsumoto and a Java-based implementation called JRuby. The two different implementations of Ruby constitute a legitimate diversification factor for the Ruby on Rail platform. (There are other implementations that are not advanced as the two. They are ignored.)

Note that multiple implementations for a language are not uncommon. For instance, Java code can be executed a number of different Java Virtual Machines (JVMs), such as Google's Dalvik VM [6]. Because Dalvik uses a different byte code from the standard Java byte code, the use of Dalvik also introduces instruction set randomization [7] at the application layer. The above observation applies to many other Restful platforms.

It must be emphasized that using different interpreters does not remove application vulnerabilities, though it does alter the attack surface of the interpreter. Conversely, diversifying an application will not necessarily fix logic design flaws or protect other server components from exploitation. For instance, if the application does not sanitize user inputs and allows for SQL injection, creating SQL queries in a different language or using a different interpreter will not resolve that problem.

## 8.3.2 Web Server Layer

We show in Table 8.1 five prominent HTTP servers and their platform compatibilities. The list is selected subjectively and by no means complete. In the table, "Open Source" indicates compatibility with many major operating systems, such as Windows, Linux, BSD, and Solaris. Except for Microsoft IIS, all others are compatible or can be ported to large numbers of operating systems.

**Table 8.1** Web server software and operating system compatibilities

| Web Server Software | OS Compabilities |
| --- | --- |
| Apache | Open Source |
| IIS | Windows platform |
| ngix | Open Source |
| lighthttpd | Open Source |
| Tomcat | Open Source |

In fact, more sources of diversification can be derived from different configurations of a given web server software to run web applications. Such web serving configurations varies with different web programming platforms and languages. Again, we will use the Ruby on Rails platform as an example. It must be emphasized that different serving configurations do not require changes in application code. Known configurations to run Rails applications are listed below. Details will ensue.

1. Apache + mod_fastcgi
2. Apache + mod_rails
3. Apache + Mongrel cluster
4. Apache + Thin cluster
5. IIS + Fast-CGI
6. Nginx + mod_rails
7. Nginx + Mongrel cluster
8. Nginx + Thin cluster
9. Lighthttpd + mod_fastcgi
10. Lighthttpd + Mongrel cluster
11. Lighthppd + Thin cluster
12. Tomcat + JRuby

We will first explain the various configurations to run Rails applications with Apache and the differences they make to increase attack surface diversity.

- The first configuration, Apache + mod_fastcgi, is the traditional approach. The ruby codes of an application are treated as CGI codes, and the mod_fastcgi plug-in is used to call upon particular ruby codes when required. In this case, Apache will have to process input URLs and its vulnerabilities are likely to be exploited. Also, mod_fastcgi is a general-purpose CGI interface that supports many other CGI languages, such PHP, Python, Perl, etc. Its vulnerabilities can also be exploited.
- The second configuration, Apache + mod_rails, uses a customized CGI interface that supports only Rails. This configuration shares the same Apache vulnerabilities with the above one. However, the CGI interface, mod_rails (a.k.a. passenger), is specialized for a single platform and most likely has a smaller set of vulnerabilities than the general-purpose mod_fastcgi. The two configurations have different sets of vulnerabilities and can be used as components of different attack surfaces.
- The third configurations, Apache + Mongrel cluster, uses Apache only as a multiplexer to forward URL requests to a cluster of Mongrel servers. Mongrel is a single-threaded server that runs only Rails applications. Its single-threaded approach and dedicated web programming platform significantly simplify the design and implementation. As a consequence, however, multiple Mongrel processes are required to handle simultaneous requests; hence the name "Mongrel cluster." With this configuration, Apache does not involve in any aspect of request processing, except for forwarding them to Mongrel processes. The likelihood of triggering Apache bugs is therefore minimized. Also, the simplicity of Mongrel keeps its vulnerability set small. The point is that this configuration has a very different vulnerability set, compared to the above two, plug-in based configurations.
- The forth, Apache + Thin cluster, configuration is similar to the Mongrel cluster but uses another small-size, Rail-only web server, called Thin. Its attack surface shares general characteristics but different specifics with the Mongrel cluster.

To conclude, all the above four configurations to run Rails applications produce different attack surfaces, even though they are all based on Apache.

Web serving configurations 5 to 11 share similar concepts described above. They will not be discussed further. However, configuration 12 (Tomcat + JRuby) is a very different approach. It uses the aforementioned alternative Ruby interpreter, JRuby, implemented in Java. The Tomcat web server is an open source software implementation of the Java Servlet and JavaServer Pages technologies [8]. The result is a web serving configuration based on a Java foundation and hence can be used to create unique attack surfaces, compared to other configurations. We point out that Tomcat is developed by the Apache Software Foundation and for this reason also called Apache Tomcat. However, Apache and Apache Tomcat are different web server solutions.

With only exception of "IIS + Fast-CGI", the other 11 configurations are based on open sourced software. They are supported or can be ported to primary operating systems. Known exceptions will be pointed out in Table 3. Because different web serving configurations produce different attack surfaces even if they use the same web server software, we will consider *twelve* sources of diversification at the web server layer, rather than just five web server programs.

## 8.3.3 Operating System Layer

Primary web server platforms include Windows, Solaris, variants of BSDs and different distributions of Linux. In this section, we will give a conservative estimate of the level of diversity that can be created at the OS level. Due to the huge number of operating systems available (a partial list at [9] gives more than 250 Linux distributions), we will use the following rules in the investigation. First, an OS must be actively maintained at the time of this writing. In particularly, there must be a company or a community in charge of timely fixing bugs and security vulnerabilities for that OS. Second, various editions or minor version numbers are not distinguished under the assumption that those variants do not increase diversity significantly. Following this assumption, the home and professional editions of, say, Windows 7, are listed simply as one OS, Windows 7. By the same token, Ubuntu 8.04 and 8.10 are listed as Ubuntu 8.

On the other hand, we do distinguish 32 and 64 versions. This is because the success of a class of advanced and dangerous attacks, such as return-oriented programming attacks [10], depends on precise address lengths. Furthermore, the differences between 32-bit and 64-bit instruction formats can be seen as a form of instruction set randomization [7, 11]. The results of this investigation are shown in Table 2. Because all the OSs in the table has both 32 and 64 bits supports, they are not listed separately.

Starting from the Windows platform, we listed both client and server OSs, because all of them support IIS and are also compatible with open source web server software. On the Solaris platform, two versions officially supported by Oracle are

**Table 8.2** Primary web server operating systems (the ×2 in the numbers stems from 32 and 64 bits supports)

| Platform | Variants | # |
|---|---|---|
| Windows | Windows XP, Vista, 7; Windows Server 2003, 2008 | $5 \times 2 = 10$ |
| Solaris | Oracle Solaris 10, 11 | $2 \times 2 = 4$ |
| BSD Family | FreeBSD (7, 8), NetBSD (4,5), OpenBSD 4 | $5 \times 2 = 10$ |
| RedHat | Red Hat Enterprise Linux 4, 5, 6 | $3 \times 2 = 6$ |
| Ubuntu | Ubuntu Server Editions 6, 8, 9, 10 | $4 \times 2 = 8$ |
| SUSE | SUSE Linux Enterprise, OpenSUSE | $2 \times 2 = 4$ |

shown. OpenSolaris is omitted for its future is not clear after Oracle obtained Sun Microsystems. For the Red Hat Enterprise Linux family, all versions before 4 are not listed for Red Hat has ceased their maintenance. Fedora distributions, though popular among some Linux enthusiasts, generally have short life cycles and are not considered stable by the authors. They are omitted in this investigation. Four Ubuntu versions are listed in the table. It may seem strange that Ubuntu 7 is not in the list, even when it has a higher version number than 6. This is because even-numbered Ubuntu server versions enjoys long term (5 years) of maintenance while odd-numbered ones have only about 1 and half years of supports. It must be emphasized that operating systems in Table 8.2 are selected at time of this writing. Candidate OSs that satisfy our selection requirements will certainly change over time. In conclusion, we have identified forty two different operating systems that contribute significantly to diversity, are stable and actively maintained. As a conservative estimation, many other lesser known/used operating systems are ignored.

### 8.3.4 Combination is the Power

Shown in Table 8.3 are the working combinations of web server configurations in Section 8.3.2 and the operating systems in Table 8.2. We now have 452 different ways of running Rails web applications on major operating systems with different web server configurations. And the effects of using different virtualization solutions have yet to be accounted for.

### 8.3.5 Virtualization Layer

Attacks at the virtualization layer have been known in practice [12, 13]. This frequently requires running code on the operating system and an unknown or unpatched vulnerability in the virtualization layer. The frequency of these vulnerabilities is far less than vulnerabilities in other layers. While the likelihood is much lower, the impact or consequence is much higher: the contamination can potentially

**Table 8.3** Compatible combinations of web serving configurations and operating systems.

| Platform | Web Serving Configurations (12 in all) | # |
|---|---|---|
| Windows | All but 2 and 6 (mod_rails does not work on Windows) | $10 \times 10 = 100$ |
| Solaris | All but 5 (IIS) | $4 \times 11 = 44$ |
| BSD | All but 5 (IIS) | $10 \times 11 = 110$ |
| RedHat | All but 5 (IIS) | $6 \times 11 = 66$ |
| Ubuntu | All but 5 (IIS) | $8 \times 11 = 88$ |
| SUSE | All but 5 (IIS) | $4 \times 11 = 44$ |

spread to all VSs on the host. This calls for diversification in a software stack of the virtualization layer itself.

As mentioned earlier, only those virtualization technologies that are used in production environments will be considered. This excludes, Qemu [14], for instance. (We understand that some parts of Qemu code are used in other virtualization technologies discussed below.) Moreover, the non-persistence requirement of MAS further restricts the options. In this investigation we search for virtualization technologies that meet the above two criteria. Before presenting the results, however, we must distinguish two types of virtualization technologies.

In general, there are two types of virtualization: hypervisor-based and OS level. The former, such as various VMware products and Xen [15, 16], is generally considered more secure because of its small code sizes and high-level isolation of VSs. The latter, such as Linux OpenVZ [17] and Solaris Zones [18], imposes lower overhead for their close integration with the host kernel. However, the integration with the host kernel raises the possibilities the attacker of a compromised VS may break out the VS through kernel vulnerabilities. The problem, however, can be mitigated by SELinux modules, such as sVirt [19], that are specifically designed for isolating virtual machines and/or containers through mandatory access control (MAC) policies. Lastly, the guests OSs of lightweight virtualization are more limited, compared to hypervisor-based ones. For instance, OpenVZ supports only Linux based VSs as guests. Solaris Zones can run Solaris or Linux guests but not other platforms.

Here we give the virtualization technologies that meet the aforementioned requirements.

- Virtualization solutions that support snapshot and revert functionalities, such as VMware Workstation, VMware ESX, and Oracle Virtualbox [15, 20]. With such supports, a newly created VS is booted up, a snapshot is taken before it serves online. The snapshot contains both memory and file system state. When the VS is brought offline, it is reverted to the pristine state snapshot. In this way the non-persistence requirement is enforced.
- OpenVZ [17]. OpenVZ is a lightweight (OS-level) virtualization technology. It does not have snapshot and revert mechanisms. However a work-around solution has been devised. The solution leverages the Logical Volume Management (LVM) on Linux [21] and works as follows.

First, an OpenVZ VS, a.k.a. container, image is created in a LVM logic volume, which will be called the template volume of the VS. The template is never mounted for direct use. Rather, a write-able snapshot volume is created and associated with it. It is the snapshot volume that is mounted. At this initial point, the data in mount point of the snapshot volume is identical to those in the underlying template volume. When the VS/container is booted up and serves online, changes to its file system is recorded in the snapshot volume. When it is brought offline, the snapshot volume is discarded, preserving the pristine state of the template volume. When the VS is needed online the next time, a new snapshot volume is created and associated with the template. The VS is then booted up again.

The above process satisfies the non-persistence requirement because all writes to the file system of a VS when it is served online are recorded in the write-able snapshot volume. The underlying template volume will not be contaminated for it is not even mounted. The use of a new snapshot volume each time guarantees that the bootstrapping of the VS starts with a clean file system and results in clean memory state. The success of this solution depends on the speed and low-overhead of LVM operations as well as the fast bootstrapping of lightweight containers. Booting up an OpenVZ container/VS takes only 1 to 1.5 seconds. Our experimental results show that the entire process takes 5 to 10 seconds, depending on the sizes of the VS file system.

**Compatibility Issues** We assume that all hypervisor-based virtualization technologies discussed above are compatible with the operating systems listed in Table 8.2. While this assumption may differ from official manuals, we believe it is well-founded for the following reasons. With the hardware virtualization supports from Intel [22] and AMD [23], essentially all i386 and x86_64 based OSs can be virtualized. When an OS is not officially listed as supported, it is usually due to lack of smooth integration, for instance, the lack of integration of guest and host desktops. This is not a problem because MAS uses virtual machines as servers. Another common issue is seamless sharing of files (called shared folders by VMware). This is actually undesired for the isolation of MAS VSs and needed to be disabled. A more relevant issue is the lack of hypervisor support for hardware emulation in the guest OS. Of particular importance for servers is the efficiency of the network interfaces. A VS with unsupported OS may not be as efficient as those with official supports in networking operations. We consider them still usable as long as the less efficient VSs constitute only a small portion of the online VSs or used in off-peak hours.

## 8.3.6 The Results

We now have three hypervisor-based virtualization technologies that meet our requirements: VMware Workstation, ESX, and Virtualbox. Combined with the 452 web serving configurations discussed above, we have 1356 different software stacks, or attack surfaces. In addition, OpenVZ supports 198 configurations in Table 3 that are based on Linux (RedHat, Ubuntu and SUSE). In total, we have $1356 + 198 = 1554$ unique attack surfaces.

To summarize, there exists the potential of very high levels of diversification, in the thousands or even more. The question of how far one should go in diversifying components is a matter of practicality and effectiveness. In practical terms, this is a function of attack surface area, likelihood and consequence. The most important issue, we believe, is the management of such a complicated and diversified system, addressed in the next section.

## 8.4 Management Complexity

It must be acknowledged that introducing a large array of diversified software increases management complexity. There are really two different issues: 1) the setup cost of such a complicated system, and 2) the challenges of continuously managing it. The creation of $N$ different VSs requires more resources and effort than a single system. This problem can be alleviated by incremental rollout. Rather than setting up all $N$ VS types before the system becomes operational, one can start with lower levels of diversity and introduce new VS types when they are ready. This will reduce time to market, but not overall effort cost. However, since most of the stack components are off-the-shelf, the effort involves integration of different off-the-shelf stacks (e.g., a LAMP stack or a Microsoft stack) with different flavors of each and porting any application code to the new stack. This effort is less than a full $N$-version programming (NVP) scheme with different teams building full-custom solutions.

For daily management tasks, the first key to reducing complexity is to use a master template VS for the management of each type of VS stack. When a patch/update is available for some component in a VS type, all VS master templates with that component are updated. Then the $K$ new VSs are cloned from each newly updated master VS. The master VS is not deployed online to keep it from being attacked. The increased work factor of the MAS then is: (a) identifying all VS types that employ an updated component, (b) applying the update to these identified master templates, and (c) deploying the newly cloned master templates on the next rotation for each VS type.

The second key is automation. The above process can be automated in many places. For instance, current asset lifecycle management tools already identify software in an enterprise that needs to be updated—step (a) above. Likewise these same tools will automatically update this software with the current patch. In our system, the update is applied to the master template image for each VS stack instance rather than to the image serving online. The updated master template then needs to be cloned and deployed in the rotation—step (c) above. This last step is standard server management staging and deployment, for which some tools already exist in the market.

In other words, with standard server management tools, the management complexity isn't far beyond current effort. From a practical standpoint, however, most

IT shops tend to be either Microsoft or Unix. Supporting diverse servers will require staff with backgrounds in multi-platform environments. In conclusion, the primary cost of complexity is in developing multiple instances of a web service on diverse platforms. The cost can be amortized over time, however, without increasing time to market.

## 8.5 The Need for New Metrics

Previous research on attack surfaces generally assumes that a small attack surface leads to increased security [24, 25, 26, 27]. The common purpose of these efforts is to define metrics in order to measure the attack surface "area" of a given system. The results are used to help administrators to identify unused components or unsafe configurations in the system to reduce its attack surface. Such an approach can be used to harden individual MAS VSs.

The proposed MAS concept, however, seems to increase total attack surface area because of its use of multiple attack surfaces. In this way, it could be argued that the MAS approach diminishes the security of the whole system. However, we believe that the existing metrics for attack surface areas are inadequate to evaluate MAS for two reasons. First, the changing nature of MAS breaks the basic assumption of existing metrics: the attack surface remains unchanged. The second reason is about the reachability uncertainty: an attacker has no control on which VSs attack packets will be directed to. This breaks another previous assumption, that is, the target attack surface is always reachable by attackers.

It is obvious that any metric to evaluate MAS must take into account its changing and unpredictable nature. While research in this direction is still in a nascent stage, we have made two basic observations.

- Because packets from a client/attacker can be directed to any one of different VSs, the present set of online attack surfaces can be considered a single "mash-up" surface. However, the sum of these surfaces is probably not accurate since probing and attack packets will be randomly distributed among $M$ present online surfaces. Likewise the uncertainty element means evaluating the security or likelihood of attack success on a single attack surface is not accurate either. Evaluating the intrusion resilience of the whole system in the context of a moving target is more appropriate but challenging.
- The unpredictable and changing nature of MAS necessities some probability/stochastic model(s) to be involved. The result is unlikely to be in the form of a single number or tuple, as in the case of previous metrics of attack surfaces. Probability can be used to determine the likelihood of a single VS instance to be targeted for a given request/attack, which is perhaps a lower bound on likelihood of success.

Although we have not completed the above tasks at the time of this writing, preliminary evaluations and results are presented for the potential of MAS in increasing intrusion resilience. Assuming that for an attack to succeed, it requires $K$ vulnerabilities in the diversified layers existing simultaneously in any one of the $N$ different VSs. We show in Table 8.4 the probabilities for such an attack to succeed, that is, all $K$ exploits arrive at the target VS out of the $N$ VSs. Precisely, we show the value of $1/C(N,K)$. We are realist in the values of $N$, starting with a small $N = 20$ to a modest $N = 100$.

**Table 8.4** Attack successful probabilities with various $K$ and $N$ values (All $N$ VSs are different attack surfaces)

| K | 20 VSs | 40 VSs | 100 VSs |
|---|--------|--------|---------|
| 1 | 5.0000000% | 2.5000000% | 1.0000000% |
| 2 | 0.5263158% | 0.1282051% | 0.0202020% |
| 3 | 0.0877193% | 0.0101215% | 0.0006184% |
| 4 | 0.0206398% | 0.0010942% | 0.0000255% |

It must be emphasized that the above figures are rudimentary. On one hand, it ignores the cases where one attack method may compromise more than one type of VSs. For instance, an attack exploiting bugs in a particular version of Apache will succeed, at least in the first step, in all VSs using the same version of Apache regardless the underlying OS and virtualization method. Moreover, an attacker typically tries more than one attack kits/paths. On the other hand, enforcing diversity in presented VS images mitigates this concern. Similarly, the presented figures ignore the beneficial impact of anomaly detection, intrusion detection systems, and our feedback-control system.

## 8.6 Related Work

Computer virtualization was first introduced by IBM in 1972 [28]. It has recently experienced a powerful revival. Representative present virtualization technologies include various VMware products [15], Xen [16], Oracle Virtualbox [20], and Microsoft Hyper-V [29].

A significant body of work in program instrumentation exists to protect servers, including web servers, against attacks, to recover after attacks, and also to make servers fault tolerant [30, 31, 32, 33]. While these techniques can tolerate the effect of a fault, they can no longer guarantee the session semantics, and the program may no longer operate correctly. For example, with Failure-Oblivious Computing [30], an invalid memory reference that could have crashed the program instead produces a "manufactured" result that at least allows the program to continue execution. However, there is no guarantee that the program will still be in a correct or consistent state.

An issue common to the above techniques is that they require access to source code and are ideally used by the developer of the code, rather than by the acquirer of the server software. While there is prominent open-source web software, such as Apache, many others are not. In contrast, the MAS architecture does not require access to source code. In addition, we are able to provide continuous service with guarantees of integrity.

Various types of randomization/diversification techniques have also been investigated to thwart attacks. Representative examples include instruction set randomization [11], address space layout permutation [34], redundant data diversity [35], design and configuration diversity [36], and randomness in operating system interface [37]. Rather than focusing on a particular aspect of the system for randomization, MAS seeks to find compatible combinations of off-the-shelf, mature technologies to create diversity and randomness.

The most similar intrusion tolerance solution to MAS is SCIT [38]; they both use virtualization, replicated VS images, reversions, and rotations. There are, however, critical distinctions. First, SCIT uses a simple rotation algorithm to revert VSs at a fixed time interval. In contrast, MAS installs anomaly detection engines in every VS to enable event-driven reversion within a fixed reversion cycle. This allows clean VS to stay online for longer fixed cycle times, resulting in lower overhead—most of the performance degradation is taken during reversions. In addition, fixed reversion cycles define windows of exposure. The longer the cycle time the longer the exposure and the lower the overhead of the system. For shorter windows of exposure, the SCIT system will experience higher overhead and potential user disruption from frequent recycling. MAS does not force reversions when they are not needed, but will provide an upper bound on persistence through a fixed reversion time that can be set according to the throughput needs of the environment. Second, SCIT uses an open source version of Terracotta [39] to share information among servers. Terracotta is a client-server memory clustering service based on the concept of Network Attached Memory (NAM). It must run on a server inside the intranet and will retain states, including corrupted/poisoned ones. SCIT therefore cannot be described as completely stateless and can continue to propagate poisoned states. MAS, in contrast, is stateless because its requirement on web applications to be RESTful. Non-persistent state of the web service is ensured on each reversion. Moreover, MAS introduces diversification/randomness to VS images.

Related research on intrusion detection systems (IDSs) are outside the scope of this chapter, but we emphasize that IDS solutions will either miss attacks (false negatives) or produce too many false alarms (incorrect detections) that tend to "numb" system administrators to real events. By removing humans from the loop and enforcing non-persistence, we address false positives and false negatives with our approach.

## 8.7  Conclusion

This chapter advocates the idea of introducing diversity and uncertainty to web serving environments so that web services will be significantly more resilient to attacks. The proposed Moving Attack Surface (MAS) concept uses virtual server stacks that are configured with different software mixes, producing diversified attack surfaces. By randomly changing the composition of online VSs and introducing uncertainty in their reachability, attackers will have to face multiple, changing, and unpredictable attack surfaces. While one cannot completely rule out their possibilities, successful attacks will be significant more difficult and damages will be limited.

We have also shown that there is no lack of diversification sources. In fact, even our conservative estimation results in thousands of different VSs, each with its own unique attack surfaces. Our next step is to evaluate the most effective way to increase and automate diversification. Management complexity is also a critical factor. We will explore automatic diversification and management techniques to aid in creating multiple diverse images of functionally equivalent web virtual servers.

## References

1. The Top Cyber Security Risks in Year 2009, http://www.sans.org/top-cyber-security-risks.
2. Yih Huang; Ghosh, A.K.; Bracewell, T.; Mastropietro, B.; , "A security evaluation of a novel resilient web serving architecture: Lessons learned through industry/academia collaboration," Dependable Systems and Networks Workshops (DSN-W), International Conference on, June 28 to July 1, 2010.
3. Yih Huang, Anup K. Ghosh, "Automating Intrusion Response via Virtualization for Realizing Uninterruptible Web Services," Eighth IEEE International Symposium on Network Computing and Applications (NCA'09), 2009.
4. Fielding, R. T. and Taylor, R. N. 2002. "Principled design of the modern Web architecture," ACM Trans. Internet Technology. 2, 2 (May. 2002), 115-150.
5. Microsoft WCF Data Service, http://msdn.microsoft.com/en-us/data/odata.aspx
6. Google Dalvik VM, http://www.dalvik.com
7. E. G. Barrantes, D. H. Ackley, S. Forrest, and D. Stefanovic. "Randomized instruction set emulation," ACM Trans. Info. & System Security, 8(1):3 40, Feb. 2005.
8. Java Servlet Technologies, http://www.oracle.com/technetwork/java/index-jsp-135475.html
9. http://en.wikipedia.org/wiki/List_of_Linux_distributions
10. Hovav Shacham, "The geometry of innocent flesh on the bone: return-into-libc without function calls (on the x86)," CCS '07 Proceedings of the 14th ACM conference on Computer and communications security. Whistler, BC, October 2007.
11. Gaurav S. Kc, Angelos D. Keromytis, and Vassilis Prevelakis. 2003. "Countering code-injection attacks with instruction-set randomization," In Proceedings of the 10th ACM conference on Computer and communications security (CCS '03). ACM, New York, NY, USA, 272-280.
12. National Institute of Standards, NIST. National vulnerability database, http://nvd.nist.gov.
13. R. Wojtczuk. "Subverting the Xen hypervisor," in Black Hat USA, 2008.
14. Fabrice Bellard. Qemu, "A fast and portable dynamic translator," In Proceedings of the USENIX 2005 Annual Technical Conference, FREENIX Track, pages 41-46, 2005.
15. VMware, Inc. http://www.vmware.com.

16. Paul Barham, Boris Dragovic, Keir Fraser, Steven Hand, Tim Harris, Alex Ho, Rolf Neuge-bauer, Ian Pratt, and Andrew Warfield. "Xen and the art of virtualization," In Proceedings of the nineteenth ACM symposium on Operating systems principles (SOSP '03). New York, NY, USA, 2003.
17. OpenVZ lightweigt virtualization, http://openvz.org.
18. D. Price and A. Tucker. "Solaris zones: Operating system support for consolidating commercial workloads," In Proceedings of the 18th Usenix LISA Conference., 2004.
19. sVirt, http://selinuxproject.org/page/SVirt
20. Virtualbox, http://www.virtualbox.org/
21. D. Teigland and H. Mauelshagen. "Volume managers in linux," In Proceedings of USENIX 2001 Technical Conference, June 2001.
22. Neiger, Gil; A. Santoni, F. Leung, D. Rodgers, R. Uhlig. "Intel Virtualization Technology: Hardware Support for Efficient Processor Virtualization". Intel Technology Journal (Intel) 10 (3): 167-178. Available at http://download.intel.com/technology/itj/2006/v10i3/v10-i3-art01.pdf
23. AMD Virtualization (AMD-V) Technology, http://sites.amd.com/us/business/it-solutions/virtualization/Pages/amd-v.asp
24. Pratyusa K. Manadhata, Jeannette M. Wing, "An Attack Surface Metric," IEEE Transactions on Software Engineering, 01 Jun. 2010.
25. Pratyusa K. Manadhata, Jeannette M. Wing and Mark Flynn, "Measuring the attack surfaces of two FTP daemons," Conference on Computer and Communications Security: Proceedings of the 2nd ACM workshop on Quality of protection; 30-30 Oct. 2006.
26. T. Newsham and J. Hoaglan. "Windows Vista Network Attack Surface Analysis: A Broad Overview," CanSecWest, 2007.
27. M. Howard. "Fending off future attacks by reducing attack surface," Available at http://msdn.microsoft.com/library/default.asp?url=/library/en-us/dncode%/html/secure02132003.asp, 2003.
28. R. J. Creasy. "The origin of the VM/370 time-sharing system," IBM J. Research and Development, 25(5):483-490, September 1981.
29. Microsoft Hyper-V Server, http://www.microsoft.com/hyper-v-server/en/us/default.aspx
30. Rinard, M., C. Cadar, D. Dumitran, D. Roy, T. Leu, and J.W. Beebee, "Enhancing server availability and security through failure-oblivious computing," in Proceedings of the 6th Symposium on OSDI, December 2004.
31. Sidiroglou, M.E. Locasto, S.W. Boyd and A. Keromytis, "Building a Reactive Immune System for Software Services," in Proceedings of the USENIX Technical Conference, 2000.
32. Qin, F., J. Tucek, J. Sundaresan, and Y. Zhou, "Rx: treating bugs as allergies—a safe method to survive software failures," in Proceedings of the 20th ACM Symposium on Operating Systems Principles (SOSP), pp. 235-248, 2005.
33. Sidiroglou, S., O. Laadan, A. Keromytis, "Using Rescue points to Navigate Software Recovery (Short Paper)," in Proceedings of the IEEE Symposium on Security & Privacy, pp. 273-278, May 2007, Oakland, CA.
34. Kil, C., Jun, J., Bookholt, C., Xu, J., and Ning, P. 2006. "Address Space Layout Permutation (ASLP): Towards Fine-Grained Randomization of Commodity Software," In Proceedings of ACSAC'06, 2006.
35. A. Nguyen-Tuong, D. Evans, J. C. Knight, B. Cox, and J. W. Davidson. "Security through redundant data diversity." In 38th IEEE/IFPF International Conference on Dependable Systems and Networks (DSN'08), Anchorage, Alaska, USA, 2008.
36. A. Bessani, A. Daidone, I. Gashi, R. Obelheiro, P. Sousa and V. Stankovic. "Enhancing Fault-/Intrusion Tolerance through Design and Configuration Diversity," 3rd Workshop on Recent Advances on Intrusion-Tolerant Systems (WRAITS 2009).
37. M. Chew and D. Song. "Mitigating Buffer Overflows by Operating System Randomization," Tech Report CMUCS-02-197. December 2002.

38. Yih Huang, David Arsenault, and Arun Sood. "Incorruptible System Self-Cleansing for Intrusion Tolerance," Performance, Computing, and Communications Conference, IPCCC 2006.
39. The Terracotta project, http://www.terrracotta.org

# Chapter 9
# Toward Network Configuration Randomization for Moving Target Defense

Ehab Al-Shaer

**Abstract** This chapter presents a moving target defense architecture called Mutable Networks or MUTE. MUTE enables networks to change their configurations such as IP address and routes randomly and dynamically while preserving the requirements and integrity of network operation. The main goal of MUTE is to hinder the adversary's capabilities in scanning or discovering network targets, launching DoS attacks and creating botnets structure. This chapter presents the challenges and applications of moving target defense and it also presents a formal approach for creating valid mutation of network configurations.

## 9.1 Introduction

The network attack cycle spans number of steps including reconnaissance, finger printing, network mapping, exploitation, coordination, reporting, and propagation (see Figure 9.1). In each step, the adversary relies on the static nature of cyber infrastructures to achieve the attack target effectively. The static nature of network configuration enables adversaries to discover and compromise network resources remotely. For instance, network configuration such as IP addresses, port numbers, platform type, service and patch version, protocols, service vulnerability and even firewall rules can be discovered using network scanning and fingerprinting tools [3, 4, 5]. In addition, the accept-by-default Internet access control makes network reconnaissance and zero-day worms inevitable. This calls for novel ideas to change the game of cyber security for the advantage of defenders in the face of ever advancing cyber attacks. MUTE attempts to archive this goal by using moving

Ehab Al-Shaer
Cyber Defense and Network Assurability (CyberDNA) Center,
College of Computing and Informatics,
University of North Carolina, Charlotte.
e-mail: ealshaer@uncc.edu

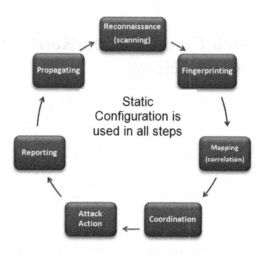

**Fig. 9.1** Attack Cycle

target defense techniques that force attackers to continuously chasing their target, deterring, and eliminating attacks without interrupting regular network traffic. This will eliminate the attacker's time and space advantage and create agility against advanced persistent threats.

As the network configuration is relatively static in the current game, the adversaries mainly rely on network reconnaissance (i.e., scanning and fingerprinting) as precursory step for lunching or propagating attacks in a network. Likewise, attack coordination assumes known and static host configuration. For instance, botnet communication and coordination depend on well-defined structure presuming static configuration such as IP address as well.

This chapter presents a new moving target defense architecture called Mutable Networks (or MUTE). The MUTE architecture allows for creating periodically alternative random configurations (called mutation), while maintaining the integrity and continuity of network operations and services. The frequently random mutation of hosts' location and identity in the network will constantly invalidate and deceive the adversary discoveries. The basic idea was initially proposed by the author in the "Moving Target" session during the National Cyber Leap Year Summit, in August 2009 organized by DoD and NITRD. In this chapter, we will present a formal approach to create random configuration mutations that satisfy the network requirements, and illustrate applications and challenges related to moving target defense.

## 9.2 MUTE Approach

Our goal is to support the dynamic and random changing of network configurations such as IP addresses, and port numbers, and response behavior to counter scanning worms, and reconnaissance and finger printing attacks, by continuously outdating the collected system information within a short time window, and deceiving attackers to fake targets for further analysis. The change has to be fast to outperform automated scanner and worm propagation, smooth to minimize service disruption and delays, unpredictable to ensure that discovering hopping IP addresses is computationally infeasible, and operationally safe to preserve system requirements and service dependencies.

### 9.2.1 MUTE Architecture

The MUTE architecture implements the moving target through the following techniques:

1. **Random Address Hopping:** Network hosts will be frequently re-assigned random virtual IP address that will be used for routing independently form the actual IP address. The selection of the random IP addresses is synchronized across the network using crypto-based function and secret random keys to guarantee unpredictability and global configuration synchrony. The random IP addresses are selected from both the private address range and the unused address space which are sufficiently large. IPv6 offers much more available space for potential randomization. In this proposed approach, networked systems (i.e., end-hosts) will be assigned different addresses frequently based on random functions. One approach to achieve synchrony is to use round robin randomization.

2. **Random Finger Printing:** Host responses will be intercepted and modified transparently to maximize the entropy in the system behavior and give a false OS and application identity. Without identifying the exact specifics of OS type and/or application servers, remotely exploitation will be infeasible. There are two mechanisms to randomize external system responses. One is to intercept and modify session control messages such as TCP 3-way handshake in order to cause false platform or service identification and deceive adversaries. Another technique is to use firewalls to deceive scanners by generating positive responses for all denies packets.

The combination of these two techniques will enable effective moving target defense approach against many attacks. During the MUTE target motion, active sessions will also stay uninterrupted and users will continue reach network services via DNS as usual. In the next section, we present a formal approach to create valid mutations of network configurations that maintain network invariants.

## 9.2.2 Configuration Mutation

In our previous work [1, 2], we show an end-to-end encoding of access control configuration based on Binary Decision Diagrams (BDDs) to model the global network behavior. This results into a single Boolean expression (BDD) that represents all configuration interactions (i.e., flows and transformation) in the network. We will summarize our modeling discussion in the following sections.

### 9.2.2.1 Modeling of Network Behavior Using BDDs

An ACL policy is a sequence of filtering rules that determine the appropriate action to take for any incoming packets: $P = R_1, R_2, R_3, \ldots, R_n$. Thus, each rule can be written in the form:

$$R_i := C_i \rightsquigarrow a_i$$

where $C_i$ is the constraint on the filtering field that must be satisfied in order to trigger the action $a_i$. The condition $C_i$ can be represented as a Boolean expression of the filtering fields, $fv_1, fv_2, \ldots, fv_k$ as follows:

$$C_i = fv_1 \wedge fv_2 \wedge \cdots \wedge fv_k$$

where each $fv_j$ expresses a set of matching field values for field $f_j$ in rule $R_i$. Thus, we can formally describe a firewall policy as:

$$P_a = \bigvee_{i \in index(a)} (\neg C_1 \wedge \neg C_2 \ldots \neg C_{i-1} \wedge C_i)$$
$$= \bigvee_{i \in index(a)} \bigwedge_{j=1}^{i-1} \neg C_j \wedge C_i$$

Similarly, we can define the routing policies as follows: let a routing rule be encoded as:

$$R_i := D_i \rightsquigarrow n_i$$

Where $n$ is integer representing the forwarding port $ID$ where $D_i$ is the destination and $n_i$ is a unique integer (id) designating the next hope in the network. Thus, the policy of the routing entries that forward to next hope $n_k$ can be defined as follows:

$$T_n = \bigvee_{i \in index(n)} \bigwedge_{j=1..(i-1)} (\neg D_j \wedge D_i) \text{ such that } index(n) = \{i | R_i = D_i \rightsquigarrow n_i\}.$$

We can then represent the entire routing table for a node j as follows:

$$T^j = \bigvee_{\forall n = next-hop} T_n.$$

The entire network is modeled as a state machine where each state determined by the packet header information and packet location on the network as follows:

$$States = Locations \times Packets$$

Thus, the **characterization function** to encode the state of the network can be represented as follows (after abstracting payload):

$$\sigma : IP_s \times Port_s \times IP_d \times Port_d \times Loc \rightarrow \{\textbf{true, false}\}$$

$IP_s$  the 32-bit source IP address.
$Port_s$  the 16-bit source port number.
$IP_d$  the 32-bit destination IP address.
$Port_d$  the 16-bit destination port number.
$Loc$  the 32-bit IP address of the device currently processing the packet.

Since network devices are modeled based on the policy semantic and packet transformation, transition relation is **characterization function**:

$$\textbf{T} : Curr\ pkt \times New\ pkt \times Curr\ loc \times New\ loc \rightarrow \{\textbf{true, false}\}$$

Therefore, the behavior **characterization function** of the network device $d$ can be model as follows:

$$\phi_d : Loc_d \times Policy_d \times T_d \rightarrow \{\textbf{true, false}\}$$

This simply means that the characterization function gives *true* if there is a traffic matching condition in $Policy_d$ of the device at $Loc_d$ that enables the packet transition/transformation $T_d$ to take place. Therefore, the Global Transitions relation of the entire network will be simply union of all network devices:

$$T = \bigvee_{i \in devices} \phi_{device_i}$$

### 9.2.2.2 Network Configuration Mutation

This BDD representation of network behavior allows for configuring mutation. A network configuration mutation is the process of creating an alternative valid configuration that satisfies the network invariants or mission requirements. For example, the reachability from $X$ to $Y$ can be via *R1, R2, R3, FW1* or via *R9, R11, R3, FW1*, which both represent two different mutations as both paths satisfy the reachability from $X$ to $Y$, yet they are not identical.

**Definition 9.1.** $\phi_1$ and $\phi_2$ are two different mutations of a network configuration with requirements **R** iff the following is true:

1. $(\phi_1 \quad \phi_2)$

2. $R \to \phi_1 \wedge R \to \phi_2$

Note that (1) shows that $\phi_1$ and $\phi_2$ represent different network configurations and (2) shows that they both achieve the same requirements. For example, changing an IP address of a server will result into a new valid configuration mutation iff this IP address change does not cause any violation of the configuration requirements.

MUTE creates a random or constrained configuration mutations periodically and then enforce them in the network dynamically. Constrained mutation is constructed based on other factors such as IDS feedback, budget or QoS constraints. Each mutation will be sufficiently different from all previous ones during a reasonable time window to invalidate the active attacker discoveries such as network scanning.

### 9.2.3 What MUTE Can Protect

- **Protecting P2P communication of critical infrastructure against scanning and DoS.** This is used for proprietary special-purpose client and server applications. Example of this includes mission-critical networks and applications. Moving target defense can be integrated in these applications to require minimal control overhead in the network.
- **Protecting from external network reconnaissance and mapping attacks.** Reconnaissance tools usually scan networks using only IP addresses and ports (host names may not be known or name scanning is not efficient).
- **Terminate or disrupt attack coordination and botnet communication.** Master and slave bots communicate using fixed IP addresses. They usually avoid connecting using host name and DNS resolution to minimize detection or tracking. However, if the infrastructure addresses is changing frequently, this will cause disconnection between botnet nodes.
- **Protecting network infrastructure from DoS attacks.** DoS attackers assume that end-hosts use fixed IP address or routes. However, this will not be the case under MUTE moving target architecture.

## 9.3 MUTE Research Challenges

MUTE architecture must address the following challenges in order to be practical and effective.

- **Fast and Unpredictable.** MUTE must be fast to outperform automated scanner and worm propagation. Also the motion speed can be dynamically adjusted and situationally-aware based on external inputs such as IDS alerts. Moreover, while the motion is highly unpredictable, its overhead or impact can be measured and minimized.

- **Operationally Safe.** MUTE must preserve the system invariants during distributed motion. In other words, network requirements must globally enforced all the time even during transition periods. Also, moving target must be *transparent* such that active sessions and running services will not face any perturbation due to changing configuration.
- **Deployable.** This means MUTE should require no changes in the network infrastructure, protocols or end-host. It can be deployed independently from end-host platforms and protocols.
- **Scalable.** The MUTE motion should scale linearly with the number of nodes, flows, moving targets and attacks. In other words, the architecture must be agile to accommodate these factors dynamically.

# References

1. E. Al-Shaer, W. Marrero, A. El-Atway and K. AlBadani, *Network Configuration in a Box: Towards End-to-End Verification of Network Reachability and Security*, In Proceedings of 17th International Conference on Network Communications and Protocol (ICNP'09), pp. 123-132, Princeton, 2009.
2. H. Hamed, E. Al-Shaer and W. Marrero, *Modeling and Verification of IPSec and VPN Security Policies*, In Proceedings of International Conference on Netwrok Communications and Protocol (ICNP'05), 2005.
3. T. Samak, A. El-Atawy and E. Al-Shaer, *A Framework for Inferring Firewall Policy Using Smart Probing*, In Proceedings of International Conference on Netwrok Communications and Protocol (ICNP'07), 2007.
4. Network Vulnerability Scanner. *http://www.nessus.org/nessus*
5. Network Mapper. *http://nmap.org*

# Chapter 10
# Configuration Management Security in Data Center Environments

Krishna Kant

**Abstract** Modern data centers need to manage complex, multi-level hardware and software infrastructures in order to provide a wide array of services flexibly and reliably. The emerging trends of virtualization and outsourcing further increase the scale and complexity of this management. In this chapter, we focus on the configuration management issues and expose a variety of attack and misconfiguration scenarios, and discuss some approaches to making configuration management more robust. We also discuss a number of challenges in identifying the vulnerabilities in configurations, handling configuration management in the emerging cloud computing environments, and in hardening the configurations against hacker attacks.

## 10.1 Introduction

As the size and complexity of data centers grows, so does the sophistication and complexity of managing its myriad resources including computational elements, storage systems, networking fabrics, software and services. The hardware and software infrastructure must be managed at multiple levels spanning from individual devices (and associated device drivers) all the way up to the entire data center infrastructure and operations. The management is needed from multiple perspectives (e.g., performance, availability, security, energy efficiency, etc.) and over the entire *life cycle* of the hardware and software. This is the scope of what is loosely referred to as "configuration management" (CM) and it involves a large variety of data obtained and stored in various ways. It is clear that such data must be protected from unauthorized access and corruption.

The Operating System, middleware, and applications often maintain configuration information in a rather primitive form, i.e., in "configuration files", which can

Center for Secure Information Systems
George Mason University
e-mail: kkant@gmu.edu

be easily misconfigured or corrupted. However, the management planes of enterprise systems use a much more organized hierarchy of databases for keeping and manipulating CM data. In the past, CM dealt mostly with configuration of physical equipment and was done in out-of-band (OOB) manner using specially designed management software running a separate processors. The resulting CM repositories were therefore relatively isolated and available only to the physically separate management infrastructure; however, the sophisticated management requires a close coordination between OOB and normal in-band management, which makes the OOB management much more vulnerable.

The recent trend of widespread virtualization significantly complicates the CM since the virtualization effectively turns "hard" assets such as a server with fixed set of resources into "soft" assets with dynamically varying parameters. For example, the set of hardware threads, physical memory, or network interface bandwidth dedicated to a virtual machine (VM) could be changed dynamically. The file based VM configuration is highly vulnerable to misconfigurations and attacks, but recent efforts to standardize VM configuration is helpful in this regard (see open virtualization format [11]). The emerging trends of outsourcing and multi-tenacy further increase the complexity and vulnerability due to configuration information flow related restrictions and lack of trust. These attributes provide new avenues for attack on CM and increase chances of misconfigurations.

In this chapter, we expose CM vulnerabilities and discuss challenges in making it secure. We also propose some mechanisms that include exploitation of the special structure of data centers and discuss diversity techniques for hardening the defenses against attacks. Although a substantial amount of literature exists on protecting specific aspects of a computer networks and systems (e.g., routing tables, databases, etc.), the research on protecting configuration management systems per se has been quite limited. We shall point out related work as appropriate in subsequent sections.

The outline of the chapter is as follows. Section 10.2 provides an overview of the configuration management infrastructure and standards in enterprise systems. Section 10.3 discusses in detail the consequences of attacks on configuration management data and the mechanisms that hackers can exploit for attacking it. Section 10.4 discusses some general security mechanisms for protecting CM data, including those that exploit the redundancy that naturally exists in data centers. Section 10.5 then discusses the challenges in securing configuration management both in traditional environments and in emerging cloud computing environments. Finally, section 10.6 concludes the discussion.

## 10.2 Configuration Management Basics

Configuration management refers to all aspects of ensuring that the data center continues to provide the desired services. It involves continuous tracking, update, and troubleshooting of HW, SW and service configurations. In this section, we discuss the evolution and current status of configuration management in enterprises.

## 10.2.1 Scope of Configuration Management

Systematic configuration management has its roots in telecommunications systems, which follow the FCAPS model specified in ITUs telecommunications network management (TNM) standards [15]. FCAPS enumerates five categories of management activities: Fault, Configuration, Availability, Performance, and Security. Although "Configuration" is only one of these, all types of management must deal with substantial amounts of data that can be loosely defined as configuration. For example, security involves a variety of configuration data such as firewall rules, authentication methods, parameters and keys, access control setup and rules, etc. In fact, configuration management is central to ensuring desirable properties for the system, be it performance, availability, security, etc. With energy (and correspondingly power and thermal) management becoming crucial in data centers, the corresponding configuration data (e.g., power states at various levels, temperature limits, airflow requirements, etc.) also needs to be maintained. We can therefore refer to an expanded FCAPSE model for modern data centers, where the "E" stands for energy.

Although "configuration" conceptually refers to system aspects that are relatively static, such a notion of configuration is inadequate in modern data centers. First, with wide-spread use of virtualization, the configuration needs to include virtual machine settings, which can change dynamically and could migrate from server to server. Second, a flexible resource management often implies that the relevant policies and parameters are explicitly specified and manipulated instead of being buried in the management code. This applies not only to the physical infrastructure and its abstractions but also to software and services as well. Consequently, configuration management becomes a truly central aspect of modern data centers.

Another aspect of configuration management is its temporal span, i.e., keeping track of assets over their entire life-span. In particular, a "hard" asset such as a server or switch, needs to be managed from the moment it is brought into the data center until it is removed (due to failure or retirement). The various stages along this temporal scale include: (a) automated discovery of capabilities and "qualification" of the asset (i.e., checking authenticity of all already installed hardware, firmware and software), (b) configuration and provisioning of the asset with desired OS and utilities to make it available for normal use, (c) provisioning of services (and their reprovisioning as conditions/needs change), (d) active performance and availability monitoring and tuning, (e) diagnosis, trouble-shooting, reconfiguration, repair, upgrade, etc. as needed, and (f) eventual removal and retirement of the asset. Fig. 10.1 pictorially shows the management attributes and life-cycle management of an asset. The life-cycle management applies to software as well since new software must be authenticated and properly configured, existing software frequently patched ("repaired" or "upgraded"), and ultimately the software must be retired (although the virtualization technology allows older and newer software versions to continue running side by side). It is also important to note that increasingly, sophisticated software and its management is crucial not only for the servers but also for other assets including switches, storage bricks, security appliances, etc.

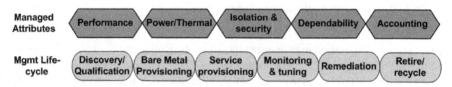

**Fig. 10.1** Illustration of Management Attributes, Life-Cycle and Activities

The organization of data centers naturally defines a hierarchy which can be exploited for configuration management. Servers are typically placed in a fixed size rack, either directly or – in case of blade servers – in a chassis that fits the rack. A chassis often has sophisticated built-in management capabilities for the blades hosted in it. Increasingly, racks also sport management capabilities for the assets installed there. The next level may be a cluster of racks and ultimately the data center level. Such a hierarchical structure simplifies management and allows for scalability of the physical infrastructure. The network – both mainstream as well as storage – also follows a similar fat-tree structure and hence can be managed in a hierarchical fashion [22]. Even in a virtualized environment, the hierarchical structure is useful in allocating all VMs for an application physically close together.

## 10.2.2 Configuration Management Infrastructure

Configuration management involves a variety of repositories that generally follow the hierarchical system structure. In particular, at the lowest HW levels, each device carries a firmware repository containing both fixed and settable parameters and their current values. At the next level, a subsystem (e.g., control plane of the router) or system (e.g., entire server) will have its own firmware or SW repository containing the appropriate parameters (e.g., amount of memory installed). The higher level parameters may or may not be related to lower level parameters simply. For example, the internal BW of the switch is usually less than the sum of individual bandwidths supported by all the ports.

Configuration repositories generally follow the standard Common Information Model (CIM) developed by the Distributed Management Task Force (DMTF) [7]. CIM is a hierarchical modeling language based on UML (unified modeling language) for defining objects and relationships between them. These relationships could be structural or more abstract, e.g., binding between virtual machines (VMs) and the physical server they run on. CIM unifies and extends existing instrumentation and management standards (e.g., SNMP, DMI, CMIP) by providing both schemas and a specification language. A CIM schema defines an object in the entity-relationship style and allows for compact representations of complex objects using concepts such as nested classes, instantiation, inheritance, and aggregation. For example, a CIM model of a switch includes its physical structure, various parameters required for configuring it (e.g. per port and shared buffer, packet formats supported, port speeds, etc.), their current settings, and methods to change the values.

DMTF has also developed Web-Based Enterprise Management (WBEM) specification that provides mechanisms to exchange CIM information in an interoperable and efficient manner. CIMOM (CIM object manager) is an open-source implementation of WBEM. The components of WBEM include access to CIM information in a variety of ways including web services based management (WSMAN), CIM query language, CIM command language interface (CLI), etc. However, WSMAN is becoming quite popular and runs atop SOAP (simple object access protocol), which itself is layered on top of HTTP. WSMAN consists of several components: (a) WS-Addressing – defines references to web service endpoints, (b) WS-Transfer – implements basic access functionality such as get, put, create, delete, (c) WS-Enumeration – allows iteration through members of a collection, (d) WS-Eventing – supports publish/subscribe interface, and (e) WS-Security – provides authentication and encryption services for SOAP communications (discussed later). The security procedures are optional and often bypassed due to performance reasons. This allows a wide variety of web-services based attacks on CIM repositories, as discussed in section 10.3.2.

CIM based models can be used for representing the configuration of entities beyond individual HW assets, such as configuration data for a rack or chassis hosting a number of servers, switch, storage boxes, etc. The configuration data in this case could involve rules for allocating power among the assets, fan control parameter, establishing share or uplink bandwidth among servers, etc. Similarly, CIM models can be specified for specifying the configuration of individual VMs or a network of VM's forming a "virtual cluster". In fact, DMTF has defined a standard CIM/XML representation of VM's called Open Virtual Format (OVF) [11]. Such a format is substantial improvement over "configuration file" based representation in that it is standard, vendor-independent and admits storage and manipulation using above-mentioned technologies.

DMTF also has some ongoing initiatives for implementing vendor and OS independent management of assets. This includes SMASH (Systems Management Architecture for Server Hardware) for managing HW assets in pre-boot state and CDM (Common Diagnostic Model) for diagnostics [12]. The Virtual Management Initiative (VMAN) provides a comprehensive OS independent VM management (creation, allocation, monitoring, etc.) capability to manage VM's (represented using OVF) that can be invoked by the OS and middleware [10]. In spite of these initiatives, the need for rich data management capabilities are often provided by vendor-specific and domain specific management packages. For example, one package may be used for provisioning OS on bare machines, while another one is used for performance monitoring. Invariably, such vendor-specific management packages (VSMPs) include their own private configuration databases that maintain relevant information in a way that they deem most suitable. The maintenance of potentially overlapping information in different databases in different formats can lead to many difficulties including misconfigurations and exploitations by malicious users.

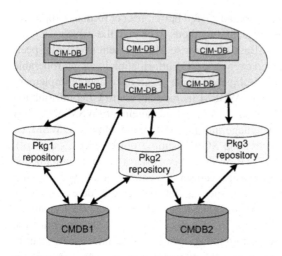

**Fig. 10.2** Illustration of repository hierarchy for management

The configuration data in a data center naturally follows a hierarchy with one or more top level configuration management databases (CMDBs) that consolidate information from all repositories. Figure 10.2 illustrates this with 2 CMDB's at the top. CMDB's typically support the federated model which can allow them to scale to large installations. CMDBs are important to capture dependencies between various packages and HW/SW components and provide a global view of the configuration. They can be exploited for global health monitoring of the data center, and are beginning to be used for top-down control by interfacing with individual packages. For example, management of the network that includes routers from multiple vendors would require engaging the management capability built into each router. Interoperability between CMDBs between different vendors is a serious issue that some recent standards efforts such as CMDBf (see dmtf.org/sites/default/files/standards/documents/DSP0252_1.0.1_0.pdf) are attempting to address. Nevertheless, working with multiple CMDBs by different vendors provides ample opportunities for misconfiguration and attacks that can exploit top-down control functionality to make the entire infrastructure unstable.

In general, management operations involve two distinct types of activities: (a) operations support and (b) resource control. The former refers to activities such as installation, configuration, patching, repair, etc. whereas control refers to dynamic resource allocation and scheduling. In servers, the control is typically handled by the "in-band" side (i.e., by OS and middleware) that runs on the main processor, whereas the operations support is handled by the out-of-band (OOB) side, which runs on a separate management processor, traditionally known as baseboard management controller (BMC). Although BMC was originally responsible for very basic functions such as temperature monitoring and fan control, it has lately evolved to perform quite sophisticated management functions [17]. A similar configuration is used in routers and switches where the control side handles route updates and the management side handles interface configuration, QoS setup, etc. The control and management sides increasingly require coordination for sophisticated management thereby making the OOB side vulnerable to attacks coming from the in-band side, hence making the configuration management security more critical. VM management is a perfect example of fusion of operations support and control. While VMs are dependent on the hypervisor that runs on the main processor, it is desirable to integrate VM management with the traditional OOB management software so that functionality like power/temperature driven VM migration can be accomplished.

## 10.3  Security of Configuration Management Data

In this section we show why the security of CM data is critical and what unique security issues arise relative to such data. We also discuss several potential attack scenarios that hackers may attempt. Although attacks on CM data have not been common in the past, much of this has to do with relative obscurity and inaccessibility of OOB based management. As the standards continue to evolve towards a truly integrated and comprehensive management CM data will increasingly become a rich target of security attacks.

### 10.3.1 Attacks on Computing Infrastructure

In this section we highlight generic attacks on or misconfigurations of repositories at various levels of the computing infrastructure. A later subsection discusses attacks more specifically crafted toward disrupting the network per se. Because of the criticality of the CIM data, low level software using it (e.g., preboot utilities, OS drivers, etc.) may check for consistency and sanity of CIM data before using it. However, the action taken in case of problems is usually not very sophisticated and may either result in panic and restart, or require management console input to correct the value and continue. A restart can clear up bad data only for static and discoverable information. Depending on the operator to fix the problem could be unreliable and even dangerous. In many cases, proper functioning requires consistency across multiple entities, and deficiencies in checks could be exploited by attackers to create undetectable corruptions. Furthermore, since different configuration parameters are used at different times (e.g., service startup time or reboot time), some corruptions may not be discovered for a long time, and when they are, it may be very difficult to track down their root cause.

Data centers typically employ large number of assets of identical type, which means that if an attacker finds a single vulnerability, he/she can use it for a large scale attack. The increasing size of data centers and the practice of using only a few unique configurations to ease management burden makes this problem easier to exploit by hackers.

Higher level repositories such as those maintained by a management package may duplicate the information contained in individual server CIM repositories to varying degrees. Such duplication is desirable from an efficiency perspective since access to firmware managed information over web-services could be extremely slow. Furthermore, allocation or migration of an application requires a global view of the entire data center. Since data copy stored in higher level repositories is unlikely to be refreshed frequently from individual repositories, a hacker can corrupt it with the assurance that the corrupted data will not be overridden for some time. Such an attack can cause the provisioning process to misbehave and result in traffic congestion, server overload, or other problems.

The most insidious attack on CM data is on the aggregate parameters maintained in the package repositories. Aggregate parameters often include simple counts (e.g., number of servers or VMs available for job scheduling) and averages/sums over multiple elements (e.g., average CPU utilization over all servers in a rack or total uplink traffic in and out of the rack). These aggregate parameters are useful for making quick decisions before examining the more detailed individual data. For example, if a provisioning request comes to a rack manager, it can be promptly rejected if its uplink BW requirements exceed the available uplink BW, or the average CPU utilization is too high. A corruption of such aggregate data can cause either underutilization of resources (e.g., no allocations take place from the rack because the used uplink BW is artificially set too high) or overutilization (e.g., congestion in the rack switch because the available uplink BW is artificially set too low). The attacker could even set the parameters to values that results in error exit or emergency shutdown (e.g., thermal limit exceeded) and thereby bring the entire rack down.

The risks posed by corruption of aggregate data become more severe as we go up the hierarchy. In particular, a corruption of a single configuration item in the global CMDB (e.g., total available bandwidth at top level switch) could bring down the entire data center. Unfortunately, the complexity of CMDB's presents a large number of such opportunities for severely disrupting the data center operations.

## 10.3.2 Attack Pathways

The most direct way of corrupting key configuration data is compromise of the servers running higher level management entities such as a cluster or rack manager. However, there are also several, presumably easier, ways of causing disruption. For example, a hacker could make legitimate requests that trigger known weaknesses of the configuration management procedures or by hiding malicious code into the requests. The latter is facilitated by the expanding use of web-services based management, which is known to be vulnerable to a host of attacks [30]. As with other web-services, WSMAN interfaces for manipulating configuration data are described using WSDL (Web Services Definition Language) and the descriptions are often automatically generated. Automatic generation often means that descriptions include *all* supported procedures including those not really intended for use by non-developers.

Hackers can exploit these as an easy mechanism to corrupt configuration data. Similarly, publication of the web services via a public directory such as UDDI simplifies the job of the hacker.

Since SOAP headers in WSMAN commands use XML and require XML parsing, it is possible to craft bogus headers that nevertheless require significant parsing effort. Also, a SAX (Simple API for XML) based parser (that extracts all relevant information in a single pass) can be easily tricked into overwriting earlier values. This is one mechanism by which a legitimate update to configuration variable can be hijacked to produce an invalid or otherwise problematic value. Another mechanism concerns the misuse of *XML external entities*, which is merely a macro facility by which one could include contents of external files in the XML stream. If the hacker can overwrite or replace such a file, it can put arbitrary XML code there. One such possibility is to open a new TCP connection with the privileges of the XML parser and perform arbitrary data transfer. A related attack is XML schema poisoning to alter control flow or otherwise cause incorrect processing of XML data. Finally, the hacker can inject arbitrary data wrapped in XML (e.g., XPATH expressions, SQL queries, LDAP requests, etc.) to achieve specific attacks related to how the configuration data is manipulated. Some of the XML manipulation attacks can even disable authentication and thereby gain unrestricted access to the configuration data.

## 10.3.3 Attacks on Network Configuration

As the management interface to switches becomes more directly engaged in supporting features such as QoS controlled virtual paths or entire virtual clusters, the corresponding configuration data becomes more vulnerable to attacks and misconfigurations. Switch configuration data includes a number of attributes including VLAN setup, size of address table and number of MAC addresses per port, QoS setup, interface speeds and corresponding parameters, etc. In particular, VLANs are often used for traffic isolation, and are being exploited to provide layer-2 QoS in the data center Ethernet context [5]. A number of VLAN related and other attacks on switches are well known and can be exploited to disrupt data center traffic flows [27]:

1. MAC flooding attacks that fill-up the hardware table that associates destination MAC addresses with switch ports. Once that happens, traffic directed to additional MAC addresses will be broadcast to all ports and can be easily sniffed. This issue is normally addressed via a configuration parameter that limits the number of unique MAC addresses per port. A corruption of this value can circumvent the protection.
2. Switch configuration anomalies or corruption can cause certain ports to start behaving like "trunk ports" that are allowed to forward traffic between VLANs.
3. Ethernet switches use some version of the spanning tree protocol (STP) to implement loop-free layer-2 routing. It is possible to corrupt the configuration data such that the bridge PDU (BPDU) messages used in the STP cause a switch to

be elected as the root of the spanning tree and thereby have the traffic directed as desired.

With increasing use of Ethernet for storage traffic, these attacks (and several others not mentioned here) can even be used for large scale exposure or stealing of stored data.

Although data centers mostly employ layer-2 switches in the network interconnection infrastructure, layer-3 routers are also needed at the periphery to connect to the external world. In addition, the emerging trend of distributed data centers to support seamless cloud computing environments also results in non-local server-to-server traffic flowing through the routers. In addition to the layer-2 attacks discussed above, routers can also be attacked at layer-3. The extensive configuration and policy setup for the interdomain routing algorithm such as BGP, coupled with the reluctance on part of ISPs to share their setups leads to plenty of chances of misconfigurations [21, 2]. Some common ailments include advertisement of route for an entire prefix which is not entirely served by the router, improperly configured alternate routes leading to packet loss and convergence issues, and incorrect packet discrimination rules that may deny desired packets or accept unwanted ones. These issues are often addressed by checking route configurations against the rules and policies expressed declaratively. Some recent research in area concerns discovering the rules and policies by data mining instead of being pre-specified [21].

Routers invariably support flexible IP flow and QoS configuration including MPLS, differentiated service (DSCP), reservations (e.g., RSVP), etc. The extensive configuration involved in this setup needs to be protected as well. There are many attacks that can be directed towards MPLS signaling [24], differentiated services [32], and reservation based QoS services [33] and mechanisms based on cryptographic authentication and encryption have been proposed. In all cases, however, the routers involved must store the necessary configuration parameters for the QoS treatment, and integrity of this data needs to be ensured.

The most common routing attacks concern perturbation of the routing table by latching on to route update messages. In particular, suppression, duplication, or change to route update messages can cause misdelivery and congestion. Such attacks have been considered extensively in the literature, and are not strictly speaking configuration attacks. Cryptographically enhanced route update protocols, such as Secure BGP (SBGP) [6]) are designed to secure updates, but require much more complex configuration. In fact, SBGP requires two PKI (public key encryption) hierarchies and is thus even more complex than DNS-SEC that requires single such hierarchy. It is to be noted that although DNS-SEC was introduced to address the vulnerabilities of DNS, its complexity makes it quite prone to misconfigurations [9].

### 10.3.3.1 Energy Related Attacks

As more powerful devices and servers are stuffed in smaller form factors, the power and thermal densities become unsustainable and effective cooling more expensive. At the same time, the increasing size of data centers makes the energy/cooling and power delivery costs dominant in large data centers. This has resulted in aggressive push towards not only energy efficient design but also active management of energy/power as a finite resource that can be shifted where needed most. Thus, configuration management includes intelligent energy management and involves keeping track of energy availability, current requirements, cooling requirements, temperature, energy states of various devices and servers, etc [19]. This provides ample new opportunities for energy related attacks, but to date very little attention has been paid towards the security aspects of power management. For example, in windows OS, although the power management can be restricted by administrators, by default any authenticated user can alter power management settings.

There are several ways to abuse power management capabilities. If the ACPI (advanced configuration and power interface) access is not tightly controlled, it may be possible for a hacker to gain access to a user account and set power states of the server to undesirable values (e.g., put an active server to sleep, run the CPU and other devices at lowest speed thereby causing congestion, prevent CPU/devices from going into lower power modes and thereby force thermal events, etc.) Another possibility is to exploit web-service security holes to corrupt the recorded values of energy states of servers in CMDBs and/or energy states of various devices (e.g., CPU, memory, IO adapters, etc.) CIM repositories. Finally, it is possible to cause power circuits to be overloaded or thermal emergencies to be triggered by simply increasing the load – that is, by a form of denial of service (DoS) attack focussed on energy consumption. It is important to note that more sustainable and energy efficient designs make data centers more vulnerable to energy attacks [18]. For example, ambient cooling, use of lower capacity power supplies, lower capacity UPS, etc. all make the energy attacks easier.

### 10.3.4 Attacks on virtualized Device Configuration

As virtualization becomes pervasive in data centers, it brings new security challenges as pointed out in [26, 14]. These challenges imply similar issues with respect to the configuration data that defines the characteristics of the virtual device. While the number of real devices is limited by monetary, space, power and other considerations, virtual devices can be created at almost no cost. Thus the number of the virtual devices within a data center can grow explosively, particularly as the virtualization overhead is driven to be negligible via proper hardware support and software mechanisms [4]. Consequently, management servers have to handle many more devices which increases the amount of configuration data and is corresponding vulnerability.

Unlike physical devices, virtual devices may appear and disappear dynamically. This makes the tracking of compromised devices quite difficult since the device may disappear before an attack is discerned. Moreover, since the states and configurations of virtual devices can be easily logged and restored later, old configurations may result in inconsistencies and conflicts. Since the virtual devices run atop physical ones, they must bind both with the underlying physical infrastructure and the management servers. When a virtual device moves from one physical system to another, these binding relations change as well, and must be properly updated. A compromised virtual device could easily "infect" the configuration of its next host and possibly even the next local management server before the compromise is detected.

As the virtualization support permeates the hardware and firmware, virtual device configuration data is beginning to migrate to the standard management repositories, as already stated and protection of these repositories becomes essential. Although, isolation is one of the most important reasons for the popularity of VM technology, it is possible for rogue processes running in a VM to escape the VM boundaries and compromise other VMs or the physical machine. Thus, it is important to protect VM configuration data against such "insider" attacks as well. The trusted virtual data center proposal from IBM [3] is designed to enforce isolation between VMs on a platform by providing a special management VM that checks access to specified resources (e.g., a virtual disk, VLAN, etc.) by a VM. The management VM interfaces with the configuration manager CIMOM and thus is able to protect the integrity of configuration data. It also proposes to virtualize the platform TPM (trusted platform module) in order to provide attestation capabilities to each VM for the software running on the VM. This work exploits the sHype mandatory access control extensions to the Xen hypervisor [28]. Reference [8] discusses how to establish trusted virtual domains for communication among a set of related VMs using existing techniques such as Ethernet encapsulation, VLAN tagging and VPNs.

## 10.4 Securing Configuration Management Data

In this section, we first briefly discuss available security mechanisms in current management standards and then introduce a novel scheme that exploits the redundancy that exists in the configuration data in order to detect updates that may result in misconfigurations or corruptions.

### 10.4.1 Existing CM Security Mechanisms

WBEM provides several mechanisms for secure access to CIM repositories. Clients can be authenticated via authentication tokens which are usually user-name/password, but could also be Kerberos tokens or public key (PKI) certificates. Message integrity is provided by including a message digest in the communication linked with the authentication token. ACLs are used for providing required access control to the clients over CIM hierarchies and must be configured manually. By default, all clients have read access over the entire name space. The auditing functionality records all authentication events (successful or not) and changes to management data made by the clients.

WS-security [34] (a part of WBEM) supports authentication, integrity and confidentiality for SOAP messages via a variety of security models including PKI, Kerberos, and SSL. Specifically, it supports multiple security token formats, multiple trust domains, multiple signature formats, and multiple encryption technologies. An extension to WS-security [35] supports secure message exchange between multiple parties by establishing a security context for the entire message exchange session.

Authentication of clients and devices via PKI certificates is clearly useful but its high overhead usually detracts from its routine use. For the most part, configuration data does not need to be kept confidential; instead, the primary requirement is its integrity. Therefore, instead of encrypting the stored or exchanged data, it is more important to address the issue of data corruption – whether intentional or accidental. Furthermore, when the corruption does happen, it should be possible to detect and possibly correct it. Suitable schemes depend on the nature of data in terms of how often it changes and the extent of damage that corruption can cause.

## 10.4.2 Exploiting Redundancy in Data

The configuration data stored in various repositories has significant amount of redundancy which can be exploited for consistency verification purposes. Let us start with the relatively static information such as hardware type, setup and raw capacities (e.g., 3.0GHz, dual-core processor, 16GB DDR3-1333 memory, etc.), installed software (e.g., Redhat EL6), etc. Data centers often deploy a large number of identical and identically configured servers, switches, storage bricks and other assets. This lack of diversity can be exploited both by the hackers for replicating attacks and by the configuration manager for detecting configuration attacks and to reduce the overhead of protection. In general, the configuration of all servers (or devices) of the same type may not be identical, instead, certain aspects of the configuration may be unique (e.g., switch port to which the server is connected) while others are either identical or admit some narrow range or set of acceptable values. We call these parts as unique configuration data (UCD) and shared configuration data (SCD) respectively. Although both types of configuration data need to be protected, it is possible to exploit the existing redundancy for protecting SCD at a lower cost. This could be done by nominating a few assets as *reference* whose SCD instance is regarded as a gold standard and used for validating others. The configuration data of the reference assets is protected aggressively using the following mechanisms:

1. Authentication of all HW and SW installed on the assets via local TPM (trusted platform module), if available, or via suitable remote authentication.
2. Extensive sanity checking of repository data both against actual configuration (obtained via discovery and enumeration procedures) and via consistency conditions.
3. Information flow related security controls such those suggested in [20] to monitor attacks on web-services that can catch and even recover from undesirable flows.

Certainly the UCD part of the data cannot be left unprotected, but to use the same mechanism, it would have to be duplicated in the reference asset. This is a reasonable approach if the amount of unique data is very small. If the unique data can be verified more directly via a direct discovery or enumeration, than such duplication is not necessary.

The configuration data from assets can be checked against that of the reference assets both periodically and at the time of significant events (e.g., just before and after a reboot, or when a potential attack/compromise is suspected). Hashing can be used to implement this efficiently in trusted management servers; i.e., the management servers only store a hash value (or more generally a hash map) of the data in each repository, and a comparison of hash maps is used to check for consistency. The hashing scheme can also admit ranges if the values are trimmed down to the lower bound of the range before computing the hash. This is an acceptable approach if the allowed ranges are rather narrow and the precise value within the range is inconsequential from a configuration robustness perspective. For wider ranges, it may be possible to divide the assets into groups and maintain a separate reference for each group.

A similar scheme can be used for virtual machines as well. Although it is possible to create VMs with arbitrary parameter values or even modify some parameters for a running VM, such an approach quickly leads to a management nightmare in large systems. Thus, using only a rather limited candidate set of VM configurations is not only a practical approach, it also allows the use of above mentioned group based protection mechanism.

When multiple groups are involved, an update to a changeable configuration parameter may require moving the entity to a different group. This can be allowed safely provided that the group membership is maintained in the secured management server that implements the authentication and verification, rather than residing with the entity itself.

### 10.4.3 Securing Aggregate Data

As stated earlier, the security of aggregate data is vital. Fortunately, aggregate data is by definition redundant and can be verified via recomputation either periodically or when the values fall outside some nominal range. If the underlying algorithms update the aggregate data lazily (i.e., not every change to individual values is immediately reflected in the aggregate values), one could not insist on exact match on verification. This could lead to false positives, whose probability can be reduced by the following measures: (a) Use of multiple verification failures to declare an attack while each time still replacing the existing value with the newly computed value, and (b) Use of historical information or "trend" to distinguish normal behavior from abnormal one. There is obviously a tradeoff between false positive probability and latency in detecting an attack.

It is important to note that attack resistance requires a somewhat different treatment of error conditions with respect to aggregate quantities: "impossible" or out of range values should not result in simply raising an exception; instead, a recovery attempt needs to be made by recomputing the aggregate value.

## 10.5  Challenges in Securing Configuration Management

In this section we discuss a number of issues that complicate configuration management and describe the security challenges brought about by them.

### *10.5.1  Configuration Dependencies*

The configuration and hence proper operation of an entity could depend on the configuration of another entity either directly or due to the way system is structured. In some cases, a common configuration instance may apply to multiple entities. The classical case for this is configuration specified via configuration files (e.g., the current situation with VMs). In this case, a misconfiguration can affect many seemingly independent entities. A similar situation arises whenever a common default configuration is used, even when each entity has its own independent configuration record. The problem here is that many instances will likely to continue to use the default configuration that may be faulty. In both of these examples, it may be possible for a hacker to deliberately cause misconfiguration by altering the common information. The practice of keeping aggregate data also creates a strong dependency in that the corruption of the aggregate value affects proper usage of the corresponding assets. Dependencies can also be indirect – for example, misconfigured network BW between two racks may prevent allocation of certain applications to these racks even if the individual servers in the racks have adequate computing and network capacity. More generally, misconfiguration of a single device (e.g., a NIC, accelerator, etc.) could substantially impact all applications that use that device or use it in a certain way.

A major challenge in configuration management is characterization and modeling of such dependencies. Although there is a substantial amount of literature on identifying program data and control dependencies [31], the dependencies from the misconfiguration impact perspective can be different, perhaps more in line with the notion of abstract dependencies that is often used in the context of program slicing [23]. New metrics and models to characterize such dependencies and to identify "critical dependencies" are the first steps to find out ways of fortifying the CM systems and enhancing the robustness of CM data. The notion of "critical dependencies" can be defined in multiple ways including dependencies that lead to most widespread impacts, most serious impact, or even those that are easiest to exploit for disrupting system functioning. A formal characterization and algorithms for finding critical dependencies remain important open problems.

A somewhat unique aspect of dependencies in configuration data is that many dependencies may not be triggered for long periods of time. For example, updates to the physical device configuration within a server will, in most cases, not take effect until the server is rebooted. In a data center environment, servers may not be rebooted for weeks or months. This means that by the time the misconfiguration or malicious update takes effect, it may be nearly impossible to track down how, when, and under what circumstances the update happened and what else might have been affected. In terms of VM configuration, certain parameters may be fixed for the duration of VM's existence (e.g., size of allocated hardware threads or main memory) while others are more dynamic (e.g., allocated disk space) depending on the design. At the application and middleware level also, different parameters may have different lifetimes. Thus, in order to properly model the dependencies, we also need to consider grouping by events that trigger them, while at the same time characterizing the relationship between various groups.

## 10.5.2 Configuration Management for Clouds

Configuration management in a cloud computing environment brings in additional challenges due to involvement of multiple parties and possibly distributed infrastructure. Although current cloud computing infrastructures are owned and operated by a single vendor (e.g., Amazon), a more general outsourced model is likely to emerge in the future as discussed in [19]. For example, several different enterprises may lease "data centers" as physical clusters from the same underlying server farm. The advantage of such a model is the economy of scale for the server-farm operator, and the ability of the leasing enterprise to easily alter the size of its data center and delegate physical infrastructure management (e.g., replacement of failed servers or patching them) to the server farm operator. These outsourced physical data centers could then be virtualized and leased to the service providers or end customers. In this model, it is possible for the same service provider or customer to lease multiple, possibly geographically distributed, resources and thereby create a distributed, virtualized data center. Fig. 10.3 shows such a 4-layer conceptual model of future data center. In this depiction, rectangles refer to software layers and ellipses refer to the resulting abstractions.

Such a model subsumes everything from a non-virtualized, centralized data center entirely owned by a single organization all the way up to a geographically distributed, fully virtualized data center where each layer possibly has a separate owner. The latter extreme provides a number of advantages in terms of consolidation, agility, and flexibility, but it also poses challenges in a number of areas including the integrity and privacy of the configuration management. In particular, an effective resource and configuration management requires that nonlocal CM data be available wherever sharing happens. This implies, for example, that the physical

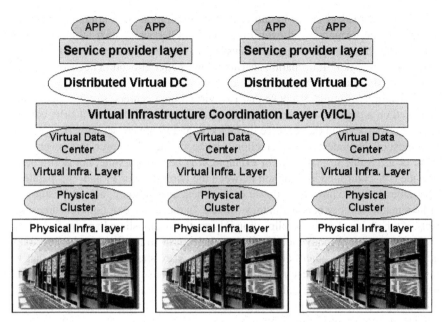

**Fig. 10.3** Logical Organization of Future Data Centers

clusters need visibility into the configuration of the networking infrastructure that happens to be shared (horizontal visibility). Similarly, a virtualized data center running on top of a physical cluster may need to know both about the configuration of the underlying physical cluster (vertical visibility) and other virtual data centers (horizontal visibility). However, such visibility needs conflict with the privacy and security needs of various layers. The latter may include the following:

1. Visibility restriction to Higher Layers: A physical cluster owner may not want to fully release configuration information to the virtual data center above, because part of this information may be considered as a "business secret".
2. Lack of Trust in Lower Layer Information: A virtual data center may not entirely trust what is being revealed by the lower layer. Generally, there is no expectation of malicious intent by the lower layer, but the lower layer may underreport or hide certain resources.
3. Lack of Trust in Sharing Information with Lower Layer: The higher layer may not give out all of its configuration data to the lower layer, because such data may be passed on to its peer by the lower layer.
4. Complete lack of knowledge or trust horizontally and hence no direct information sharing among the peers.

Achieving effective configuration management while respecting the privacy/security needs of various layers is a challenging problem that has not been examined in the past. It is important to note here that since arbitrary parties may be sharing the infrastructure, there is a far greater chance (than in a traditional data center environment) of inadvertent or intentional misconfigurations that affect other parties in terms of performance and even functionality. Of course, such an environment also provides ample opportunities for customers to actively launch security attacks. Note that while more information sharing allows better allocation decisions, it also increases risk of uncooperative behavior.

As a simple example, suppose that two virtual data centers, say, $V_1$ and $V_2$, are deployed on a physical cluster $P$ consisting of two racks. If there is a strict control over all resources, and the resource limits for $V_1$ and $V_2$ are conservatively specified, then most of the undesirable interactions can be avoided. However, this is very difficult or infeasible in practice. For example, it is neither possible, nor desirable to provide BW controlled virtual path between the two racks for $V_1$ and $V_2$ separately. The same applies to how much power draw or heat dissipation $V_1$ and $V_2$ are allowed or how much memory bandwidth they can use. In the absence of tight resource controls, if the physical resource allocation information is not shared among $V_1$ and $V_2$, each of them could inadvertently allocate their tasks so as to stress the inter-rack network BW. On the other hand, if the allocations are shared, it is possible that $V_1$ (or $V_2$) intentionally squeeze inter-rack communications of the other either to gain performance for their applications or to hurt others. Note that the reason why this is a unique problem for clouds is because the task allocation decisions are no longer done by a single central authority.

In addition to the problem of multiple virtualized data centers sharing common resources, the model in Fig. 10.3 also admits truly large, geographically distributed data centers (virtualized or not). Configuration management in such an environment becomes challenging because of potential lack of uniformity among the configuration management structures and practices used by different server farms, which further increases chances of misconfigurations. Reference [13] describes a distributed configuration management approach for routers in a large ISP network using a specifically designed template based configuration management language. There are proposals to simplify management of large scale systems by partitioning the management responsibilities either physically (as in[25]) or logically (as in [1] where data plane presents a standard management interface to the management plane). However, in general, scalable and secure configuration management in large heterogeneous distributed environments remains an open problem.

### 10.5.3 Hardening Configurations Against Attacks

Configuration management can be made more robust both by reducing the attack surface and by changing it dynamically. The attack surface can be reduced by making the configuration data less accessible via a variety of techniques including authentication, encryption, access controls, and information flow controls, as already discussed. The change of attack surface can be done by exploiting moving target defense (MTD) or more generally by introducing diversity. In particular, the scheme discussed in section 10.4.2 can be hardened by rotating the reference nodes according to a randomized scheme, so that brute force attacks on the reference server have less chance of success.

The most generic diversity technique is to change in-band and OOB IP addresses and port numbers for each machine in the management hierarchy according to some schedule. However, there are other configuration management specific ways of using MTD as well. One potentially weak link in CM is the interaction between OOB and IB sides which is usually via the IPMI (intelligent peripheral management interface). Hardening of IPMI messages by techniques similar to instruction set randomization (ISR) and consistency checking could be useful in foiling attacks that target IB-OOB interaction.

It was commented in earlier sections that the dynamism brought in by virtualization (e.g., on-the-fly resizing of VM resources and migration) complicates configuration management and enhances opportunities for attacks and misconfiguration. However, the same dynamism can also be exploited to fortify the defenses. For example, a deliberate VM migration or changes to resources allocated to the VM can make it harder to target the VM. This also makes attempts to poison VM configuration data harder. However, there is currently no formal model that provides a basis for choosing one technique over another. Similarly, quantification of the benefits of dynamism remains an open problem.

Randomization of memory addresses, or more generally address space layout randomization (ASLR) is a well known defensive technique that has also been implemented in some current operating systems. The same principle can be used for CIM objects representing configuration. The base offset of CIM objects can be randomized relatively easily, but a finer grain randomization of individual attributes within a CIM object is harder. Once again, quantitative models for guiding design of good randomization techniques and techniques for assessing their effectiveness remain largely unexplored.

It was mentioned earlier that configuration errors/corruption can be particularly insidious since configuration data is often used on special events (e.g., reboot of machine or restart of service). A more proactive use of configuration data can detect problems early, but needs to be applied carefully to avoid inconsistencies and early failures. For example, a systematic approach to testing out altered configurations in a continuous but limited way could be a useful way to provide *timing diversity* that spreads the risk across time.

MTD can be potentially useful in resolving the conflict between usefulness and risks of sharing configuration data horizontally or vertically in the context of the general cloud computing model discussed in section 10.5.2. In particular, the non-local configuration data can be fuzzified before sharing so that various entities can make good allocation decisions without having to share their detailed configuration data. This fuzzification cannot be a simple aggregation; it needs to change dynamically so that the information less useful for abuse. Once again, coming up good mechanisms for fuzzification and how to achieve balance between usefulness and privacy remain open problems.

## 10.6 Conclusions

In this chapter, we examined the problem of securing configuration management (CM) within data centers. We discussed CM related vulnerabilities in a data center in general, including servers and network nodes. It was noted that the web-services based management – although increasingly popular – can harbor attacks that can seriously disrupt data center operations. We then presented some simple mechanisms to ensure integrity of CM data. However, the general problem of CM security remains unsolved, particularly in the emerging cloud computing environment. We presented the challenges of securing CM and pointed out several approaches that use the principle of moving target defense.

## References

1. H. Ballani and P. Francis, "CONMan: taking the complexity out of network management", Proc. of ACM SIGCOMM Workshop on Internet Network Management, Sept 2006, pp41-46
2. L. Bauer, S. Garriss, M.K. Reiter, "Detecting and resolving policy misconfigurations in access-control systems", In Proc. of 13th ACM Symposium on Access Control Models and Technologies, June 2008, pp185-194.
3. S. Berger, R. Cceres, D. Pendarakis, et al., "TVDc: managing security in the trusted virtual datacenter", SIGOPS Oper. Syst. Rev. 42, 1 (Jan. 2008), pp 40-47.
4. K. Biswas and A. Islam, "Hardware Virtualization Support In INTEL, AMD And IBM Power Processors", available at arxiv.org/abs/0909.0099.
5. IEEE task group 802.3.az, "Energy Efficienct Ethernet", www.ieee802.org/3/az/public/nov07/hays_1_1107.pdf.
6. K. Butler, T. Farley, T. McDaniel, J. Rexford, "A Survey of BGP Security Issues and Solutions", to appear in Proc. of IEEE, 2010.
7. "Common Information Model", Available at www.wbemsolutions.com/tutorials/CIM/cim-specification.html
8. S. Cabuk, C.I. Dalton, H. Ramasamy, M. Schunter, "Towards automated provisioning of secure virtualized networks", Proc. of 14th ACM CCS conference, Oct 2007, pp 235-245.
9. C. Doccio, J. Sedayao, K. Kant and P. Mohapatra, "Quantifying and Improving DNSSEC Availability", to appear in proc. of ICCCN conference, Aug 2011.
10. "Virtualization Management (VMAN) Initiative : DMTF Standards for Virtualization Management", Available at http://www.dmtf.org/standards/vman
11. "Open Virtualization Format", Available at dmtf.org/sites/default/files/standards/documents/DSP2021_1.0.0.tar
12. J. Crandall, "DMTF Technologies Overview", Available at www.snia.org/events/storage-developer2008/presentations/wednesday/JohnCrandall_DMTF_Profiles_for_Storage.pdf
13. W. Enk, T. Moyer, P. McDaniel, et.al., "Configuration management at massive scale: system design and experience", IEEE Journal of Selected Areas in Communications, April 2009, Vol 27, No 3, pp323-335.
14. Tal Garfinkel and Mendel Rosenblum, "When Virtual Is Harder than Real: Security Challenges in Virtual Machine Based Computing Environments", USENIX Association, 2005
15. P. Goyal, R. Mikkilineni, M. Ganti, "FCAPS in the business services fabric management", Proc. of 18th IEEE Intl. workshop on Enabling Technologies, 2009.

16. R.C. Merkle, "Protocols for Public Key Cryptosystems", In Proc. of 1980 IEEE Symposium on Security and Privacy, 1980.
17. Intel Active Management Technology. Available at en.wikipedia.org/wiki/Intel_ Active_Management_Technology
18. K. Kant, "Distributed Energy Adaptive Computing", Proc. of International Conf. on Communications (ICC), May 2010.
19. K. Kant, "Data Center Evolution: A Tutorial on State of the Art, Issues, and Challenges", Elsevier Computer Networks Journal, Dec 2009.
20. M.S. Lam, M. Martin, B. Livshits, J. Whaley, "Securing Web Applications with Static and Dynamic Information Flow Tracking", Proc. of ACM sigplan symp. on partial evaluation and semantics based program manipulation (PEPM), 2008.
21. F. Le, S. Lee, T. Wong, et. al, "Detecting network-wide and router-specific misconfigurations through data mining", IEEE/ACM Trans. on networking, vol 17, No 1, Feb 2009, pp 66-79.
22. C. E. Leiserson, "Fat-Trees: Universal Networks for Hardware-Efcient Supercomputing", IEEE Trans. on Computers, Vol 34, No 10, pp892901, 1985.
23. I. Mastroeni and D. Zanardini, "Data Dependencies and program slicing: from syntax to abstract semantics", Proc. of ACM sigplan symp. on partial evaluation and semantics based program manipulation (PEPM), 2008.
24. F. Palmieri and U. Fiore, "Enhanced security strategies for MPLS signaling", Journal of Networks, Vol 2, No. 5, Sept 2007.
25. L. Pasquale, J. Laredo, H. Ludwig, et.al., "Distributed Cross-Domain Configuration Management", Proc of ICSOC 2009, LNCS 5900, pp622-636.
26. J.S. Reuben. A Survey on Virtual Machine Security. Helsinki University of Technology, 2007. Available at http://www.tml.tkk.fi/Publications/C/25/chapters/ Reuben_final.pdf
27. S.A. Rouiller, "Virtual LAN security: weaknesses and countermeasures", available at uploads.askapache.com/2006/12/vlan-security-3.pdf
28. R. Sailer, T. Jaeger, E. Valdez, et al, "Building a MAC-based Security Architecture for the Xen Opensource Hypervisor", 21st Annual Computer Security Applications Conference (ACSAC), Dec 2005.
29. F.T. Sheldon and C. Vishik, "Moving toward trustworthy systems: R&D Essentials", IEEE Computer magazine, Sept 2010, pp 31-40.
30. A. Stamos and S. Stender, "Attacking Web Services: The Next Generation of Vulnerable Enterprise Applications", Proc. of Defcon XIII. Available at www.isecpartners.com/.. ./iSEC-Attacking-Web-Services.DefCon.pdf.
31. W. Stanley, J. Laski, "Program Dependencies", in Software Verification and Analysis, springer-verlag, 2009, pp125-142.
32. A. Striegel, "Security Issues in a Differentiated Services Internet", Proc. of HiPC workshop, 2002.
33. V. Talwar, K. Nahrstedt, S.K. Nath, "RSVP-SQOS : A SECURE RSVP PROTOCOL," Proc. of IEEE Intl. conf. on Multimedia and Expo (ICME'01), 2001
34. Web service security specification, available at docs.oasis-open.org/wss/2004/ 01/oasis-200401-wss-soap-message-security-1.0.pdf
35. Web services secure conversation specification, available at specs.xmlsoap.org/ws/ 2005/02/sc/WS-SecureConversation.pdf

# Author Index